best
restaurants®
san francisco
bay area

OTHER BOOKS IN BEST RESTAURANTS SERIES

best restaurants®
san francisco
bay area

published in cooperation with

San Francisco Focus

The City Magazine for the San Francisco Bay Area

Jacqueline Killeen
Sharon Silva
Carol Warren
Mary Gottschalk
George Starke

Illustrations by Roy Kileen

101 Productions
San Francisco

Some of the material in these reviews has been previously published in the restaurant columns of *San Francisco Focus,* a publication of KQED, Inc. The selection of restaurants for this book was totally the opinion of the authors. KQED, Inc. as a matter of policy declines to endorse, explicitly or implicitly, all commercial ventures.

Best Restaurants is the trademark of 101 Productions, registered with the United States Patent and Trademark Office.

Published by 101 Productions, 834 Mission Street, San Francisco, California 94103.

Distributed to the book trade
by the Macmillan Publishing Company, New York.

Library of Congress Cataloging-in-Publication Data

Killeen, Jacqueline,
     Best restaurants, San Francisco Bay Area.

     Includes index.
     1. Restaurants, lunch rooms, etc.--California--San Francisco--Directories.   Restaurants, lunch rooms, etc.--California--San Francisco Bay Area--Directories.   I. Silva, Sharon.   II. Title.
TX907.K4835   1986   647'.95794'6   86-2434
ISBN   0-89286-260-2

CONTENTS

INTRODUCTION

What's next: Blackened goat cheese? We live in an era of culinary cliché; hundreds of restaurateurs have jumped on the California, Cajun, or whatever bandwagon, without ever looking back. This is an age in which the ABCs of salad making have been redefined as arugula, balsamic, and chèvre, and superchefs receive the kind of media attention once reserved for movie stars.

In the midst of this madness, it's difficult to distinguish the definitive dining experience from the derivative, to sort out the trend setters from the trend followers. Certainly San Francisco is as guilty of faddishness as any other American city, but we like to think we create trends more often than we follow them. The San Francisco Bay Area unquestionably boasts more good restaurants per capita—and a greater diversity of ethnic cuisines—than any other area of the country.

When we first started writing a guide to Bay Area restaurants back in the less-faddish late sixties, the selection of "best restaurants" was fairly straightforward. Despite San Francisco's reputation as an international dining mecca, not that many choices really existed. Now, to eat a daily meal in each of the city's restaurants would take approximately eleven years and nine months. These numbers clearly make a comprehensive guide impossible.

Instead, we have presented what we consider to be the "best" in each particular type of dining experience. Our choices are based upon eighteen years of actively reviewing the restaurants of this area, most recently for *San Francisco Focus,* and upon our personal tastes and prejudices.

The selections range from luxurious dinner houses where triple-digit checks for two are the norm, to ethnic storefront cafés where bargain prices prevail. Yet throughout we have applied one criterion: the food must be outstanding and worth the price. Our bottom line for including a restaurant in this book is: would we ourselves return there?

To help you find a restaurant to match your budget for the evening, we have divided our selections into categories of inexpensive, moderate, and expensive, using the symbols shown below. We have based the ratings on the price of an average three-course dinner in that restaurant, food only; cocktails, wine and tips would be extra. In many restaurants, you could end up spending more if you splurged or less if you tightened your belt. Prices quoted in this book were in effect at the time of publication and are subject to change at any time.

$ **UNDER $12** The food will be good as well as economical, but atmosphere and smooth service may be lacking at some of these restaurants. Dress is most always casual.

$$ **UNDER $25** In this price range of $12 to $25, we expect charm and atmosphere in addition to excellent food.

$$$ **OVER $25** At this price, we demand perfection in every department. The food must be exceptional, the service flawless, and the surroundings magnificent.

It should go without saying that our visits to restaurants are anonymous, that we always pay our own restaurant check, that there is no charge to a restaurant to appear in this book. In fact there is absolutely no way a restaurant could buy or bribe its way into our book.

SAN FRANCISCO

San Francisco: Richmond District
ACROPOLIS BAKERY
& DELICATESSEN
Russian **$**

The Acropolis Bakery and Delicatessen shows signs of being almost as durable as its namesake. After 45 years, the Greek owners of this beloved Russian café and bakery retired, but not before assuring that their traditions would continue. Kitty Quon, the new owner, thought that cotton tablecloths would be an improvement over the old oilcloth, but soon learned from her customers that this change would not be tolerated; since that one lapse she has let well enough alone. Amazingly though, as fresh menus are printed, the modest prices don't change either. Part of the charm of the Acropolis is the relaxed feeling of family dining in the kitchen of an old-country cook. The Russian soups served with freshly made breads should not be missed. Rassolnik is an intriguing blend of chicken giblets and pickles with sour cream. Pelmeni, the small Russian ravioli, is a marvel of delicacy and its chicken broth has a lightness and subtlety that does not argue with the sour cream and fresh dill topping. Veal cutlets, chicken, beef, and fish dishes are lovingly prepared and served with kasha and vegetables. Searniki, a fried cottage cheese and egg pancake served with sour cream, will make displaced New Yorkers looking for a good dairy restaurant happy. Other house specialties are piroshki, both meat and cabbage, and galubtsy, a very filling but ever-so-light stuffed cabbage. (Most house specialties can be ordered in half portions, another tradition well worth preserving.) Blintzes are served year-round, and for about one month before lent each year blini with caviar, thin slices of herring, and smoked salmon with sour cream are offered. The printed menu is only a guide. If you wish, a plate of cold salads, meats, and cheeses will be prepared for you from the abundant deli counter. And it is a rare diner who leaves without taking home samples—the eggplant salad is superb. Pastries from the Acropolis kitchen are second to none. Maya, the pastry chef, emigrated from Russia seven years ago and works from the old Russian recipes that came with the restaurant. Kitty's only menu change was requested by some faithful customers who for years had been agitating for pot stickers. These had become part of the diet of White Russians who came here by way of China. Kitty Quon obliged and it looks as though the Acropolis Bakery and Delicatessen is going to be around another 45 years.

ACROPOLIS BAKERY AND DELICATESSEN, 5217 Geary Boulevard, San Francisco. Telephone: (415) 751-9661. Hours: 8:30 am–9 pm Monday–Saturday, 9 am–7 pm Sunday. Cards: AE, CB, DC, MC, V. Reservations not accepted. Wine and beer only. Street parking.

San Francisco: Richmond District
ALEJANDRO'S
Latin American/Spanish $$

Alejandro Espinosa is a native Peruvian who has been cooking in some of San Francisco's top Mexican restaurants for the past quarter of a century. Now he has his own place and mixes traditional Mexican fare with a few Peruvian classics, an interesting array of Spanish dishes and some astoundingly good Alejandro creations. One of these is called Alejandrinos, an appetizer of Monterey jack cheese, jalapeños, and eggs stuffed in a Japanese gyosha skin. Don't miss it. Another winner is the ensalada de nopales, a large goblet filled with diced cactus, red bell peppers, sliced onions, and shredded lettuce dressed with a hint of cilantro. Notable among the entrées are a traditional Peruvian dish of rabbit simmered in a sauce of peanuts and cilantro and a classic Spanish zarzuela de mariscos, a seafood stew cooked with shallots, tomatoes, herbs, and sherry. Some entrées are marked "a lo macho." If you don't have an asbestos mouth, beware of these; they are fiery hot. Alejandro's Mexican fare is some of the best in town, and the restaurant has the commendable policy of letting you compose your own combination plato from a selection of eight typical dishes. Alejandro's dining room is more formal than most Mexican restaurants, with whitewashed walls, hand-crafted gilt-framed mirrors from Peru, and white napery on the tables. A rather noisy bar occupies one side of the front dining room, but there's a quieter room in the rear.

ALEJANDRO'S, 1840 Clement Street, San Francisco. Telephone: (415) 668-1184. Hours: 5–11 Monday–Thursday, 5–midnight Friday–Saturday, 4–11 Sunday. Cards: AE, CB, DC, MC, V. Reservations advised; not accepted for parties of two on Friday and Saturday. Full bar service. Street parking.

San Francisco: North Beach
AMELIO'S
French/International $$$

A new life was breathed into this historic restaurant in 1985 when Jacky Robert, formerly of Ernie's and one of the country's most talented French chefs, became a partner and took over the ailing kitchen. Now Robert's dazzling contemporary-yet-classic style is packing in those who truly appreciate creative cooking. Robert describes his style as "the cuisine of tomorrow" because he believes that 50 or 100 years from now the cuisine, like the races of people, will be an international blend. Classically trained in Normandy and later at such famous restaurants as Maxim's in Paris, this young chef has also embraced Italian influences, like a seafood ravioli with basil broth, and even his own version of cioppino. Oriental accents are found in a Korean-style warm salad of jumbo shrimp marinated in soy, sesame, and garlic, or a rack of lamb sauced with soy and honey. Presentation, however, is his hallmark. He uses china of different patterns to enhance his designs, which are always beautiful, sometimes dramatic, and often whimsical. (A jaunty parasol, made from woven shoestring potatoes, tops sesame-glazed sautéed rabbit.) Desserts are also spectacular, to wit the "two-chocolate mousse" that looks for all the world like a medieval castle. Amelios's has an à la carte menu, but to appreciate truly Robert's style you should order the four to six-course fixed-price dinner, which assures a balance of flavors and a contrast of textures and colors throughout the meal. Though Robert's cooking is as bright as tomorrow, the setting is yesteryear. Amelio's started as a 1920s speakeasy and it still looks that way, with banquettes upholstered in floral brocade and crystal chandeliers.

AMELIO'S, 1630 Powell, San Francisco, Telephone: (415) 397-4339. Hours: 5:30–11 daily. Cards: AE, CB, DC, MC, V. Reservations required. Full bar service. Valet parking. Private banquet facilities: 6–55.

San Francisco: Cow Hollow
ARCHIL'S
Russian $$

Good Russian restaurants in San Francisco have always been as scarce as beluga caviar and, in some cases, almost as expensive. But when Archil Merab opened his homey little place off Union Street some years back and put his mother Ina in charge of the kitchen, there was finally a spot to enjoy good Russian (actually Georgian) cooking at modest prices. Neither Archil nor Ina were strangers to the restaurant business; he is the son and she is the ex-wife of and one-time executive chef for the founder of Alexis. Their menu offers a nod to a few all-too-familiar dishes like stuffed cabbage rolls and beef stroganoff, but many of the other entrées are seldom encountered. Some newcomers include a chakhokhbili (Georgian stew) of rabbit and onions in white wine scented with garlic, chicken tamara in a walnut sauce (walnuts play an important role in Georgian cooking), and kufta (lamb meatballs in a piquant tomato sauce). Entrées are served with rice pilaf and a vegetable, and the dinner price includes borscht, a romaine salad, and a choice of desserts ranging from an unusual coffee cheesecake to kisel, a traditional Russian sweet of puréed fruits. All in all, that's noble dining on a proletarian budget.

ARCHIL'S, 3011 Steiner, San Francisco. Telephone: (415) 921-2141. Hours: 5:30–10 Tuesday–Saturday. Cards: MC, V. Reservations suggested. Wine and beer only. Street parking.

Archil's

IKRA 5.50
baked eggplant, served cold

PASHTET 5.50
liver paté served with sauteed onions

MATJES HERRING 5.75
served in our house dressing

EGGPLANT SVETLANA 5.75
in pastry shell with sourcream sauce

Dinner

BORSCHT
ROMAINE SALAD

———•———

FILET OF BEEF STROGANOFF 16.95
prepared in sour cream sauce with mushrooms

FILET MIGNON MARCO POLO 16.95
crushed black peppercorns in cream sauce

BITKI SMETANA 12.75
ground beef kutlets, sauteed onions and sour cream

GOLUBTSY 11.75
stuffed cabbage rolls in tomato sauce

RABBIT CHAKHOKHBILI 14.75
prepared in white wine, onions and touch of garlic

KUFTA 12.50
lamb meatballs in tangy tomato sauce

SHASHLIK ARCHIL 16.95
marinated skewered lamb, Georgian style

LAMB TONGUE PROVENCALE 12.75
poached and served in herb sauce

CHICKEN TAMARA 14.75
Georgian specialty in garlic walnut sauce

CHICKEN ODBIVNAYA 13.75
boneless breast, breaded and sauteed in butter

KOTLETY POZHARSKY 12.50
ground chicken kutlets served with drawn butter

* BONELESS SQUAB ST GEORGE 18.00
stuffed with rice, pine nuts and currants

FISH KOTLETY 12.75
ground fish kutlets served with mustard sauce

All Entrees served with Pilaf And Fresh Vegetable

———•———

COFFEE 1.25   **TEA 1.00**

San Francisco: Downtown
BARDELLI'S
Continental $$

Time seems to stand still at this historic restaurant as you savor the atmosphere of old San Francisco. Crystal chandeliers hang from the high coffered ceilings supported by gigantic marble columns, and at noontime a rosy glow bathes the foyer as light streams in through a spectacular stained-glass mural of a peacock. Bardelli's started its long history as an oyster house in 1906, and it's still run with the no-nonsense approach characteristic of the city's turn-of-the-century restaurants: starchy white napery on the tables and efficient service by formally attired waiters. Some of the house specialties were instigated by former owner Charles Bardelli, a noted Italian chef who gave his name to the place in 1949: Chicken Jerusalem in a mushroom-sherry sauce with baby artichokes, and fillet of sole Bardelli in a white wine sauce laden with crab and shrimp. But one of the best bets here is the daily seafood special, especially the delicately poached salmon when it's in season. Bardelli's is conveniently close to the Geary and the Curran for pre-theatre dining; however, at night it lacks the vitality of the lunchtime hours when its patronage consists largely of regulars seeking an oasis of serenity from the downtown hurly-burly.

BARDELLI'S, 243 O'Farrell Street, San Francisco. Telephone: (415) 982-0243. Hours: 11:30–10 Monday–Friday, 5:30–10 Saturday. Cards: AE, CB, DC, MC, V. Reservations advised. Full bar service. Discounted parking at Downtown Center Garage. Private banquet facilities: 25–40.

FROM THE SEA

Shrimp Curry or Creole 9.75
Calamari Livornese or Fried 9.75
Red Snapper with Capers 9.75
Filet of Sole au Vin Blanc, Bardelli 10.95
Fried Filet of Sole, Tartar Sauce 9.75
Broiled Petrale or Meuniere 12.25
Prawns, Fried or Meuniere 11.75
Scallops, Sauté Meuniere 11.75
Fresh Salmon, Grilled or Poached 12.75
Abalonett Steak Dore 11.75

VEAL SPECIALTIES

Veal Scaloppine Bardelli 12.75
Veal Piccata 12.75
Veal All'agro 12.50
Veal Parmigiana 11.75
Veal Saltinbocca 12.95
Veal Cutlet 11.50

POULTRY

Baked Chicken with Gnocchi 9.50
Chicken Sauté Florentine with Mushrooms, Artichokes and Green Olives 11.75
Chicken Sauté with Mushrooms 10.25
Chicken Jerusalem 11.75

OTHER ENTREES

Sweetbreads Sauté with Mushrooms 10.50
Filet of Beef Tips, Sauté au Champignons 12.75
Calves Liver Steak 10.50
Tripe, Espagnole or Poulette 9.75
Calves Brains in Brown Butter & Capers 10.75
Paillard a la Marchand de Vin 12.95
Medallion of Beef Bardelli 12.95

FROM BROILER

Broiled Lobster Tail 21.50
Double French Lamb Chops 16.25
New York Cut Petit Steak 12.50
New York Cut Steak 15.75
Double New York Steak, for Two Served with Potato, Artichoke and Mushroom 35.50
Please Allow Us 30 Minutes To Prepare

San Francisco: Lower Pacific Heights
BON TEMPS
Cajun-Creole   **$$**

Long before Paul Prudhomme put Louisiana cooking on the culinary map, Brad Borel was cooking Cajun-Creole at his family home in Breaux Bridge, Louisiana. In fact, in the late 1970s, before there were any Creole eateries in San Francisco, Borel was catering dinners at the homes of friends, who all encouraged him to open a restaurant. That he did, in late 1985, and those who had become accustomed to the upbeat hype of blackened redfish et al welcomed the unpretentious, untrendy quality of the food. "I just want to do good, straight-up natural cooking," Borel says. No endangered redfish blackens the skillet here. Instead, the menu presents a range of traditional Louisiana dishes—barbecued shrimp, coubouillon (poached catfish in a piquant sauce), gumbo, jambalaya, shrimp Creole, and such, accompanied with rice, vegetables, and hot corn muffins. The house specialty, however, is a Borel original: chicken breast with a cornbread dressing perked with andouille sausage and crayfish tails. He has named it chicken Larré after his wife Larré, who serves as hostess. The dessert list is brief and yummy: fruit cobbler, pecan pie, and a bread pudding with whiskey sauce to die over. The two small, candlelit dining rooms are decorated with the same unassuming grace that characterizes the food: black-and-white etchings and photographs by local artists repose on the restful, neutral-colored walls. Although it's a new restaurant, one has a feeling that Bon Temps has been here awhile and might be around forever.

BON TEMPS, 1963 Sutter Street, San Francisco. Telephone: (415) 563-6300. Hours: 6–11 Tuesday–Saturday. Cards: AE (MC and V being applied for). Reservations advised. Wine and beer only. Street parking.

Appetizers and Salads

Jambalaya	$4.50	Gumbo Cup	$3.95
Bar-b-Qued Shrimp	5.25	Shrimp Remoulade	4.95
Stuffed Shrimp	4.95	Green Salad	2.50

Entrees

• **Bar-b-Qued Shrimp** 12.95
  (Shrimp glazed with Chef Borel's own Bar-b-Que
  Sauce. Served with Savory Rice & Fresh Vegetables)

• **Chicken Larre'** 9.50
  (Chicken Breast, Stuffed w/ a Savory Cornbread Dressing
  w/ Andouille Sausage & Crab Meat. Topped w/ a Creamy Butter
  Sauce. Served w/ Fresh Vegetables.

• **Coubouillon** 11.00
  (Louisiana Catfish Poached in a Spicy-tangy Sauce
  Piquante. Served over Steamed Rice & w/ Fresh Vegetables).

• **Crawfish Etouffée** 13.95
  (Succulent Louisiana Crawfish Tails Sauted in a Spicy
  Brown Roux Sauce. Served Over Steamed Rice and
  w/ Fresh Vegetables).

• **Gumbo** 7.50
  (Louisiana Gumbo with Chicken, Andouille
  Sausage and Shrimp).

• **Jambalaya** 8.50
  (Traditional Louisiana Rice Dish Baked with Cajun
  Tasso Ham, Chicken and Shrimp. Topped with a
  Spicy Sauce Piquante. Served with Fresh Vegetables).

• **Shrimp Creole** 11.95
  (Shrimp Poached in a Rich Spicy Tomato Sauce. Served
  Over Steamed Rice with Fresh Vegetables).

• **Shrimp Etouffée** 12.95
  (Shrimp Sauteed in a Spicy Brown Roux Sauce.
  Served Over Steamed Rice with Fresh Vegetables).

• **Stuffed Pork Chop** 9.75
  (Double Pork Chop Stuffed w/ a Spicy Dressing of
  Apples, Pork and Bread Crumbs. Topped w/ a Sherry
  Sauce. Served w/ Fresh Vegetables).

Desserts

Fruit Cobbler	2.00
Bread Pudding with Whiskey Sauce	2.50
Pecan Tart	2.75

1963 SUTTER STREET   SAN FRANCISCO, CA 94115   (415) 563-6300

San Francisco: North Beach
BUCA GIOVANNI
Italian
$$$

After 18 years as chef at Vanessi's, Giovanni Leoni opened his own place with the intent of bringing to San Francisco the dishes of his native Tuscany—particularly the rural cooking of the Serchio Valley. His wealth of experience and knowledge virtually guarantees an outstanding gustatory experience at Buca Giovanni. The dining room is located in the cellar of an unpretentious North Beach building and resembles the grotto-type restaurants found in Italy. The brick walls and structural columns have been sandblasted, and the effect produced is warm, cozy, and romantic. The cooking is done upstairs at street level and the food transported by dumbwaiter. Antipasto misto alla Buca is a shareable plate containing bresaola, a beef bottom round cured in the Italian Alps, smoked salmon, tender calamari, olives, and chewy sun-dried tomatoes in olive oil. Insalata di funghi sul crostone is an unusual offering with country overtones: A thick slice of italian sourdough is toasted and covered with a cold sliced mushroom mixture, the juices of which penetrate the bread. The pasta here is unsurpassed anywhere in the city and is made daily in a very fancy pasta machine. Tortelli alla lucchese are extra-large raviolis filled with several different meats and served in a rich and lusty sauce of rabbit, chicken, and tomatoes. In contrast, panzerotti salsa de noci is a light, white sauce containing ground walnuts and delicate seasonings served over veal-filled

LE CARNI, LA SELVAGGINA, IL PESCE

(Different Meats, Birds, Fish)
Sauteed to Order, Served with Vegetable of the Day.
BUCA GIOVANNI uses Provimi Veal Rib Eye only — Eastern Beef.
Ask your waiter for Fresh Fish of the Day.

Petti di Pollo al Cartoccio 8.95
(Boneless Breast of Chicken with Natural Sauce, Mushrooms and Prosciutto in Parchment Paper)

Pollo alle Olive 9.50
(Chicken sauteed with Black Olives, Rosemary, Garlic, Onions, Red Peppers and White Wine)

Bistecchine di Agnello a Scottadito 15.95
(Lamb Chops sauteed with Herbs, Garlic and Wine) or (Olives, Oregano, Capers)

Medaglioni di Filetto al Pepe Verde e Barbaresco 13.95
(Beef Filet sauteed with Green Peppercorns)

Piccatine di Vitello Aglio e Salvia (Garlic and Sage) 12.25

Piccatine di Vitello Salsa al Peperone Rosso 12.25
(Red Pepper Sauce)

Piccatine di Vitello Prosciutto and Avocados 12.45

Piccatine di Vitello Zingara 13.60
(Prosciutto, Onions, Mushrooms and Red Pepper)

Piccatine di Vitello al Funghi Porcini 17.75
(Italian Porcini Mushrooms)

Quaglie al Ginepro 14.95
(Quails sauteed with Juniper Berries, Herbs and Gin)

Quaglie alla Toscana 14.95
(Quails sauteed with Herbs and Mushrooms in a Light, Tasty Sauce)

Pollo Marinato alle Erbette (Broiled) 8.95

Bistecchine di Agnello (Broiled) 15.65

Medaglioni di Vitello ai Funghi Porcini 18.75

Filetto (Broiled) 13.95
(Beef Filet)

Gamberoni allo Zenzero 11.95
(Jumbo Prawns sauteed in a Ginger Sauce)

Medaglioni di Cervo 14.95
(Salsa Bruna al Barbaresco)

Scampi allo Spumante 12.25
(Sauteed Baby Lobster Tail with Italian Sparkling Wine)

Medaglioni di Filetto all'Erbette dell'Orto 13.95

Piccatine di Vitello ai Carciofini 13.60

CONTORNI
(Vegetables)

Fagioli alla Toscana 1.75
(Beans sauteed with Garlic and Sage)

Fagiolini Verdi Saltati 2.25

Zucchini Impanati Fritti 2.75

Verdura del Giorno 1.90

Patate Fritte 1.50

Funghi Saltati Aglio e Salvia ... 2.95

13

ravioli. Linguine marinara, with clams, calamari, and tomatoes, combines the best of the two worlds of seafood and pasta. Prime beef and veal sautés are prepared with the deftness that owner-chef Leone perfected in his years at Vanessi's. If you feel you have room for a sweet, take the zabaione alla Gerardina, a cold Italian concoction that somewhere back in the closet has a distant English trifle relative. Except in rare medically proscribed diets, do not skip the best coffee in town, either regular or espresso. Bellissimo!

BUCA GIOVANNI, 800 Greenwich Street, San Francisco. Telephone: (415) 776-7766. Hours: 5:30–11 Monday–Saturday. Cards: MC, V. Reservations advised. Wine and beer. Street parking.

San Francisco: Moscone Center Area
CADILLAC BAR
Mexican/Seafood $$

Most new "hot spots" have a tendency to turn cold when the novelty wears off. Not the Cadillac Bar, however. Even though some potential customers are turned off by the wall-to-wall sea of yuppies, the Cadillac's popularity seems to grow each year. The restaurant's only a half block from Moscone, but it is locals, not conventioneers, that stand six deep at the bar during the long, wet wait for lunch or dinner. The Cadillac is patterned after a similar establishment in Nuevo Laredo that has been whetting the thirsts of Texans since 1926. It's big, barnlike, barren of "decor," and so noisy that it's a perfect candidate for a lunch date with someone you're not speaking to. What, then, makes it so popular? The answer is simple in this town where people will suffer almost any indignity for good seafood: some of the freshest fish around, impeccably grilled over mesquite charcoal and served with a creamy, slightly piquant sauce whose formula is as securely guarded as were Pancho Villa's hideaways. A number of pescado choices appear on the printed menu, along with grilled meats, chicken, and milk-fed kid, but the best bet is always the catch of the day: salmon, sea bass, snapper, or whatever. If you're hungry for a taste of old Mexico, do share an aperitivo of quesadillas scented with cilantro, but be sure you're really hungry or a party of three or more because the *plato es muy grande.* There are several ways to get around the lunchtime wait too: Go early or late, or make up a party of eight and you'll get a reservation.

CADILLAC BAR, One Holland Court (off Howard west of Fourth Street), San Francisco. Telephone: (415) 543-8226. Hours: 11:30–11 Monday–Friday, 5–midnight Saturday. Cards: AE, CB, DC, MC, V. Reservations accepted only for parties of eight or more; no reservations Friday and Saturday nights. Full bar service. Parking at Fourth and Mission garage.

San Francisco: North Beach
CAFE AMERICAIN
California Cuisine $$

This bright café skillfully blends the looks of a proper grill (starchy white tablecloths, stark white walls, a big open kitchen) with the aura of a North Beach coffeehouse. And while old-time Italians might raise their eyebrows over carpaccio made from American buffalo loin, most North Beach residents find the Americain's California-style cooking and mesquite-grilled seafood a pleasant alternative to the neighborhood's heavy trattoria fare. Although chef Daniel Malzhan changes his menu daily, you will often find among the appetizers (in season) the delicious little Hog Island sweetwater oysters from Tomales Bay, served with a champagne or horseradish mignonette, and a salad composed of avant-garde produce—radicchio, arugula, frisée, escarole, and suchlike. Among the entrées, there's most always a pizza fresh from the oak-fired brick oven. One day you might find a filling of duck confit, sautéed red cabbage, roasted shallots, walnuts, fontina, and provolone. Another day, it might be pork sausage, roasted eggplant, tomatoes, mozzarella, and asiago. Grilled seafood is the restaurant's signature dish, but often baked fish or a shellfish ragout is offered as well. Veal, rabbit, and duck—in many guises—make frequent appearances on the menu, as does baby chicken: sometimes fried in a buttermilk batter and sometimes sautéed with oysters, ham, and leeks. In short, versatility and surprises are the hallmarks of this café. But you don't have to order a full meal to enjoy the Americain: There's a café section in front where you can drop in for coffee and pastry or a glass of wine and a snack any time from 7 am until midnight.

CAFE AMERICAIN, 317 Columbus Avenue, San Francisco. Telephone: (415) 981-8266. Lunch: 11:30–2:30 Monday–Friday. Dinner: 6–10 Sunday–Thursday, until 11 Friday–Saturday. Open for Continental breakfast or pastries 7 am–midnight daily. Cards: MC, V. Reservations advised. Wine and beer only. Street parking.

San Francisco: Mission District
CAFE GITANES
Tunisian   **$**

The facade brings to mind the distinctive blue French cigarette pack from which the restaurant takes its name. The cuisine is that of a former French colony, and, yes, most of the staff are French-born Tunisians who have never set foot in the home of their ancestors. But the Tunisian restaurants of Paris are not to be dismissed, and neither is Gitanes. To date, this is the only place in San Francisco where you can enjoy a couscous dinner for a reasonable price, plus you don't have to endure a surfeit of rich courses, rosewater-sprinkled palms, and stiff knees from sitting on the floor—all required at the city's high-priced Moroccan couscous restaurants. Brik, the flaky, deep-fried pastries that enclose an egg and/or tuna, are delicious and generous enough to split between two; try them on the combination plate with merguez, the homemade spicy Tunisian sausage that is a specialty of this restaurant. A pair of salads—mechouia and tunisienne—are offered and, of course, there is the couscous, steamed semolina "beads" served with vegetables, lamb, chicken, fish, or merguez. The desserts vary, and are more French than North African, but you can accompany your meal with a bottle of Tunisian wine. Breakfast (omelets and other egg dishes, on Saturday only) and lunch (European and Tunisian sandwiches) fill the daylight hours at this modest eatery, where the French language will serve you better than English—or Arabic.

CAFE GITANES, 3214 16th Street, San Francisco. Telephone: (415) 431-5838. Hours: 11–10 Monday–Friday, 10–10:30 Saturday. No cards. Reservations accepted. Beer and wine only. Street parking.

San Francisco: Richmond District
CAFE RIGGIO
Italian $$

John Riggio's chic trattoria has played to a full house practically every night since it opened some years back, and even a seat at the long bar is often difficult to grab. But the inevitable wait (no reservations) doesn't keep the crowds away, because Riggio offers some very good food at affordable prices, especially if you share courses, which seems to be encouraged here. A standout among the antipasti is a skillet with chunks of Sicilian caciocavallo sizzling in garlicky olive oil. The house salads are composed of crisp romaine garnished with anchovy fillets or antipasto, and a marinated squid salad is a meal in itself. The pastas are also recommended, especially the unusually plump tortellini with little bits of bacon mixed into a creamy, slightly pungent sauce. Veal—tender and white—is the café's specialty, and the selections range from scaloppine al Marsala and a very lemony piccata to saltimbocca. Good choices for dessert are an exceedingly rich chocolate mousse torte or cannoli, and you can depend on the latter to have a crispy shell—the house-made ricotta filling is stuffed to order. Limited offerings of California and Italian wines are moderately priced. Service here is excellent and unrushed—even when standees are awaiting their tables—and the setting is uncluttered and attractive. The chief adornment on the stark white walls that rise above wood-paneled wainscotings are gigantic blow-ups of recipes hand-printed in Italian.

CAFE RIGGIO, 4112 Geary Boulevard, San Francisco. Telephone: (415) 221-2114. Hours: 5–11 Monday–Saturday, 5–10:30 Sunday. Cards: MC, V. Reservations not accepted. Full bar service. Parking in French Hospital lot across the street.

Café Riggio

Specializing in Italian Cuisine

Antipasti

Chiocciole 4.30
(Escargots in Garlic Butter)

Formaggio all' Argintera 4.00
(Cheese Sauté)

Carciofi 2.95
(Fresh Marinated Artichoke Hearts, Bed of Spinach)

Minestrone: Cup 1.25 – Bowl 1.95
(Italian Vegetable Soup)

Antipasto Italiano 3.95
(Assorted Cold Appetizers)

Salads

Insalata della Casa 2.25
(Hearts of Romaine with Antipasto Garnish)

Insalata di Pomodoro con Cipolla 2.95
(Sliced Tomatoes and Onions Vinaigrette)

Insalata di Acciughe 3.35
(Hearts of Romaine with Anchovy Filets)

Insalata di Calamari Marinata 4.25
(Marinated Squid Salad)

Pastas

Fettucine all' Alfredo 6.75
(Fresh Noodles with Cream, Butter and Cheese)

Spaghetti al Pesto 6.50
(Spaghetti with Garlic and Sweet Basil)

Vermicelli con Sugo di Carne 5.95
(Thin Pasta with Meat Sauce)

Conchiglie con Sugo di Carne 5.75
(Pasta Shells with Meat and Tomato Sauce)

Tortellini alla Panna 6.75
(Stuffed Pasta with Cream, Butter, Cheese and Meat)

Cannelloni Imbottiti 7.50
(Baked Stuffed Pasta with Meat and Spinach)

Entrées

— Ask Your Waiter About Our Daily Specials —

Bistecca alla Pizzaiola 11.50
(N.Y. Strip Steak with a Tomato Sauce and Cheese)

Scaloppini di Vitello al Marsala 9.95
(Sliced Veal Sautéed with Marsala Wine and Mushrooms)

Vitello alla Parmigiana 8.75
(Veal Cutlet Topped with Tomato Sauce and Cheese)

Scaloppini di Vitello Piccata 9.75
(Sliced Veal Sautéed with Lemon, Wine and Capers)

Saltimbocca alla Romana 10.25
(Escalopes of Veal Sautéed with Prosciutto Ham and Cheese)

Costolette alla Milanese 8.75
(Milanese Veal Cutlet)

Petti di Pollo al Marsala 7.75
(Breast of Chicken with Marsala Sauce and Mushrooms)

Calamari alla Cacciatora 7.75
(Squid with Tomato Vegetable Sauce)

Calamari Fritti 7.75
(Fried Squid with Lemon, Garlic and Butter)

Filetto di Petrale, Meunière 8.75
(Filet of Sole with Lemon Butter Sauce)

Gamberi con Aglio e Burro 12.25
(Prawns with Garlic, Butter and Lemon)

Vongole alla Fiorentina 8.95
(Steamed Clams, Tomato, Sweet Basil and Garlic)

Side of Vegetables 1.75

CAFFE SPORT & TRATTORIA
Italian (Sicilian) $$

There is scarcely an inch of wall or table space that is not ornately carved or covered with collages of old posters or assemblages of seashells, statuary, or cookware in this haven of Sicilian seafood. Caffé Sport is literally a floor-to-ceiling collection of memorabilia, where bottles, lanterns, Italian coppa, and cheeses hang from the beams to create a perfect rendition of a down-home Sicilian trattoria struck by high kitsch. The kitchen, small by most restaurant standards, and quite plain in comparison to the dining room, is the origin of a long list of southern Italian seafood and pasta creations. Calamari is honorably treated as a salad, fried, or covered with a rich tomato sauce. Scampi are served on a huge plate in a wine-garlic-caper sauce, while a magnificent whole lobster (sufficient for two) is bathed with lemon, garlic, and wine. Combination plates bring a mountain of calamari, prawns, and clams or scallops, and the simply prepared petrale sole is a perfect partner to a dish of pasta con pesto. Clams, sardines, a seafood combination, or eggplant are additional pasta offerings. There are three dinner seatings, at 6:30, 8:30, and 10:30 pm. Come with a party of four or more; reservations are not accepted for smaller groups, and the place is as packed with people as it is with artifacts. Portions are very large (no understatement here), and priced rather high, so be prepared for a good-size tab. Caffé Sport does a turnaround midday though, when its lunch proves one of the best bargains in North Beach. The menu is limited, but two people can split a platter of fried calamari and one of pasta con pesto, each have a glass of wine, and walk out for no more than $15.

CAFFE SPORT & TRATTORIA, 574 Green Street, San Francisco. Telephone: (415) 981-1251 Lunch:

noon–2 pm Tuesday–Saturday. Dinner: 6:30 pm–11 pm
(three seatings) Tuesday–Saturday. No cards. Reservations accepted for parties of four or more. Beer and wine
only. Street parking.

San Francisco: Civic Center
CALIFORNIA CULINARY ACADEMY
French   **$$**

Culinary theater at its best is found at the restaurant of
this noted training school for professional chefs. The
restaurant is actually located in a restored turn-of-the-
century theater where light filters down from skylights
in the high vaulted ceiling. The proscenium arch,
flanked by massive Corinthian columns, frames a bilevel
glassed-in stage that offers a continuous show: The
lower level is a working kitchen for the students; above
is a demonstration classroom. In addition, large windows
on one side of the dining area open into more kitchens.
On the main floor, three-course prix-fixe lunches and
dinners are served with four choices of appetizer,
entrée, and dessert that change weekly; on the horseshoe-
shaped balcony above, à la carte lunches are served at
two tiers of tables—everyone has a view of the stage.
The cooking is in the classic French tradition espoused
by the academy and its European-trained instructors.
But the most dramatic feast occurs on Thursday and
Friday nights and Friday noon when a grand buffet is
presented. The huge tables are laden with dozens of
elaborately garnished terrines, pâtés, galantines, salads,
and roasts. A hot entrée is served at table before a visit
to a second buffet of luscious desserts, pastries, fruits,
and cheeses. The student servers might not be experi-
enced, but they are eager to please: Their performances
are being graded by the professional maître d's who
supervise the dining room.

CALIFORNIA CULINARY ACADEMY, 625 Polk Street, San Francisco. Telephone: (415) 771-3500. Main dining room hours: seatings at noon, 12:30, 6, 6:45, and 7:30 Monday–Friday. Balcony hours: noon to 1 Monday–Friday. Cards: AE, MC, V. Reservations required in main dining room; not accepted in balcony. Wine only. Valet parking at night. Private banquet facilities: up to 300.

San Francisco: Richmond District
CAMBODIA HOUSE
Cambodian $

In 1985 after several years in San Francisco working in restaurants at every level from busboy to sous chef, personable Sonn Pok opened this handsomely decorated place offering traditional Cambodian fare. For any lover of a pungent fish flavor, one of the defining traits of this cuisine, there is prahok katih, a dish of ground pork with coconut milk and anchovy sauce. A more subtle preparation is an appetizer called thei phart, fried slivers of sundried fish tossed with garlic, sugar, and salt, and served with fresh lettuce and grapefruit. "In Cambodia, everyone loves barbecued chicken; the best comes from the area surrounding the famous Angkor Wat," explains Pok. His San Francisco version is a respectable presentation of this classic dish: first marinated in spices, the chicken is then grilled until wonderfully moist on the inside and delightfully charcoally on the outside. Pickled vegetables and a brilliant orange chili sauce are served alongside. Also outstanding is pompano expertly deep-fried and served with a garlic, chili, and onion sauce; a blend of ground pork, bay shrimp, and smoky-flavored eggplant, lightly seasoned with green chili and scallions; a simple vegetable dish of watercress with brown bean; and chicken in a red curry sauce. "That curry is really our national dish," says Pok. "It is eaten all over Cambodia." Visible here too is China's influence on the dining traditions of Cambodia, with certain noodle and stir-fry dishes obvious adaptations of Chinese plates. "In my country, as in those of many of our neighbors, Chinese people have always been the restaurateurs," observes Pok. "You didn't go out for real Khmer food in Pnomh Penh; you ate it in someone's home." In San Francisco, fortunately "home" can mean the Cambodia House.

CAMBODIA HOUSE, 5625 Geary Boulevard (near 20th), San Francisco. Telephone: (415) 668-5888. Hours: 11–10 daily. Cards: MC, V. Reservations advised. Beer and wine only. Street parking.

San Francisco: Downtown
CAMPTON PLACE
New American   **$$$**

Chef Bradley Ogden has probably done as much as anyone in this country to elevate American cooking to its present level of respect. But his style is not exactly all-American steak and apple pie, although he does do those things too, with a creative finesse that marks all his dishes. Only American ingredients are allowed in the kitchen—even cheeses like provolone, brie, and parmesan are domestic—and he buys the best from all over the country: Kansas City beef, Missouri cured ham, eastern scallops. He also relies heavily on foods indigenous to this continent: Corn is used in a creamy soup and in blue corn cakes topped with poached spiny lobster for an appetizer. Cranberries are combined with apples for a relish that accompanies smoked duck breast. Grated zucchini is layered with grits and custard for an airy timbale that's served with grilled veal chops with morels. Sweet potatoes are cut into shoestrings to serve as a nest for grilled quail with bacon. Though apples are not native to America, Ogden uses them to garnish a number of dishes—such as the outstanding pheasant sausage and grilled calf's liver that often appear on the lunch menu. Pecans play a big role in desserts that would astound a typical down-home cook, such as a soufflélike chocolate-pecan cake, and old-time rhubarb becomes quite sophisticated combined with strawberries in a luscious pastry crisp. Campton Place is about the only top restaurant in San Francisco to serve breakfast, and Ogden's imaginative touch is felt here, too, in items like pecan waffles, apple-cheese pancakes, and Missouri-cured ham with poached eggs and orange hollandaise. But whatever time of day you dine at Campton Place, you'll find the atmosphere elegant and understated. The walls are upholstered in peach fabric, velvet-covered banquettes line one wall (with seats too close for privacy), and the tables are set with Wedgwood china, which might well be the only imported thing in the place.

CAMPTON PLACE, 340 Stockton Street, San Francisco. Telephone: (415) 781-5555 or (800) 647-4007. Breakfast: 7–11 Monday–Friday, 8–11 Saturday, 8–10 Sunday. Brunch: 10–2:30 Sunday. Lunch: 11:30–2:30 Monday–Saturday. Dinner: 6–10 daily. Cards: AE, CB, DC, MC, V. Reservations required. Full bar service. Valet parking.

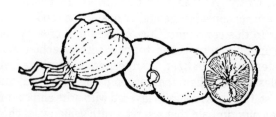

San Francisco: Jackson Square
CIAO
Italian (Northern) $$

It's difficult to take a restaurant seriously when it has as its main decorative features a magazine rack of Italian publications, a wall-mounted motor scooter, an over-abundance of mirrored walls and brass railings, a cold case of food to rival a good delicatessen, and all of the fresh house pasta, in a rainbow of colors, on display. Add a crowd of fashion trend-setters to the dining room, and you begin to wonder whether Ciao is a restaurant or a movie set. But there is little worry over superficiality once you've tried the dishes that make up the unconventional menu: no listing of 14 veal dishes, or the usual round of commonplace pastas. For a first course, there is carpaccio, paper-thin slices of raw beef dressed with a mustard sauce; grilled marinated radicchio; buffalo mozzarella on tomato slices, graced with a basil leaf; or, one evening on the specials board, porcini mushrooms and wedges of parmesan splashed with olive oil. The pastas include fettuccine, with everything from a simple fresh tomato and basil sauce to an elaborate seafood mixture of shrimp, clams, squid, scallops; pappardelle (a wide noodle) dressed in a superb sauce of porcini and cream or one of walnuts and cream; and linguine, prepared alla carbonara or alle vongole. Meat and fish entrées are simply prepared: charcoal-grilled pork or lamb chops; baby veal; Milanese-style sausages; brochettes of quail; a mixed grill of pork sausage, veal, chicken, and quail. Bollito misto, one of the house specialties, is three boiled meats—often tongue, brisket, and chicken breast—served with three sauces, including a very good olive oil, parsley, and caper one. Save room for dessert; the fruit ices—lemon, papaya, orange, banana, melon—are delicious. There may be a lot of "fashion" here, but there is also considerable substance—and imagination.

CIAO, 230 Jackson Street, San Francisco. Telephone: (415) 982-9500. Hours: 11–midnight Monday–Saturday, 4–midnight Sunday. Cards: AE, MC, V. Reservations advised. Full bar. Street parking or in nearby garage; free valet parking at MacArthur Park, around the corner.

San Francisco: Mission District
CUBA RESTAURANT
Cuban and Spanish $–$$

The Cuba bills itself as a Cuban and Spanish restaurant, and owners George and Ana Portugal deliver. They offer such traditional Cuban specialties as boliche machada, a masterfully seasoned and simmered "pot roast" of costly beef rib eye. Then, for those dreaming of the far side of the Atlantic, there is a full-blown paella (a dish that Cubans have, however, adopted for their own). Among the other Carib favorites is the sopa de los siete mares, a seafood soup-cum-stew that is a match for the most elaborate bouillabaisse; fork-tender slices of beef tongue with a robust tomato sauce; and slices of roast pork laced with garlic and served with boiled yucca. Those who treasure bacalao, the salted cod that is a mainstay of the Portuguese diet and popular in Italy, Spain, and Greece as well, should try the bacalao a la Viscaina, a large ramekin of pleasantly salty cod chunks in a rich mixture of tomatoes, potatoes, and onions. Fluffy white rice and rich, flavorful black beans accompany most of the dishes. This longtime Mission District institution usually has a subdued salsa beat going in the background, and a friendly, lively crowd in attendance.

CUBA RESTAURANT, 2886 16th Street (near South Van Ness), San Francisco. Telephone: (415) 864-9871. Hours: noon–10 daily. Cards: AE, DC, MC, V. Beer and wine only. Street parking.

San Francisco: North Beach
DES ALPES
Basque $

These five-course, family-style dinners might well be the best bargain in town, and the wood-paneled dining room with its tables topped with checkered oilcloth is a very pleasant setting. A tureen of soup and lots of crunchy bread start the meal. Next comes an outstanding vinaigrette of string beans with chopped onions and hard-cooked eggs. Then, in the Basque tradition, *two* entrées follow in turn, the second served with fried potatoes and a green salad. Ice cream and coffee top off the meal. The entrées change nightly on a preset schedule: Tuesday brings a choice of sweetbreads or rock cod, plus roast beef; Wednesday, beef tongue with mushrooms or veal stew, plus roast lamb or roast pork; Thursday, oxtail stew, plus chicken with rice or roast lamb; Friday, fish (such as trout) or steamed clams with rice, plus strips of beef fillet; Saturday, lamb stew or fillet of sole, plus roast beef; Sunday, sweetbreads plus chicken or roast beef. The quantity would keep any trencherman happy, the quality is above average, and the price is eminently affordable: $8.50 to $9.00.

DES ALPES, 732 Broadway, San Francisco. Telephone: (415) 391-4249. Hours: 5:30–10 Tuesday–Sunday. Cards: MC, V. Reservations advised on weekends. Full bar service. Parking difficult.

San Francisco: Downtown
DONATELLO
Northern Italian $$$

Donatello has become so famous that the small luxury hotel in which it's located has changed its name from the Pacific Plaza to The Donatello. The restaurant's two dining rooms are elegant and intimate, all done up with mirrors, marble, and exquisite tapestries. The food, which many consider the city's best Italian fare, focuses on the Emilia-Romagna region of Italy, which is known for the cheeses and hams of Parma and the pastas of Bologna. Donatello makes and serves some of the more familiar Bolognese pastas, such as tortellini and tagliatelle, along with esoteric varieties like garganelli (a ridged, tubular noodle that's sauced here with tomatoes, prosciutto, and peas). Chef Michael Hart looks north to Piedmont, however, for the inspiration of his delicate pâté of liver and white truffles. Donatello's à la carte menu emphasizes veal, along with some unusual entrées like venison with porcini mushrooms and broiled rabbit with chestnuts and brandy. But there's also a daily prix-fixe menu that includes Italian wines especially chosen to complement the food. A typical dinner (if there is such a thing here) might start with risotto drenched with butter and parmesan, and a fish course of sea bass sautéed with lemon and garlic, accompanied with an Italian Riesling; a main course of medallions of veal with a thyme-infused lemon sauce, paired with a hearty Barbera d'Alba; and, for dessert, white chocolate mousse with fresh raspberries, and sparkling Asti Spumante.

DONATELLO, 501 Post Street, San Francisco. Telephone: (415) 441-7182. Hours: 11:30–2:30, 6–10:30 daily. Cards: AE, CB, DC, MC, V. Reservations advised. Full bar service. Valet parking. Private banquet facilities: 20–50.

San Francisco: Lower Pacific Heights
THE ELITE CAFE
American (Creole)   **$$**

This classy café opened in 1981, before the country
went crazy over New Orleans cookery. A long bar/
counter extends down one side of the narrow room,
partitioned booths are lined up on the other side, and
tables topped with white napery are crammed in between.
The place, which was built in the 1920s, has an art deco
look with blond wood paneling and lighting fixtures of
the period; revolving fans are hung from the high ceiling.
The fans and the lack of frills are reminiscent of
Galatoire's in New Orleans, as is the no-reservations
policy. But there's a bar of freshly shucked Gulf oysters
to keep you happy while you wait, along with some
typical Southern drinks such as plantation milk punch
and sazerac (a mixture of bourbon and Pernod). The
menu is studded with classic Creole dishes which
include gumbo and shrimp remoulade among the starters
and a number of redfish dishes in which the method and
seasonings come smack out of Louisiana, even though
local rock fish has been substituted for the Gulf fish.
The Elite introduced to San Francisco blackened redfish, in which the fillets are quickly sizzled in butter
and spices at extremely high temperatures. Other Gulf
seafood is flown in, however, such as crawfish, speckled
trout, and stone crab claws. Although seafood is emphasized here, some other down-home dishes are offered,
such as roast pork loin with sweet potatoes and cornbread
dressing. And desserts are right out of the bayous: Try
the bread pudding with bourbon sauce or the sinfully
rich chocolate-pecan pie. Brunch is a big occasion in
New Orleans and so it is at the Elite, especially on a
clear morning when the sun streams in from the large
skylight. For a modest price, the complete brunch
consists of a plate of fresh fruit, a marvelous hot and
crumbly cornbread with honey, and a choice of eight

Creole entrées. One of these is grits and grillades, a Louisiana breakfast staple composed of strips of veal in a hot Creole sauce with buttered grits on the side. A number of poached egg dishes with New Orleans origins are also served, like eggs Sardou (with creamed spinach, artichokes, and hollandaise), eggs Hussarde (with Canadian bacon and two sauces: marchand du vin and béarnaise), and even the ubiquitous eggs Benedict, which supposedly came from New Orleans, too.

THE ELITE CAFE, 2049 Fillmore at California, San Francisco. Telephone: (415) 346-8668. Dinner: 5–11 Monday–Saturday, 5–10 Sunday. Sunday brunch: 10–3. Cards: AE, MC, V. Reservations not accepted. Full bar service. Street parking.

San Francisco: Richmond District
EL SOMBRERO
Mexican $

Aficionados of Mexican food can be certain of three things at El Sombrero: They will have to wait for a table during normal dinner hours; the food will be of uncompromising quality and freshness; and the portions will be gargantuan. Even though Mexico was San Francisco's motherland, consistently good Mexican restaurants are difficult to find here. But for four decades El Sombrero has maintained its standards, as its peers rise and fall (including El Sombrero's own branch at the Cannery). Rival restaurateurs have tried to copy El Sombrero's superb green chili sauce, but none can duplicate it. Do try the enchiladas verdes with this sauce, topped with sour cream. The chicken and avocado tostada is spectacular here, looking as beautiful as it tastes. Tacos burst with mounds of shredded chicken or beef. And even the tortillas are freshly made on the premises. The dining room has a hacienda look with whitewashed walls, heavy wooden furniture, wrought-iron detailing, and a small bar that almost never has enough stools for the waiting throng. But the margueritas make even the wait enjoyable.

EL SOMBRERO, 5800 Geary, San Francisco. Telephone: (415) 221-2382. Hours: 11:45–10 Tuesday–Saturday. No cards. Reservations not accepted. Full bar service. Street parking.

San Francisco: Mission District
EL TAZUMAL
Salvadorean $

When you open the menu at El Tazumal, your loyalties are immediately divided. On the left side are the Salvadorean specialties, while the right lists the Mexican offerings. Stick with the former, because the Salvadorean food is exceptional and distinct from most Latin American fare you'll encounter. The portions are large here, so control your consumption of the delicious tortilla chips and salsa that automatically arrive when you are seated. The carne deschilichada, a combination of shredded meat, peppers, tomato, and ribbons of egg; beef tongue in a sauce of wine, tomato, peppers, garlic, and spices; lomo de puerco asado, moist, flavorful pieces of pork smothered with fried potatoes and ringed with fried banana slices; lomo saltado, strips of beef, sweet pepper, and fried potato; and the deep-fried red snapper are all to be recommended. Most entrées are accompanied with fluffy, lightly seasoned rice and cheese-topped refried beans. The dining area is comfortable, the brown-and-white tablecloths and decorative plants giving the place more polish than most of the restaurants in the neighborhood. Service is friendly and prompt, but never so quick that care in the kitchen is compromised, and when you order an espresso at meal's end, don't worry about being rushed. Just relax and enjoy. Owner Rigo Pacheco has also solved the dining problems of those with no time to spare, with the opening next door of a fast-food place offering such items as tacos, pupusas, and burritos.

EL TAZUMAL, 3522 20th Street (between Mission and Valencia streets), San Francisco. Telephone: (415) 550-0935. Hours: 10 am–midnight daily. Cards: AE, MC, V. Reservations accepted. Beer and wine only. Street parking.

San Francisco: West Portal
EL TOREADOR
Mexican **$**

For nearly three decades this little café has featured the regional cooking of Jalisco, home of the original owners. Esperanza and Laurence Mahan now own the place and have added a lot of pizzazz—piñatas, bright paper flowers, posters, and whatnot—while wisely retaining the time-tested recipes such as soup scented with cilantro and bittersweet-chocolate molé seasoned with seven spices. Among the Jaliscan specialties are gorditas (plump tortillas topped with chorizo or chicken, green sauce, sour cream, guacamole, and chopped onions), carne asada de Jalisco (steak cooked in ranchera

sauce topped with green sauce and sour cream), chalupas de Chapala (four small tortillas with shredded cheese, green tomatillo sauce, sour cream, and guacamole), and machaca Guadalajara (shredded marinated beef scrambled with eggs.) Dinners are priced about $6 for soup, entrée, refried beans, Spanish rice, salad, and freshly made tortillas. A dozen typical combination plates are also offered, as well as single selections; these include another Jaliscan dish: empalmada, which might be described as a tortilla sandwich filled with chopped ham and melted cheese. El Toreador's loyal patronage is attested by the lines waiting to get in during peak hours and scores of love notes from satisfied customers pinned to the walls.

EL TOREADOR, 50 West Portal Avenue, San Francisco. Telephone: (415) 753-9613. Lunch: 11:30–2:30 Tuesday–Friday. Dinner: 4–9 Tuesday–Sunday, until 9:30 Friday and Saturday. Cards: AE, CB, DC, MC, V. Reservations accepted only for parties of six or more. Wine and beer only. Street parking or in nearby city lot.

San Francisco: North Beach
ERNIE'S
French $$$

Ernie's offers the best of two worlds: the opulent aura of turn-of-the-century San Francisco and the contemporary cooking of a classically trained French chef who is not afraid to break the bonds of tradition. Ernie's looks like a Barbary Coast bordello: mahogany paneling, red-silk-brocade wall coverings, gigantic gilt-edged mirrors, tables set with ornate silver and elegant crystal. But the food, which long suffered from being overly heavy and traditional, has entered the age of the 1980s. This trend was begun by chef Jacky Robert, who started introducing lighter, more innovative dishes here in the late 1970s.

But in 1983, when Robert left for Amelio's, the transition was completed by his successor, Bruno Tison, who had worked in France with such culinary legends as Roger Vergé, Michel Guérard, and Alain Chapel. Tison credits these mentors for inspiring some of his dishes, such as a Chapel-type hors d'oeuvre of preserved black turnips topped with foie gras and an authoritative port wine sauce. But he claims as his own other dishes like an entrée that assembles sliced loin of lamb with breast of rabbit, garnished with eggplant and roasted garlic cloves. These unusual combinations are Tison's signature. Take, for example, a lovely salad that composes chilled slices of Maine lobster and squab with black truffles and a vinaigrette spiked with Dijon mustard and a bouquet of green herbs. Original touches are found, too, in the desserts, where a dash of acacia honey flavors the sauce of a frothy lime soufflé. One wonders what Ernie's founders would think about all of this. The place started as a humble Italian trattoria, but was raised to its present plateau by Victor and Roland Gotti, whose family has owned the restaurant since 1934.

ERNIE'S, 847 Montgomery, San Francisco. Telephone: (415) 397-5969. Hours: 6:30–10:30 daily. Cards: AE, CB, DC, MC, V. Reservations required. Full bar service. Valet parking. Private banquet facilities: 20–60.

San Francisco: Financial District
565 CLAY
California Cuisine $$

From Zen priest to financial-district restaurateur sounds like a radical career change. But for David Cohn, this was a natural transition. As manager of the Zen Center's businesses, he had been in charge of Green Gulch Farms, the Tassajara Bakery, and Greens at Fort Mason. But he felt a need to try something on his own and, in 1985, bought a restaurant across from the Transamerica Pyramid at 565 Clay, Cohn realized that the vegetarian formula of Greens would not work with a business-lunch clientele, but he does incorporate the Zen commitment to fresh, natural ingredients into popular dishes such as jambalaya and grilled meats and seafood. Portions are generous, attractively presented, and accompanied with pommes frites or seasonal vegetables. Cohn personally selects his produce each day, much of it from organic farmers. The bread is from Tassajara and only range-fed chickens are used. In the latter department, a spectacular creation is the salad of smoked chicken and grapefruit segments garnished with feta cheese, black olives, *peeled* tomatoes, and fresh fruits. An elegant starter here is the creamy saffron-scented mussel chowder and there's a grand selection of pastries to top off your meal. Changing exhibits of contemporary paintings from Paule Anglim's gallery brighten the otherwise stark walls of the bar, dining room, and the private banquet rooms. Cohn is particularly proud of his banquet service where everything is cooked to order. No steam-table rubber chicken here.

565 CLAY, 565 Clay, San Francisco. Telephone: (415) 434-2345. Hours: 11:30–3, 5–9 Monday–Friday. Cards: AE, CB, DC, MC, V. Full bar service. Reservations advised. Parking in nearby lots; ample street parking at night. Private banquet facilities: 10–100.

San Francisco: Downtown
FLEUR DE LYS
French   **$$$**

The biggest culinary news of 1986 was Hubert Keller's move from Sutter 500 to become a chef and co-owner at Fleur de Lys. Keller, who has cooked at a number of three-star restaurants in France, was brought to San Francisco by Roger Vergé to open Sutter 500 in 1982. Despite changes in ownership and problems in management, Keller stayed on and gained a loyal following for his striking nouvelle cuisine. Now, in the romantic ambience of Fleur de Lys, he has found a suitable setting to showcase his cooking. The dining room is tented with hundreds of yards of red and gold paisley fabric that cascades down to frame mirrored panels. Service is under the watchful eye of partner Maurice Rouas, who has operated the restaurant for many years. Keller's menu, with a debut date of September, 1986, incorporates a few of his signature dishes from Sutter 500: a delicate soup of mussels and escargots cooked in white wine with fresh basil; and spinach-wrapped medallions of Norwegian salmon roasted with lobster and leeks. Desserts are served on large plates that contain not one, but a trio of goodies. Most of the dishes, however, were developed especially by Keller for Fleur de Lys.

FLEUR DE LYS, 777 Sutter Street, San Francisco. Telephone: (415) 673-7779. Hours: 6–10:30 Monday–Saturday. Cards: AE, CB, DC, MC, V. Reservations advised. Full bar service. Valet parking. Private banquet facilities: up to 20.

San Francisco: Jackson Square Area
FOG CITY DINER
American $$

Hark *the* restaurant success story of the mid-1980s. Fog City Diner opened to a grand fanfare of publicity in 1985 and before anyone could blow a fog horn, the wait for a weekend table was six weeks. But the reason for this instant popularity was not just the cutesy name or the media blitz. Fog City is a terrific place with very good food and the appealing concept of an unstructured menu. An assortment of "small plates" is offered: steamed clams, baked buffalo mozzarella, quesadilla, grilled eggplant with ginger-watercress vinaigrette, crab-cakes, garlic custard, and the like. It's great fun to taste and nibble and share, without ordering a full dinner. But for those who prefer more traditional ordering, "large plates" are listed with full entrées ranging from grilled sausages and polenta to dry-aged New York steak. Among the breads, don't miss the jalapeño corn muffins. The hot meaty black bean chili is a sure winner, too. Fog City was designed to emulate a luxurious railroad dining car, with dark wooden paneling, brass fittings around the huge windows, and ultracomfortable booths lining both sides of the long, narrow room.

FOG CITY DINER, 1300 Battery, San Francisco. Telephone: (415) 982-2000. Hours: 11:30–11 Sunday–Thursday, 11:30–midnight Friday–Saturday. Cards: MC, V. Reservations advised. Full bar service. Street parking or at nearby lots.

San Francisco: Chinatown
FORTUNE RESTAURANT
Chinese (Chao Chow) $

Fortune Restaurant owner Jack Lai is particularly enthusiastic and knowledgeable about Chao Chow food, the highly respected cuisine of south coastal China. Though he hails from Bangkok, his roots are in the city of Swatow (Shantou, in Mandarin), about 180 miles north of Canton, and it is his ancestors' culinary traditions that he is carrying on at his small Chinatown restaurant. Two dishes should not be missed here, for they are the cuisine's trademarks: braised duck served with a garlic-vinegar sauce, and oyster cake, a crispy circular egg "omelet" studded with oysters and Chinese chives and accompanied with two sauces, both Thai in origin: a fiery siracha chili blend and a mild fish sauce. Fortune's chicken foot soup, a flavorful, deep-colored broth loaded with Chinese red dates and an unspecified array of herbs, is precisely the type of complexly seasoned preparation for which the Chao Chows (or Chiu Chows, in Cantonese) are famed, as is a clay pot of lamb shoulder chunks in a rich braising liquid of aromatic spices. Naturally enough, seafood makes up an important part of this coastal cuisine, and the pomfret, a spiny, round flat fish related to the pompano, is one of its primary menu entries. Lai serves it deep fried with a brown bean sauce or a shower of golden garlic. His prawn balls, another specialty, are works of art: finely minced prawns, crab, pork, and water chestnuts are mixed with spices, formed into walnut-size rounds, wrapped in a bean-curd sheet, individually tied, and then deep fried. For a vegetable dish, try the kangkong (water spinach) in a sauce of tiny preserved brown beans and a generous measure of garlic, or with tiny flakes of salted fish. In addition, there are satays, stir-fries of fresh conch or geoduck clam, the classic Chao Chow rice soup called congee, bean thread noodles with seafood, and more. The critical thing to remember when dining at this temple of Chao Chow food is to stay with the regional dishes the staff does best.

FORTUNE RESTAURANT, 675 Broadway, San Francisco. Telephone: (415) 421-8130. Hours: 11–11 Thursday–Tuesday. Cards: MC, V. Reservations accepted. Wine and beer only. Street parking.

San Francisco: Nob Hill
FOURNOU'S OVENS
Continental $$$

Fournou's Ovens, in the stately Stanford Court hotel, is one restaurant by day and quite another by night. At lunchtime, tables are informally set in the light and airy "greenhouses" that flank the hotel's east side. Floor-to-ceiling windows open to a small flower-filled area, while cable cars clang along Powell Street below. The lunch menu offers a broad selection ranging from light snacks to pretty salads to filling entrées such as slices of herbed lamb. Dinners are also served here, but the choice seating is in the formal three-level dining room that focuses dramatically on the giant ovens where meats are roasted on the open hearths. Some guests prefer to sit above and gaze down upon the ovens, while others prefer a hearthside table. But for romance and privacy, request one of the semi-enclosed alcoves on the lowest tier. The dinner menu features richly sauced classics, with some variations on traditional themes. Escargots, for example, are served sans shells in a clay pot, sauced lightly with garlic and a hint of tarragon, and topped with puff pastry. Standouts among first courses are an ultra-rich crab bisque and a chived oyster ramekin in a creamy saffron sauce. A devoted cult swears that Fournou's Ovens serves the finest rack of lamb in San Francisco. For dessert concentrate on the pastries, especially the dacquoise, a mocha butter cream pie with hazelnuts. But whatever you eat and wherever you sit, you will probably agree that Fournou's Ovens provides two of the most beautiful dining settings in town.

FOURNOU'S OVENS, Stanford Court, 905 California Street, San Francisco. Telephone: (415) 989-1910. Lunch: 11:30–2:30 Monday–Friday, Dinner: 5:30–11 daily. Reservations required. Cards: AE, DC, MC, V. Full bar service. Valet parking at Stanford Court, if space available. Jackets required for men at dinner. Private banquet facilities: 12–16.

appetizers

Terrine of Duck Liver with Apple and Pistachio 5.75   Langoustine Bercy 7.50
Louisiana Style Prawn Rémoulade with Red Pepper-Corn Relish 6.75
House-made Fettucine or Spaghettini 7.95   Golden Caviar in New Potatoes 8.25
Marinated Season's Mushrooms with Olives and Shallots 5.75
Chived Oyster Ramekin in a Saffron Cream Sauce 6.75   Little Snails in Clay Pots 7.50
Smoked Scottish Salmon with Capers 7.95   Ginger Limed Bay Scallops 6.75
Fresh Hudson Valley Foie-Gras with Mousse of Artichoke 9.95

soup

Crab Bisque 5.50   Consommé Cultivateur 3.95
Chilled Cream of Watercress 4.25   Cream of Artichoke with Hazelnut 4.75

from the ovens

Roast Rack of Lamb, Choice of Aromatic Herb Sauce or Pesto Dressing 22.50
Roast Filet of Beef with Roasted-Garlic Butter 19.75   Roast Squab with Garden Peas 18.25
Roast Prime Rib of Beef au Jus with Fresh Horseradish Sauce 19.95
Roast Loin of Veal, Pan Gravy 19.50   Roast Solano County Chicken with Crushed Coriander 16.50

from the cuisine

Sautéed Scaloppine of Veal. Sauce Moutarde 20.50
Medallion of Veal. Sorrel Sauce 20.50   Broiled or Poached Pacific Salmon
Piccata of Veal al Limone 20.50   Sauce Hollandaise or Choron 17.50
New York Sirloin Steak au Poivre or Broiled 21.00   A Select Seasonal
Phyllo-Spinach Sweetbread,   Seafood Specialty 17.25
    Mustard-seed Sauce 16.25   Petrale Sole with Bay Shrimp Sauté
                                              Belle Meunière 16.95

salads

Belgian Endive and Watercress 4.95   Bibb Lettuce Vinaigrette 4.50   Mary Good's Salad 4.75
Garden Green Salad with Garlic Croutons 3.95   Hearts of Romaine Roquefort 4.25

San Francisco: Richmond District
GARDEN HOUSE
Vietnamese $

A pleasantly appointed dining room, quiet surroundings, fresh table linens, and a menu that explores the cuisine of Vietnam with imagination and finesse make the Garden House a good destination for an exotic dinner out. To begin there are feather-light crab beignets; the classic lemon-beef salad of raw beef in a harmonious mix of lemon, chilies, onion, and mint; rice-paper-wrapped shrimp and pork rolls with a rich brown-bean dipping sauce; or a shrimp-and-vegetable-filled Vietnamese "pancake." Soft-shell crab in a clay pot fragrant with spices was a special one evening, a superb treatment of this too-seldom-seen shellfish. There is flaming beef, a truly showy table presentation; grilled meats and shellfish served with coriander and mint sprigs, lettuce leaves, and rice paper sheets for diners to combine and eat out of hand; delicate complex curries; and wok-cooked dishes of ginger- or lemon-grass-scented pork, chicken, or beef. An occasional dish disappoints: the sour soup with shrimp is made too sweet by an overly generous addition of pineapple and sugar. But the minuses are few. Fried bananas and a tropical "soup" with coconut milk and lotus seeds are among the desserts, and there is rich Vietnamese-style drip coffee to finish. And if you need anything more, the always-attentive staff promptly acts on your request.

GARDEN HOUSE, 133 Clement Street, San Francisco. Telephone: (415) 221-3655. Hours: 5–10 Monday–Thursday, 10:30–10:30 Friday–Saturday, 10:30–10 Sunday. Cards: AE, MC, V. Reservations advised on weekends. Beer and wine only. Street parking.

San Francisco: Ghirardelli Square
GAYLORD
Indian

$$

Gaylord—a cousin of the famous Gaylords in New York, London, and Chicago—introduced tandoori cooking and the subtly seasoned dishes of northern India to San Francisco. Now a number of restaurants offer similar cuisine—including Gaylord's own branch at Embarcadero Center—but none has such an extensive menu as Gaylord's and only the Ghirardelli Square site offers a spectacular view of San Francisco Bay. The dining room blends East with West by mixing potted palms, Indian paintings and artifacts with tables set with pink cloths and sparkling silver. The food ranges from mild to spicy: Don't expect mouth-searing curries. Although tandoori fare (from a clay-lined oven) is the house forte, the kitchen produces a wide range of sautéed, deep-fried and sauced dishes as well. If the 66-item menu overwhelms you, consider the pre-planned feasts, each of which provides a sampling of seven to ten different dishes from $19.00 to $24.75. If you do order à la carte, plan to share the dishes around the table. You will want to include at least one dish from the tandoor oven, such as chicken marinated in yogurt or sauced with tomatoes and spices; plus one lamb entrée, perhaps the lamb pasanda in a mildly spiced cream sauce with nuts; and a seafood dish like spicy prawns cooked with green peppers and onions. Among the meatless choices you will find some Hindu classics: cubed paneer cheese stir fried with fresh peas, or cauliflower and potatoes sautéed with herbs and spices. And most certainly you will want to include some of the appetizers like the crisp samosa patties or pakora fritters; the tandoori-baked Indian breads; and some soothing side dishes like raita (yogurt with cucumbers). Gaylord also provides one of the city's most exotic brunches with a buffet of some ten dishes—another good way to sample the menu—accompanied with an array of chutneys and tandoori breads. And there's another plus at brunch here: In a corner three musicians play the sitar and other Indian instruments, while a kathak dancer charms the diners.

GAYLORD, Ghirardelli Square, San Francisco. Telephone: (415) 771-8822. Lunch: 11:45–1:45 Monday–Saturday. Dinner: 5–10:45 daily. Sunday brunch: 12–2:45. Cards: AE, CB, DC, MC, V. Reservations advised. Full bar service. One hour free parking in Ghirardelli Square garage. Private banquet facilities: 25–100.

San Francisco: Marina
GELCO'S
Yugoslavian $$

Pity the hordes of tourists who drive by Gelco's and never know that its unlikely motel locale shelters a superb restaurant with one of the best racks of lamb in town. The four-course dinners begin with a lavish antipasto tray laden with cold poached calamari, julienned celery root in a creamy sauce, marinated artichoke hearts, and more, accompanied with a light salad. For entrées you can't go wrong with any of the lamb choices, which range from a roast saddle en croûte to shish kebab to sautéed medallions. But why pass by the splendid rack, laved in a devastatingly rich sauce? Seafood is a good choice here also and always fresh. Owner Vlaho Buich knows how to buy fish. He is a Yugoslav-born cousin of the owners of Tadich Grill, and he worked there for eight years before buying Gelco's. Desserts are also included in the dinner price; one of the best is an ambrosial chocolate mousse cake sauced with crème de cacao. The atmosphere is romantic, with several dimly lit dining areas up the stairs from a small, convivial bar.

GELCO'S, 1450 Lombard Street, San Francisco. Telephone: (415) 928-1054. Hours: 5:30–11 Monday–Saturday. Cards: AE, CB, DC, MC, V. Reservations advised. Full bar service. Parking available at no charge in motel garage. Private banquet facilities: 32.

San Francisco: North Point
THE GOLDEN EAGLE
International   **$$**

The Golden Eagle has been flying around town in recent years. In 1982, it soared from its long-time home on Front and California streets to a new roost in Embarcadero Center. Prices, seating capacity, and the size of the menu soared as well, resulting in a sorry, short-lived move for owner-chef John Hadley. But now Hadley has found a new roost for the Golden Eagle in a tiny café on Hyde Street, just up the hill from Aquatic Park. The place is pretty and bright with windows offering a glimpse, over flower boxes, of the cable cars clanging by. The best news, however, is that the prices and the size of the menu have de-escalated. Here you will again find most of the dishes that made the original Eagle so popular: beef vinaigrette (cooked in white wine, shallots, capers, and dry mustard), fisherman's prawns (enhanced with horseradish, orange marmalade, wine, and lemon juice), and sheepherder's lamb, sauced with anchovies. Lunch offers simpler fare: salads, sandwiches, hamburgers, and fettuccine with sausage. Hadley—and the rest of us—hopes he has found a permanent home for the Golden Eagle.

GOLDEN EAGLE, 2721 Hyde, San Francisco. Telephone: (415) 771-5229. Hours: 11:30–10 Monday–Saturday. Cards: AE, MC, V. Reservations accepted. Wine and beer only. Street parking.

San Francisco: Marina District
GREENS AT FORT MASON
California Cuisine

$$

Operated by members of the San Francisco Zen Center, Greens occupies a beautifully refurbished one-time pier at Fort Mason, the nationally acclaimed arts complex that forms part of the Golden Gate National Recreation Area. The dining room of this excellent vegetarian restaurant looks out over the marina, the Golden Gate Bridge, and the Marin headlands—the kind of view that dazzles even the most jaded of San Franciscans. The regular menu includes brochettes of marinated bean curd, mushrooms, bell pepper, and seasonal vegetables grilled over mesquite charcoal; a spinach salad with Greek olives and feta cheese, dressed with a hot blend of sherry vinegar and olive oil; and a spicy Mexican black bean chili with crème fraîche. An equally tantalizing "daily specials" list regularly features a pasta (fresh noodles from Fettuccine Brothers), a pizza (one favorite

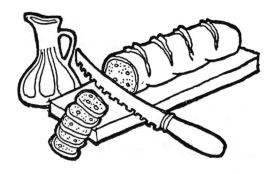

is topped with provolone, gorgonzola, fontina, and Parmesan, plus niçoise olives and herbs), a soup (the sorrel and spinach is superb), and two or three other items. The carefully chosen wine list will satisfy the most particular California wine connoisseur. Breads and desserts—a slice of irresistible poppy-seed cake or chocolate macadamia tart, for example—are from the famed Tassajara Bakery, an outlet of which is located at the restaurant's entrance; take-out cups of chili and of soup and prepared sandwiches can also be purchased at this counter.

GREENS AT FORT MASON, Building A, Fort Mason, San Francisco. Telephone: (415) 771-6222. Lunch: 11:30–2:30 Tuesday–Saturday. Bakery and take-out counter: 10:15–4:30 Tuesday–Saturday. A la carte dinner: 6–9 Tuesday–Thursday. Prix fixe dinner: 6–8:30 (seatings every 15 minutes) Friday–Saturday. Sunday brunch: 10–2. Cards: MC, V. Reservations advised for all meal hours; call between 9:30 and 4:30. Beer and wine only. Parking lot.

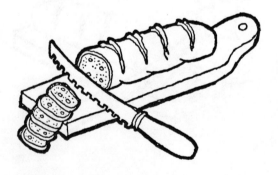

San Francisco: Richmond District
HAN IL KWAN
Korean $

Located on a quiet corner in the Richmond District, Han il Kwan stands in the midst of one of San Francisco's newest Asian neighborhoods—a "little Korea" boasting its own grocery stores, beauty parlors, doctors' offices, and videotape rental shops. Each dinner here begins with a delicate seaweed soup, surrounded by a feast of the famous prepared vegetable dishes that traditionally accompany every Korean meal. These include a hot, chili-laced fermented cabbage, a more soothing sesame-flavored spinach or bean sprout salad, and a pickled turnip kim chee that rivals the cabbage in explosiveness. Soon, the main course arrives, accompanied with a metal bowl of short-grain rice. Chief among the entrées are the celebrated bul kolgi and bul kalbi, the former sirloin strips and the latter short ribs marinated in a garlic, sesame, soy, and green onion mixture, and then broiled. The taste is flavorful but not fiery. Han il Kwan is also justifiably noted for its generous noodle dishes, tossed with broiled or stewed meats and served in a broth spiced to personal taste with chili paste. For seafood lovers, fried yellow croaker is a must, and somewhat more adventurous diners may select from two excellent entries: beef intestines fried with vegetables and chili or small octopuses prepared in the same manner. Service may be uneven in this modestly decorated family-run establishment, which is heavily patronized by local Koreans, but it is always friendly and, whenever the language gap allows, determinedly helpful.

HAN IL KWAN, 1802 Balboa Street, San Francisco. Telephone: (415) 752-4447. Hours: 11 am–11 pm daily. Cards: MC, V. Reservations accepted. Beer and wine only. Street parking.

San Francisco: Richmond District
HAPPY FAMILY
Northern Chinese $

Sixteenth-century Ming emperors imported cooks from the sea across from South Korea, to oversee the stoves of the Forbidden City. Their job was to create, in effect, the diet of China's high-level bureaucrats, or mandarins. Since then, the term "Shandong chef" has been a synonym for kitchen genius in China. San Franciscans are fortunate to have their own talented Shandong chef at work in the small, unpretentious Happy Family restaurant. What Chef Chong prepares is not the elaborate fare of the emperors, but rather that of the northern Chinese common man: shui jiao, wonderful "boiled dumplings" that arrive filled either with shrimp and chives, pork and cabbage, or beef; appetizer plates of delicately seasoned seaweed ribbons, cold wine-scented chicken; chili-and-sesame-doused slivers of pig's ear; or spicy jellyfish. Chong also produces a hearty wheat noodle that is served in soup, or generously topped with thick, ingredient-laden sauces, such as one of shrimp, pork, and sea cucumber in a matrix of sesame paste, ginger, and chili pepper. The high volume of sauce is not the dish's only distinguishing feature, however. Chong makes the noodles, popularly called "pulled noodles," *completely* by hand, transforming a mound of dough into long, uniform strands by twisting, stretching, and doubling actions, but never with the aid of a knife. Other fine Chong creations include dry-cooked green beans, sea cucumber with garlic sauce, braised whole fish, crispy chicken, and dry-fried squid.

HAPPY FAMILY, 3727 Geary Boulevard, San Francisco. Telephone: (415) 221-5095. Hours: 11:30–midnight daily. Cards: MC, V. Reservations accepted. Beer and wine only. Street parking.

San Francisco: Van Ness
HARRIS'
Steaks

$$–$$$

No one is more qualified than Ann Harris to run the city's foremost steakhouse. Daughter of a Texas cattleman, she married California beef magnate Jack Harris and later originated and supervised the stunning restaurant at his Harris Ranch near Coalingua—the first civilized wateringhole on the bleak stretch of highway between Los Angeles and San Francisco. Harris', which opened in San Francisco in 1984, is also no wild-and-woolly western steakhouse. The place is as genteel and gracious as Ann Harris herself, with handsome wood paneling, comfortable leather booths, ultrahigh, sky-lighted ceilings, and, in the rear, an open kitchen emitting the aroma of mesquite-grilled beef and seafood. Only the gigantic Barnaby Conrad murals of the Harris ranchlands remind you that this is the West. Service is impeccable, as are the appointments with fresh flowers and pale pink cloths gracing the tables. But it's the beef that really matters here and Harris' serves only dry-aged beef (with crusty, marbled sirloin strips hanging in the window to prove it). Pride of the kitchen is the Harris steak, a 15-ounce featherbone cut from the sirloin and grilled to perfection. A delicious alternative is the pan-sautéed pepper steak, a filet mignon sauced with cream and brandy. For calorie counters Harris' accompanies the steaks with steamed red potatoes and

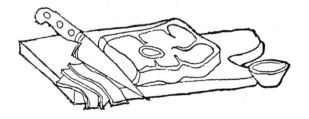

crispy fresh vegetables. But for traditionalists the usual steakhouse trimmings are available à la carte: fried or baked potatoes, creamed spinach, fried onion rings, and sautéed mushrooms. Be sure to save room for a selection from the cart of scrumptious pastries, baked in house.

HARRIS', 2100 Van Ness, San Francisco. Telephone: (415) 673-1888. Lunch: 11:30–2 Monday–Friday. Dinner: 5–11 Monday–Saturday, 4–10 Sunday. Cards: AE, DC, MC, V. Reservations advised. Full bar service. Valet parking. Private banquet facilities: 10–70.

Appetizers

Our Own Beef Paté 4.75

Blue Points-on the Half Shell 6.75	Fried Zucchini 3.75
Smoked Salmon 6.75	Fried Mushrooms 4.00
Sturgeon Caviar 22.00	Raw Vegetables 3.75
Country Ham with Seasonal Fresh Fruit 4.75	

Soups

Onion Soup 3.50   Soup of the Day 3.00   Cold Soup of the Day 3.00

Salads

Fresh Spinach 4.50   Limestone Lettuce 4.75   Mixed Greens 3.75
Crabmeat, Grapefruit & Avocado 5.75   Celery Root 4.75   Caesar (for two) 9.00
Sliced Tomato, Onion & Green Chile 4.50

Dine With Beef
Accompanied by Fresh Vegetables and Texas-Red Potatoes

The Harris Steak 17.95

Filet Mignon 17.50	Brains in Brown Butter 13.50
Petit Filet 14.50	Broiled Sweetbreads 13.50
Ribeye Steak 17.50	Ground Sirloin 12.50
Calf's Liver 13.95	T-Bone 18.95
Sliced Roast Filet, Bordelaise 15.50	

Roast Prime Rib
With our freshly grated Horseradish
Harris Cut 15.95   Executive Cut 18.95

Harris Selections

Our chef prepares a fresh catch from the sea each day

Domestic Lamb Chops 18.50   Grilled Breast of Chicken 13.50   Roast Duckling à la Boje 14.95
Mixed Grill : Petit Filet, Lamb Chop, Calf's Liver 18.50   Steak Tartare 13.50

San Francisco: Civic Center
HAYES STREET GRILL
Seafood

$$

This exceedingly popular restaurant has been a pace-setter in several respects. It was one of the first mesquite grills that now proliferate the state, and it was the first civilized dining place to open within walking distance of the Performing Arts Center. Hayes Street Grill started out as a small and plain storefront dining room with an open kitchen. Then, as the crowds kept increasing, it burst its seams into the adjoining space to make room for a bar and more tables. (A few years ago, the restaurant annexed a building on the alley behind it that's exclusively devoted to serving pizza.) A perfect start for dinner here is one of the appetizers listed on the blackboard such as smoked tuna or baby leeks in a vinaigrette perked with feta. Or you might prefer a salad, such as blood oranges and fennel. Then choose from one of the 8 to 15 seafood offerings chalked on the large blackboard. The day's catch might be snapper or rock cod, rex sole, sea bass, or salmon, even grouper or sturgeon. But whatever the fish, it will be extremely fresh and simply grilled, served with a choice of sauces. Béarnaise, beurre blanc, and tartar are always available, but the chef also concocts a few special sauces each night, varying from a blend of butter and dill to a spicy Szechwan peanut sauce. Often a seafood stew, such as cioppino, is offered as well. Entrées are accompanied with crisp homemade pommes frites, bearing no resemblance to the average restaurant's greasy french fries. Non-seafood choices are limited, but the boudin blanc—a superb, subtly seasoned sausage of chicken and pork—in itself would justify a visit here. House pastries are the grand finale at Hayes Street Grill. Intricate and extravagant, they provide the perfect contrast to the other simple fare.

51

HAYES STREET GRILL, 324 Hayes Street, San Francisco. Telephone: (415) 863-5545. Lunch: 11:30–3 Monday–Friday. Dinner: 5–10 Monday–Thursday, 5–11 Friday, 6–11 Saturday. Cards: MC, V. Reservations suggested. Wine and beer only. Street parking or in nearby lot.

San Francisco: Richmond District
HEUNG HEUNG
Cantonese $

Every now and then a modest restaurant opens that seizes the attention of hard-to-please diners. That's what happened in 1985 when the Yang family opened Heung Heung, far out in the Richmond. Word spread quickly that a first-rate Cantonese chef was turning out an array of tantalizing dishes. Among them is an extraordinary teppan creation in which a mixture of pork and shrimp is wedged between eggplant slices and then the "sandwiches" are doused with a marvelous fermented bean curd sauce; a fragrant claypot of chicken, bean curd, cabbage, and salted fish and another one of fresh oysters and roast pork; a taro root basket piled high with scallops, squid, shrimp, and vegetables; and such delicacies as duck webs in the style of your choice and cubes of blood stir-fried with garlic chives. These particular dishes only appear on the Chinese language menu, which lists some 50 specialties, but the staff will help you uncover the secrets. There are banquets for from four to ten persons, with each menu carefully chosen and very reasonably priced. The seafood dinner features whole fish from the tank, clams with black bean sauce, lobster with ginger and onion, double mushrooms with braised sea cucumber, and three more dishes, all for what a single diner would pay at many a French restaurant. Heung Heung is also renowned for its housemade noodles and won ton skins, and the place is packed at midday with folks working their way through great bowls of broth loaded with plump dumplings and firm fresh mein.

HEUNG HEUNG, 3608–3610 Balboa Street (near 38th Avenue), San Francisco. Telephone: (415) 221-9188. Hours: 11–9 daily. Cards: MC, V. Beer and wine only. Street parking.

San Francisco: Golden Gate Park
HOG HEAVEN
American (Southern) $–$$

Some like it hot, but the folk down in Memphis prefer their barbecue sauce mild, according to Hog Heaven's owner Andrea Martin, who is trying to re-create the tastes she remembers from her childhood in Memphis. Her meats—pork shoulder, sausage, chicken, pork and beef ribs—are even smoked over mesquite and hickory coals in a replica of the brick oven at Leonard's, one of Memphis's best barbecue restaurants. As promised, the sauce is very mild, although a hotter version is available. But the fixin's are superb, especially the cornbread and the crock of beans that accompany the barbecue, and the à la carte offering of thinly sliced french-fried onion rings. Recently other dishes from the deep South have been added to the menu, such as Creole seafood and Cajun gumbo. As you might guess, Hog Heaven—unlike most BBQ joints—is a genteel place with real plates (no paper and plastic) and steak knives to slice the ribs politely. And for those who prefer to dig in with their hands, finger bowls are provided.

HOG HEAVEN, 770 Stanyan Street, San Francisco. Telephone: (415) 668-2038. Hours: 11–10 daily. Cards: AE, MC, V. Reservations advised for parties of eight or more. Full bar service. Street parking or in Kezar Stadium.

San Francisco: Chinatown
HUNAN RESTAURANT
Chinese (Hunanese) $

Hunan proprietor Henry Chung may rightly be said to have fathered an American dynasty. When his establishment first appeared on Kearny Street in the mid-seventies, it was reputed to be the only restaurant in the Western hemisphere featuring the hot, pungent cuisine of the central Chinese province where Mao Zedong was born. Then an article in *The New Yorker* called the Hunan "the best Chinese restaurant in the world," and imitators proliferated overnight. Today there are seemingly thousands of Hunanese restaurants sprinkled across the face of Manhattan, and several within a few blocks of Henry's. This latter development has forced Henry to include his given name on the restaurant's sign to distinguish it from the fast-encroaching competition. Of course, some eaters will quibble with *The New Yorker*'s extravagant claim, but few lovers of spicy food will easily dismiss the Hunan's handling of the hot pepper. Try it in harvest pork, a stir-fried dish laced with fiery oil, chilies, shredded carrot, and bamboo shoots. Two longtime favorites here are the cold eggplant salad, deliciously steeped in garlic and vinegar, and the chicken salad, flecked with red pepper. Smoked ham (or chicken), a classic of Hunanese cuisine, is house-prepared and an unusual and satisfying dish, but it also can leave one gasping for water. On the milder side are fresh bacon, Hunan style; onion cakes, fried, unleavened wheat dough rounds studded with scallions; and plump meat-stuffed dumplings, an excellent appetizer. A number of seafood preparations, including snow-white scallops with hot chili-bean sauce, are featured on the menu. (You can even purchase a jar of the house hot sauce to take home.) The original Hunan is an amazingly tiny place, seating no more than a couple dozen people or so, and a waiting line is usually a given. The second location, on Sansome Street, although scorned by some because of its barnlike, very basic interior, serves the same fine spicy food and promises the same wait, but the full bar and plenty of chairs make it a more comfortable one. But Henry Chung has not been resting. A third Hunan Restaurant (oddly enough called Hunan No. 1) has recently opened on Geary in the Richmond District, San Francisco's second Chinatown.

HUNAN RESTAURANT 853 Kearny Street (between Jackson and Washington), San Francisco. Telephone: (415) 788-2234. Hours: 11:30–9:30 Monday–Saturday. No cards. No reservations. Beer and wine only. Street parking. HUNAN RESTAURANT, 924 Sansome Street, San Francisco. Telephone: (415) 956-7727. Hours: 11:30–9:30 Monday–Saturday. Cards: AE, MC, V. Dinner reservations taken until 6 pm. Full bar service. Parking on street and in nearby garages.

Time stands still at Jack's. Even though the building was destroyed by the fire of 1906, it looks just like it did in the 1860s because the owners rebuilt an exact replica. And no one since has dared to change a detail in the high-ceilinged, well-lit dining room. White walls with gold filigree, white tablecloths, plain wooden chairs, and coat hooks around the room still prevail. Jack's is a no-frills masculine type of place, and the lunchtime clientele is still predominately businessmen, many of whom—like the late Louis Lurie who ate here every day for over 50 years—would not dream of lunching elsewhere. Service by tuxedoed waiters is efficient, though sometimes brusque. And the food favored by the regulars is no-nonsense, too. Jack's English mutton chop is a time-honored tradition. Rex sole or sand dabs meunière should be ordered early, because when they run out, they are out—no day-old or frozen fish here. A variety of stews, from Irish to ragout, changes daily. And the french bread is some of the freshest, crustiest and sourest in a city famed for its sourdough. Jack's almost seems haunted by the spirits of Bonanza kings setting up million-dollar deals some hundred years ago, as their successors still do today in the private upstairs rooms where secrecy is guaranteed. In fact, these rooms are even guarded by a separate entrance so that two company presidents on the verge of a merge will not be seen arriving together.

JACK'S, 615 Sacramento Street, San Francisco. Telephone: (415) 986-9854. Hours: 11:30–9:30 Monday–Friday, 5–9:30 Saturday–Sunday. No cards. Reservations advised. Full bar service. Parking lot nearby. Private banquet facilities: 4–55.

San Francisco: Chinatown
JADE GARDEN
Chinese (Cantonese)

$

The block of Broadway between Stockton Street and Grant Avenue has experienced a Chinese restaurant shakedown in the last few years. The less successful efforts have disappeared; the solid neighbors, such as Ton Kiang and Yuet Lee have dug in stronger than ever; and some new entrants have made impressive showings. Jade Garden, a large, comfortable Hong Kong-style Cantonese restaurant with a seafood emphasis, fits the last category. The chef here, Ho Sun, is long famous in Chinatown; he manned the stove at the modest A-1 Cafe on Clay Street, where his talent with seafood was the well-kept secret of a discriminating Chinese clientele. At Jade Garden, two approaches to ordering are possible: The regular menu lists some good dishes, but better yet, ask for a translation of the several special banquet menus. The latter range from very modestly priced set dinners with six dishes, suitable for a party of four, to elaborate—and more expensive— arrays for ten that must be ordered in advance and include such delicacies as shark's fin soup, thinly sliced stuffed pig's trotter, and deep-fried crab claw encased in shrimp paste. The lower-priced banquets, among the best deals in Chinatown, feature fresh lobster or crab with ginger and green onions, crisp shrimp balls with peppery spareribs, deep-fried rock cod cubes with pickled vegetable, fresh oysters with a Dubonnet sauce, dried squid with pork kidney and livers, and right-from-the-tank catfish steamed with black beans. On the regular menu, Jade Garden offers three jellyfish dishes: with shredded duck, with ham and pork, and with lychee. In addition, there is fried milk, a mixture of evaporated and coconut milks and egg white prepared with and without shrimp and scallops; duck soup seasoned with dried orange peel; filleted rock cod stir fried with bok choy; and an assortment of clay pot dishes. Manager Charles Ho has included translations of a few of his father's many specialties on the inside of the menu cover, and this list, along with the Chinese-language menu, is changed seasonally. For a quick lunch, choose from the large selection of rice and noodle plates and noodles in soup.

JADE GARDEN, 674 Broadway, San Francisco. Telephone: (415) 956-4027. Hours: 11 am–midnight daily. Cards: MC, V. Reservations accepted for four or more. Beer and wine only. Street parking.

San Francisco: Telegraph Hill
JULIUS CASTLE
Continental $$$

For over 60 years this towered and turreted landmark has clung to the precipitous cliffs of Telegraph Hill. Built in 1923 by Julius Roz, a former restaurant counterman, the Castle was constructed with fine redwood and maple and for many decades was regarded as one of the city's finest restaurants, both for its food and its unsurpassed view. In the '60s and '70s, however, this grand old relic began to suffer from old age—the premises looked shoddy and the kitchen was unreliable. Then the place was purchased by Jeffrey Pollack and restored to its original splendor. The menu holds no surprises: It's traditional, competently prepared Franco-Italian fare that has changed very little over the years. A long-time favorite with Castle regulars is the appetizer of agnolotti, little crescents of stuffed pasta in a light cream sauce. The fettuccine is also freshly made and comes in Alfredo and pesto versions. Sautéed veal is usually a good bet here, whether in a simple piccata sauce or prepared in the style of saltimbocca with prosciutto and mozzarella. Roast duck with Grand

LES ENTRÉES

Ecalope de Veau Julius 18.75
Thin Slices of Veal Sauté in White Wine and Mushrooms

Escalope de Veau Piccata 18.75
Thin Slices of Veal Sauté, Capers, Shallots, Lemon Butter Sauce

Escalope de Veau Saltimbocca Romana 18.75
Thin Slices of Veal Sauté, Prosciutto and Mozzarella

Le Canard Rôti aux Oranges (for 2) 38.00
Roast Duck, Orange Sauce Flamed with Grand Marnier

Pigeon Grillé à l'Américaine 19.00
Broiled Squab with Mustard

Chateaubriand Garni (for 2) 42.00
Roast Double Filet of Beef with Bearnaise Sauce

Carré d'Agneau au Romarin (for 2) 42.00
Roast Rack of Lamb with Rosemary

Double Côtes d'Agneau Grillées 21.00
Broiled Double French Cut Lamb Chops

L'Entrecôte Grillée, Béarnaise 19.50
Broiled Sirloin Steak with Bearnaise Sauce

L'Entrecôte au Poivre 19.50
Sirloin Steak Sauté, Peppercorn Sauce

Tournedos Rossini 19.75
Two Small Filets Foie Gras Madeira, Truffle Sauce

LES POISSONS ET CRUSTACÉS
Fresh Fish of the Day

Specialité de Poisson Frais
Fresh Fish of the Day

Coquille St. Jacques Doré au Citron 17.50
Scallops in Eggbatter Sauté, Lemon Sauce

Filet de Sole de Petrale Grille 17.50
Fresh Filet of Sole with Lemon Butter Sauce

Gamberi "Luigi Nono" 19.00
Jumbo Prawns Sauté, Lemon and Garlic Butter Sauce

LA SPECIALITÉ DU JOUR

LES LÉGUMES

Epinard Sauté à l'Italienne 4.25
Spinach Sauté in Olive Oil and Garlic

Champignons Sautés au Vin Blanc 5.50
Fresh Mushrooms Sautés, Glazed with Chablis

Riz Sauvage 5.50
Wild Rice

Fresh Asparagus (in season)

Légumes Variées 12.50
Vegetarian Plate

Champignons des Bois 6.50
Wild Mushrooms (in season)

Applicable Sales Tax will be added to all charges

NO PERSONAL CHECKS

All major Credit Cards accepted

— PRIVATE PARTIES —

*With sufficient notice, our chef is pleased to prepare
any special request*

Marnier, chateaubriand with béarnaise, broiled squab, lamb chops, steaks, and seafood round out the menu. The view, however, is a kaleidoscope of surprises, as ships pass by and sailboats heel over on the bay below, as the ever-changing pattern of fog and clouds casts shadows on the waters, and as sunlight reflects upon or lights twinkle on the islands and the East Bay shore beyond. On busy nights or for private parties, the top floor of the restaurant is opened to diners and if you really want to feel like the king of the castle, request a table in the top turret there.

JULIUS CASTLE, 1541 Montgomery, San Francisco. Telephone: (415) 362-3042. Lunch: 11–3 Monday–Friday. Dinner: 5–10 daily. Cards: AE, CB, DC, MC, V. Reservations required. Full bar service. Valet parking. Private banquet facilities: 25–65.

San Francisco: Richmond District
KHAN TOKE THAI HOUSE
Thai $

Success forced Khan Toke to expand into the adjoining building space a couple of years ago, but little else has changed here since then. This remains the place to sample the exotic cuisine of Thailand in elegant surroundings for amazingly low prices. Start with the fried fish cakes served with a cucumber sauce; pork spheres that you tuck into rice paper and season with peanuts, ginger, chili, and herbs; or squid salad with lemon grass, onions, chili, and mint. The tom yam kung soup is a chili-pepper-spiked clear broth sour with lemon and punctuated with pink shrimp and bits of red tomato. There is a substantial list of curries, including the classic mus a mun of beef, potatoes, and peanuts; roast duck with spinach in a rich coconut-milk base; beef flavored with basil; chicken with potatoes. Also recommended are pork with garlic and pepper; deep-fried butterfish; a Thai-style omelet filled with ground pork, onions, and bamboo shoots; pad thai, rice noodles fried with egg and shrimp; and mee krob, noodles with pork and shrimp in a lightly sweetened sauce. Accompany your meal with Singha beer, a first-quality brew from Thailand, and finish the evening with perfectly cooked fried bananas and good Thai coffee. On Sunday evenings there is classical dancing and travel movies of Thailand, creating a particularly festive air in this always-pleasant setting.

KHAN TOKE THAI HOUSE, 5937 Geary Boulevard (at 24th Avenue), San Francisco. Telephone: (415) 668-6654. Hours: 5–11 daily. Cards: AE, MC, V. Service charge of 15 percent on parties of six or more. Reservations recommended. Beer and wine only. Street parking. Private banquet facilities: 10–20.

San Francisco: Jackson Square
LAFAYETTE
California Cuisine/French   **$$**

In this light-splashed bistro on Pacific, tables are jam-packed into a cheery room with rosy brick walls rising to a high sky-blue ceiling studded with skylights. Owner Jacques Charmant's credentials include stints at Paris' Plaza Athenée and New York's Four Seasons. But the cooking is more in the style of the new California cuisine than classic French. Time-honored favorites include a subtle cream of artichoke soup embellished with hazelnuts, the marinated rack of lamb, and plump East Coast mussels steamed with white wine, cream, shallots, and herbs. The mussels may be ordered as an appetizer or main course, as may a daily-changing pasta or a warm spinach and bacon salad. Among Lafayette's new menu selections are a hearty casserole of white beans topped with spicy sausage from Sonoma, and legs of duck with a

61

rich Zinfandel sauce, garnished with paper-thin slices of potatoes, zucchini, and tomato, as are a number of other entrées. Lafayette offers the same menu at the same prices—for both lunch and dinner. The skylight of course adds to the midday ambience, but at night there's a pianist in the tiny bar/foyer, and the prices, which might seem a little high for lunch, look like a bargain for dinner.

LAFAYETTE, 290 Pacific Avenue, San Francisco. Telephone: (415) 986-3366. Hours: 11–10:30 Monday–Thursday, 11–11 Friday, 5–11 Saturday. Cards: AE, MC, V. Reservations advised. Full bar service. Valet parking. Private banquet facilities: 10.

Lafayette
On Pacific

Appetizers

Chilled Gazpacho Soup with Condiments	2.75
Artichoke Soup with Hazelnuts and Cognac	2.95
Mixed Green Salad, Vinaigrette	3.50
Bacon, Spinach and Curly Endive Salad	3.95
Duck Liver Pate with Plum Wine and Prunes	3.95
Fresh Pasta of the Day	4.25
Green Salad with Baby Shrimps	4.75
Baked Clams with Garlic Butter	4.50
Confit of Duck Salad with Walnut Oil	5.50
Carpaccio, Mustard Sauce, Capers, Lettuce Chiffonade	5.95
Fresh Oysters in the half shell	5.75

Entrees

Sauteed Vegetarian Plate	6.95
Bacon, Spinach, Eggs and Curly Endive Salad	7.50
Summer Salad Mixed with Shrimps, Avocado and Tomatoes	8.75
Fresh Pasta of the Day	8.75
Sonoma Sausages with Country Style Baked Beans	8.95
Boneless Breast of Chicken, Raisins and Almond Sauce	9.95
Legs of Duck Simmered in Zinfandel Sauce	9.95
Sauteed Filet of Fresh Petrale Sole, Lemon Butter	10.75
Steamed Fresh Salmon With Herbs Sauce	11.75
Cold Fresh Salmon With Basil Sauce	11.75
Filet of Beef, Red Wine Sauce	14.95

San Francisco: Ghirardelli Square
LANZONE AND SON
Italian $$

Modesto Lanzone's son Eugene has been working in his father's restaurants since he was 15 years old. Now Modesto has made his son a partner and manager of his place in Ghirardelli Square and changed the name to Lanzone and Son. The name is not the only change. The restaurant was remodeled, but still has its handsome terra-cotta tile floors and views of Ghiradelli's plaza and the bay. The menu has also been updated to feature lighter fare: more salads and pastas. Among the latter are some unusual varieties such as guanciali, plump pillows stuffed with ricotta and sauced with mushrooms and fresh tomatoes. Ricotta is also used to stuff ravioli served with a walnut sauce and ravioloni topped with pesto. Eugene intends to change the menu more frequently than in the past, but veal will continue to be emphasized, especially the two house favorites: veal piccata and veal with mushrooms. Italian pastries, spumone, and zabaglione are included in the dessert list. As at Modesto Lanzone's in the Opera Plaza (q.v.), the restaurant displays contemporary artworks, but at Ghirardelli, the main dining areas and bar are used to exhibit the work of a single artist at a time.

LANZONE AND SON, Ghirardelli Square, San Francisco. Telephone: (415) 771-2880. Hours: 4–11 Monday, 11:30–11 Tuesday–Saturday, 11:30–10 Sunday. Cards: AE, CB, DC, MC, V. Full bar service. One hour free parking in Ghirardelli Square garage. Private banquet facilities: 17–60.

San Francisco: Mission District
LA RONDALLA
Mexican

$

This friendly Mission District standby, its orange facade a welcome beacon along busy Valencia Street, enjoys the steady patronage a consistent kitchen deserves. Take a seat at the counter and watch the chefs turn out such memorable Mexican grilled classics as adobada, marinated pork topped with a marvelous mixture of onions, potatoes, and just a touch of tomato; and fajitas, strips of beef that you pile into warm corn tortillas along with chopped onions and tomatoes, guacamole, and fiery salsa. Or try the chile verde, fork-tender chunks of pork in a complex green chili sauce; or the lomo saltado, a pan-fried blend of beef, onions, and bell peppers in a vibrant tomato sauce. Beyond the counter, flanked by a row of booths, are three more small rooms, including two dining rooms and a bar where you can sometimes hear live mariachi music. The decor is unusual and charming: everything from stuffed wild ducks hanging from the ceiling (snapshots of family hunting parties cover one wall) and colored lights shining out from simulated pine boughs, to a Jerry Mahoney dummy and posters advertising every conceivable Mexican beer. This is the perfect place for late-night cravers of south-of-the-border fare: You can satisfy those Mexican food fantasies right up until three o'clock in the morning.

LA RONDALLA, 901 Valencia Street (at 21st Street), San Francisco. Telephone: (415) 647-7474. Hours: 11:30–3 am daily. No cards. Reservations accepted. Full bar service. Street parking.

San Francisco: Mission District
LA TRAVIATA
Italian $$

In the past few years, the most notable change at this favorite dinner house of opera lovers has been the installation of a "sky" of tiny bulbs that bathes the room in "starlight." The photos of famous opera stars still line the walls, most of them affectionately inscribed to charming owner-maître d' Zef Shllaku, and the plates of food that originate in this kitchen remain as fine as ever. And don't think you have the address wrong when you find yourself in the heart of the Latino Mission District. The loyal clientele of La Traviata has been passing taco parlors for years to reach this shining example of high-quality Italian food at reasonable prices. Start with octopus in vinaigrette or an attractive antipasto. A house specialty is, deservedly, sweetbreads sautéed with tomatoes and mushrooms. There are nine veal dishes, with veal La Traviata, prepared with prosciutto and cheese, among the stars. Entrées are accompanied with fresh vegetables and pasta; the tortellini with an expertly light cream sauce is recommended. If you prefer a main course of pasta, there are several choices, including a good linguine with clam sauce and a superb gnocchi. Service is attentive, and the staff's advice on wine selection has always been worth heeding. You may even find yourself seated next to a well-known diva here, or, at the very least, the taped operatic music will sustain the mood.

LA TRAVIATA, 2854 Mission Street, San Francisco. Telephone: (415) 282-0500. Hours: 4 pm–10:30 pm Tuesday–Sunday, closed Monday. Cards: MC, V. Reservations advised. Wine only. Street parking.

San Francisco: Mission District
LA VICTORIA
Mexican $

One of the problems with La Victoria is that loyal customers get in a rut. They discover that this is where birría (goat stew) is unbeatable, and then fail ever to try anything else on the menu. The chiles rellenos produce the same lack of imagination in the regular visitor; the white-cheese-packed peppers encased in an airy, soufflé-like covering are an irresistible rendition for those who savor this traditional dish. The pork in green sauce, the flautas, the enchiladas—they all have their followers, and have for years. La Victoria is a steady place. It spruced itself up modestly some time ago and has changed little since. The waitresses still don shower caps to assure restaurant hygiene, and, inexplicably, there is no beer and wine license. The tortilla chips and salsa are as good as ever, and the service remains uneven—which is to say getting waited on isn't always easy. Finding the restaurant isn't always easy either. La Victoria Bakery & Grocery (the name the "complex" goes by) sits on a corner, with the bakery, which looks like any panadería on a Guadalajara street corner, facing 24th Street. The main restaurant entrance is around the corner on Alabama Street, but no prominent sign marks it (you can also enter through the bakery). Once you have found it though, you will probably develop your own "favorite-dish" loyalty.

LA VICTORIA, 1205 Alabama Street, San Francisco. Telephone: (415) 550-9309. Hours: 10:30 am–10 pm daily. No cards. No beer and wine. Street parking.

San Francisco: Presidio Heights
LE CASTEL
French

$$$

This delightful restaurant, located in an old Victorian house, is owned and operated by Fritz Frankel, one of the city's most respected restaurateurs. Connoisseurs are attracted here by some hard-to-find classics that appear as appetizers: calves' brains au beurre noir and bone marrow with toast. But in general the cooking at Le Castel is quite innovative. Creativity abounds in preparations such as marinated fish (à la ceviche) vividly garnished with spikes of papaya and endive. Another dish that looks as beautiful as it tastes is the loin of pork (roasted at very high temperatures according to a traditional French method, so that the meat is juicy and pink); slices are interspersed with sections of kiwi and sauced with port wine. In addition to the regular menu items, several specials are offered each night: An oft-repeated favorite is roast veal with a creamy sauce of horseradish and shallots. And don't miss the desserts: a choice of luscious pastries such as a kiwi and strawberry tart and a devastatingly rich chocolate meringue cake. Despite Le Castel's Victorian heritage, the two small dining rooms have a Moorish nuance about them, with arches and niches carved out of the stucco walls and a rosy ceiling embellished with striped friezes. Tables are set with pretty pink cloths, and the service is so attentive that it seems your every wish is guessed before you express it. In fact, one of the biggest pluses here is that—unlike at many $$$ French restaurants—every one is treated like a king at Le Castel.

LE CASTEL, 3235 Sacramento, San Francisco. Telephone: (415) 921-7115. Hours: 6–10 Monday–Saturday. Cards: AE, DC, MC, V. Reservations advised. Wine only. Valet parking. Jackets required for men.

San Francisco: Financial District
LE CENTRAL
French $$

This is one of San Francisco's most popular downtown restaurants and the reason is obvious: Le Central has all the Gallic charm of a Left Bank bistro right down to its à la carte blackboard menu. This is a regular stop for a sophisticated crowd, many with familiar faces. A wait at the bar for your table could find you rubbing shoulders with columnist Herb Caen, financier Dick Blum, or San Francisco's powerful state assemblyman, Willie Brown. Aproned waiters thread their way through the always-busy dining room carrying trays heavy with the restaurant's popular fare: appetizers of garlicky pâté and leeks vinaigrette, and entrées of choucroute alsacienne, grilled blood sausages with crispy french fries, fresh salmon with hollandaise, and ramekins of cassoulet. Fruit tarts, fresh strawberries in cream, and chocolate mousse may be among the dessert offerings. The wine list is nicely balanced between French and California bottles, and the prices reflect the accepted markup for an eatery of this caliber. Overflow crowds prompted the owners to open a second bistro, Le Candide, a half block down the street.

LE CENTRAL, 453 Bush Street, San Francisco. Telephone: (415) 391-2233. Hours: 11:45 am–10:30 pm Monday–Friday, 6 pm–10 pm Saturday, closed Sunday. Cards: DC, MC, V. Reservations advised. Full bar service. Street parking or in nearby garages.

San Francisco: Cow Hollow
L'ESCARGOT
French

$$

L'Escargot seems to respond to galloping inflation at a snail's pace. At this writing you could still enjoy an excellent three-course dinner here, in charming, intimate surroundings for less than $15. But that's if you resist ordering the escargots and the parsley-studded rack of lamb—two of the best choices on the menu. Your bill with these will more likely be about $23. Still a bargain in these times. And no true garlicophile could resist the perfume of the escargots that wafts through this small storefront restaurant. The dining room is picture pretty with sparkling wineglasses and pink napery on the candlelit tables. Included with dinner is a homemade soup, most often a vegetable crème, and a butter lettuce salad. Besides the lamb, other memorable entrées include quail with grapes and Madeira sauce, and rabbit cooked in white wine sauce. Only fresh seasonal fish is served. For dessert, the chocolate mousse is sinfully fudgy and bittersweet. And there is usually a fresh-fruit dessert, varied with the season: Perhaps strawberries with cold zabaglione sauce or raspberries in heavy cream. Inquire. Here is a rare restaurant where quality is not compromised but prices are extremely fair.

L'ESCARGOT, 1809 Union Street, San Francisco. Telephone: (415) 567-0222. Hours: 5:30–10:30 daily. Cards: AE, CB, DC, MC, V. Reservations suggested. Wine and beer only. Street parking.

San Francisco: Nob Hill
L'ETOILE
French **$$$**

For years L'Etoile was the city's high temple of classic haute cuisine. But now owners Claude Rouas and Henri Barberis have thrown out the book (L'Escoffier, that is) and encouraged their long-time chef to devise his own presentations and variations à la nouvelle cuisine. Stuffed quail now appears on the hors d'oeuvre menu, along with a pretty pink lobster pâté sauced with green watercress mayonnaise. The former encyclopedic list of entrées has been pared down to 16 and includes such colorful dishes as breast of chicken in a raspberry vinegar sauce served with a chiffonade of spinach and glazed turnips, and breast of duck with pears, blueberries, and orange sauce. A garlicky fillet of lamb is paired with pasta, and veal is laved with a creamy sauce and wild mushrooms. L'Etoile has long been famous for its hot dessert soufflés, which remain on the menu, but now there's also a cold soufflé of hazelnuts and almonds with a rum-coffee sauce. L'Etoile's dining room is one of the most beautiful and most formal in the city, with large urns of flowers towering above the curved banquettes, and a small army of captains, waiters, and busboys hovering over the tables. L'Etoile also is a candidate for San Francisco's most expensive restaurant, with entrées in the $24 range and hors d'oeuvre about $10. If this is beyond your budget, you might still want to drop by the chic little bar for a drink and the nostalgic piano playing of Peter Mintun.

L'ETOILE, 1075 California Street, San Francisco. Telephone: (415) 771-1529. Hours: 5:30–10:30 Monday–Saturday. Cards: AE, CB, DC, MC, V. Reservations required. Full bar service. Valet parking. Coat and tie required for men. Private banquet facilities: 15–60.

Hors - d' Oeuvre Froid

Foie gras et aiguillettes de canard
a la gelée de porto   20.00
Fresh Goose Liver, Duck Filet and Port Aspic

Mousse de foie de canard a L'Armagnac
salade de papaya confite   10.00
Mouse of Duck Liver in Aramagnac

Terrine de canard au poivre vert
et truffles   10.00
Pate of Duck

Pate de homard et poissons fins aux herbes
sauce émeraude   10.00
Cold Pate of Lobster and Watercress Mayonaise Sauce

Saumon fumé du Pacific   12.00
Smoked Salmon

Huitres Blue Point   10.00
Blue Point Oysters

Entrees

Gourmandise de saumon aux petits légumes et aneth   23.50
Poached Salmon with Dill Sauce

Paillarde d'espadon au confit d'échalottes et éfilochée d'endive   23.50
Swordfish with Shallots and Endive

Filets de sole et huitres au champagne   23.50
Filet of Sole and Oysters with Champagne Sauce

Quenelles de poissons truffees Cardinale   23.50
Mousse of Fish, Truffle and Lobster Sauce

Fricasee de poulet au vinaigre de framboises   24.00
Chicken in Raspberry Vinegar Sauce

Salmis de pigeon a L'Armagnac et son gateau de foie   23.00
Squab with Armagnac Sauce and Liver Pate

Emincé de canard et son foie au vinaigre de miel et gratin de pommes de terre   24.00
Filet of Duck Breast with its Liver in Honey Vinagar

Eventail de canard au poire et mirtilles sauce à l'orange   24.00
Breast of Duckling, Pear, Blueberries, Orange Sauce

Mignons de veau à la moutarde ancienne et champignons sauvages   24.00
Noisette of Veal with Mustard Sauce and Wild Mushrooms

Medaillons de veau et ragout de morilles   24.00
Veal with Morrel and Champagne Sauce

Filets d'agneau à la creme d'ail doux et pâtes fraiches   24.00
Filet of Lamb with Garlic and Fresh Pasta

Marinade d'agneau aux deux baies sauvages "façon chevreuil"   24.00
Medallions of Lamb in Game Sauce

Carré d'agneau roti servi avec son jus aux herbes de Provence   24.00
Roast Rack of Lamb with Herb of Provence

Coeur de filet de boeuf au Medoc avec son ragout de möelle   23.00
Filet of Beef in Red Wine Sauce with Marrow Stew

Filet de boeuf aux deux poivres et Armagnac   23.00
Filet Mignon Flambe in Armagnac with Pepper Sauce

Steak Tartare   20.00
Steak Tartare

LE TRIANON
French $$$

The distinguished gentleman with the towering toque who strolls among the tables is none other than René Verdon, the much-publicized chef to the John F. Kennedys during their White House days. For over a decade now he has tantalized San Franciscans with the grand cuisine of France, resisting culinary fads to present a menu that is both classic and innovative and changes little. Oysters baked in a curry sauce are an auspicious introduction, unless you are tempted by the quenelles of pheasant or the baked-in-the-shell clams Hyannisport, a nostalgic salute to Camelot. Verdon also imparts a touch of magic to the entrées with unexpected seasonings—a dish of chives and saffron in the coquilles St. Jacques, and a glazing of honey on the sensational rack of lamb. A recent addition to the menu is a fillet of spring lamb served with a mousse of pheasant. Desserts, such as chocolate mousse in a Grand Marnier sauce, demand to be ordered. Unlike many French restaurants, Le Trianon features an extensive collection of California wines, along with those of France. In fact, it was the first French restaurant in San Francisco to place local wines ahead of the Europeans on the wine list. Le Trianon also has a homier, more hospitable feeling than most of the city's other temples of haute cuisine. Madame Verdon greets and seats the guests, reminding you that this is indeed a family affair.

LE TRIANON, 242 O'Farrell Street, San Francisco. Telephone: (415) 982-9353. Hours: 6–10 Monday–Saturday. Cards: AE, MC, V. Reservations required. Full bar service. Parking in nearby garage. Coat and tie required for men. Private banquet facilities: 24.

GRILLADES
RÔTS

LE CHÂTEAUBRIAND, SAUCE BÉARNAISE
(For Two)   44.00

LE CARRÉ D'AGNEAU AU MIEL   20.00
Rack of lamb roasted with honey

LES ÉMINCÉS DE BOEUF BORDELAISE   19.00
Thin Filet Mignon Slices, Sauce Bordelaise

LES NOISETTES D'AGNEAU POÊLEES À L'AIL CONFIT   20.00
Filet of Spring Lamb, Mousse of Pheasant, Sweet Garlic

SPÉCIALITÉS

CIVET DE CANARD AU CABERNET   19.00
Duck In Red Wine Sauce, Olives Mushrooms

MIGNONS DE VEAU AUX TROIS CHAMPIGNONS   21.00
Veal Loin with Three Varieties of Mushrooms

FILET D'AGNEAU EN CROÛTE TRIANON (For Two)   44.00
Our Lamb Specialty

FILET DE BOEUF WELLINGTON (For Two)   44.00
Roast Filet In Pastry Shell, Truffles Sauce

LA DODINE DE FAISAN ST HUBERT   20.00
Our Pheasant Specialty

LICHEE GARDEN
Chinese (Cantonese)   **$**

Cantonese food too often conjures up the image of crimson sweet and sour pork, shapeless stir-fry vegetables heavy on celery, and oil-laden egg rolls. Lichee Garden defies these mistaken culinary stereotypes, and in a comfortable setting that counters the usual good-food-in-a-Formica-hole-in-the-wall atmosphere as well. The shredded roast duck and jellyfish salad is superb, its lightly scented sesame-soy dressing the perfect complement to the rich fowl and pleasantly chewy sea life. Spiced salt spareribs arrive crisp and pungently seasoned, and the steamed shrimp-stuffed bean curd is silky and light. A fine-mesh taro-root basket holds a variety of seafood—shrimp, scallops, squid—and vegetables, and an order of double squid (fresh and dried) is a delight of flavors and textures. You will need to decode the Chinese menu to try the delicious clay pot dishes here; anise-scented lamb and bean curd sticks, and roast pork, rock cod, and garlic are just two of your choices. Also secreted away on this sheet is a minced squab dish, to be wrapped in lettuce leaves and eaten out of hand, and boned duck webs stir fried with snow peas. Lunchtime brings an interesting array of noodle dishes and rice plates, and quiet surroundings. There is often a line here, so be prepared for a wait.

LICHEE GARDEN, 1416 Powell Street, San Francisco. Telephone: (415) 397-2290. Hours: 11:30 am–9:30 pm daily. Cards: MC, V. Reservations suggested. Beer and wine only. Street parking.

San Francisco: North Beach
LITTLE CITY ANTIPASTI BAR
International $$

When it opened a few years back, Little City introduced to San Francisco the tapas bar concept: making a full meal from an assortment of "little dishes." But unlike the tapas bars of Spain, Little City's selection of appetizers traverses the globe, with a dozen or so selections ranging from baba ghannouj to Manila clams in black bean and ginger sauce, from quesadillas to baked camembert or brie, from raclette to grilled Italian sausage. You can still make a meal of antipasti here, but the restaurant has expanded its offerings. Usually a half-dozen pastas are available, such as spinach and ricotta ravioli or penne with fennel sausage, artichoke hearts, chilies, and asiago cheese. Entrées might include grilled yellowfin tuna with tomatillo salsa, bass baked in parchment, chicken breasts stuffed with mozzarella, or Oriental pot roast with shiitake mushrooms and snow peas. Little City's large windows offer peeks at nearby Washington Square, a crowded bar occupies about a third of the main room, and the tables sit on a dais next to it—noisy, but fun, just like a tapas bar should be. A rear dining room offers some respite from the usual din.

LITTLE CITY ANTIPASTI BAR, 673 Union Street, San Francisco. Telephone: (415) 434-2900. Antipasti service: noon–midnight daily. Lunch: 11:30–2 daily. Dinner: 6–11 Sunday–Thursday, until midnight Friday–Saturday. Cards: AE, MC, V. Reservations accepted only for parties of six or more. Full bar service. Street parking or at nearby garages.

This tiny neighborhood café is so popular that sometimes there is standing room only in the center aisle for those queued, awaiting a table. But the regulars don't seem to mind if someone's purse is hanging over their bread basket. The food is wonderful, the prices are quite reasonable, and proprietors Rolf and Louise Tschudi strive to please. Luzern offers high-quality, four-course dinners priced from $10 to $15. Chef Tshudi's soups are always a delight—perhaps leek and potato or watercress or vegetable barley. And the butter lettuce salad is coated with a delightful herb-scented dressing. Veal dishes dominate the entrée selections—tender scallops sautéed with artichokes and mushrooms, or laved in a brandied cream sauce with slivers of morels, or in the classic Swiss presentation called geschnetzeltes, to name a few. The rack of lamb here is excellent, as is the duck with orange sauce. Desserts are simple—crème caramel, ice cream, or sherbet. But after the rich main courses, who needs more? There are two reminders that this is indeed a Swiss restaurant: two fondue selections are offered with soup or salad and a giant photo mural of Lucerne dominates the red-flocked walls.

LUZERN, 1431 Noriega Street, San Francisco. Telephone: (415) 664-2353. Hours: 5–10 Wednesday–Saturday, 4–9 Sunday. No cards. Reservations advised. Beer and wine only. Street parking.

<u>Dinners</u>
Soupe du jour
Salade

1. Rack of Lamb — 15.²⁵

2. Saumon poché Nantua — 11.²⁵
   Poached Salmon with shrimp sauce

3. Poulet Sauté Grand Mère — 9.⁷⁵
   Chicken sauté

4. L'Escalope de Veau Murat — 11.⁷⁵
   Veal with artichoke and mushrooms

5. Ris de Veau Financière — 11.⁰⁰
   Sweetbreads in Brandy, Cream and mushrooms

6. Veau Cordon Bleu — 11.⁷⁵
   Breaded veal stuffed with Ham and cheese

7. Médaillons de Bœuf Luzern — 13.²⁵
   Filet of beef with Herbs-butter sauce

8. Emincée de Veau a la Crème — 10.⁵⁰
   Veal in delicious Cream Sauce - geschnetzeltes.

9. Coquille St Jacques — 11.⁷⁵
   Crab-Scallops and Shrimps in a Sea Shell

10. Escalope de Veau aux Morilles — 12.⁷⁵
    Veal in mushroom sauce

11. Canard a l'Orange — 12.⁷⁵
    Duck with Orange sauce

12. Wienerschnitzel — 11.⁷⁵
    Breaded veal Cutlet

13. Steak au Poivre — 14.⁰⁰
    Pepper steak

Desserts

Crème Caramel ~ Ice Cream or Sherbet

Minimum Charge : 4.⁰⁰ per person

San Francisco: Jackson Square
MACARTHUR PARK
American $$

Ribs are practically synonymous with MacArthur Park
to many San Franciscans, but this wasn't always the
case. In 1972, Jerry Magnin and Larry Mindel (who had
started their small restaurant chain with Chianti in Los
Angeles) opened MacArthur Park in an abandoned pre-
earthquake warehouse near Jackson Square. At first
locals thronged here to gawk at the stunning decor—
exposed brick walls, skylights, multilevel seating—but
the menu seemed to have no identity of its own. Then an
oakwood smoker and an all-American menu were installed
and the Park became famous for its lean, marinated
baby back ribs smoked in oak and finished over a
mesquite grill. But ribs are only a small part of the story
here: From the smoker also come chicken and pork
chops and Petaluma duck, and from the grill come
exceptional spicy sausages made in house, fresh Sierra
rabbit, dry-aged New York steaks, a fabulous whole
sizzling catfish, and more. Much more, for instance
appetizers of grilled pasilla peppers stuffed with three
cheeses, grilled escarole with smoked ham and Sonoma
goat cheese, or even a salad of grilled skirt steak with
baby leeks, Anaheim chilies, and a lemony dressing.
MacArthur Park makes a mean chili served with grilled
flat bread. And the desserts are terrific: Try Judy's mud
pie or the sensational turtle pie—chocolate genoise in a
pecan butter crust slathered with a rich caramel sauce.
This restaurant is one of those rare old-timers that
improve markedly as the years roll by. The latest
improvement is an honest-to-God breakfast (*not* brunch),
with the likes of slab bacon cured in honey and smoked
in oakwood, oatmeal with dates and raw sugar, waffles
with black walnuts and real maple syrup, and juices
freshly squeezed to order. Enough to make the laziest
Sunday sleeper get out of bed.

MACARTHUR PARK, 607 Front Street, San Francisco. Telephone: (415) 398-5700. Breakfast: 7–10 Monday–Friday, 9:30–2 Sunday. Lunch: 11:30–2:30 Monday–Friday. Dinner: 5:30–11 Sunday–Thursday, 5:30–midnight Saturday. Cards: AE, MC, V. Reservations advised. Full bar service. Valet parking. Private banquet facilities: 60.

OAKWOOD SMOKER

Baby Back Ribs
   Full Slab 11.95
   Half Slab 7.90
Ribs and Chicken 11.95
Half Chicken 7.40
Ribs, Chicken and Sausage 11.95
Fresh Petaluma Duck with Lingonberry Sauce 11.80
One Pound Pork Chop (split on request) with Shoestring Sweet Potatoes . . 8.90

FRESH FISH

Fresh Fish #1 . . . . 7.45
Fresh Fish #2 . . . . 10.80
Fresh Fish #3 . . . . 12.95
Whole Sizzling Catfish 11.95
Live Maine Lobster . . . . A.Q.
Grilled Fresh Shrimp, Fennel, Lime 11.80

MESQUITE CHARCOAL GRILL

Grilled Homemade Sausages with Tomato Chutney or Baked Beans 6.95
Hamburger or Cheeseburger 4.95
Filet Mignon Steak Sandwich "Harry's Bar" 9.25
Grilled Duck Breast with Braised Red Cabbage and Smoked Bacon 10.50
Pounded Double Breast of Chicken 7.75
Fresh Game Hen, Lime and Thyme 8.95
Calf's Liver Steak with Oakwood-Smoked Bacon 8.95
Fresh Sierra Rabbit, Rosemary 9.85
California Lamb Chops with Fresh Mint 14.50
Aged Eastern Porterhouse Steak with Onion Strings 14.95
Dry-Aged New York Steak with Onion Strings 15.95

DESSERTS

Judy's Mud Pie 3.25
New York Cheesecake 2.75
Green Apple Pie 2.50
   a la mode 3.50
Fresh Berry Shortcake 3.00
Pecan Pie 2.75
Fresh Berries with "Our Cream" 3.00
Turtle Pie 3.80
Vanilla Ice Cream 2.00
   with Homemade Hot Caramel or Fudge Sauce 3.00

In terms of Vietnamese-restaurant longevity, Mai's is an old-timer. The original location on Clement Street was opened in the late 1970s and has been attracting a loyal Vietnamese and non-Vietnamese clientele ever since. There is a second branch, on Union Street in Cow Hollow, and a third on Ninth Avenue in the Sunset, but the original remains this writer's favorite. Mai's popularity is deserved, for the food is well prepared, reasonably priced, and consistent. The three major noodle soups of Vietnam—Hanoi, Center (Hue), and Saigon style–are offered, as is the less frequently encountered preparation of rice topped with mildly seasoned chicken and mushrooms cooked in earthenware. You can make your own Vietnamese "tacos" by ordering the platter of grilled pork balls, rice paper sheets, mint sprigs, lettuce, etc.; tuck a bit of everything into the rice paper, then dip the "package" into the accompanying thick soybean-based sauce before eating. Vinegar beef, beef in lot leaf, pork kebab, shrimp balls, a variety of mild curries, and the beef and shrimp salads are all fine examples of this kitchen's abilities. The Clement Street Mai's is modestly decorated and always crowded on weekend nights. The blossoming of Vietnamese restaurants throughout the city doesn't seem to have phased Mai's devoted customers.

MAI'S No. 1, 316 Clement Street (between Fourth and Fifth Avenues, San Francisco. Telephone: (415) 221-3046. Hours: 11–10 Sunday–Thursday, until 11 Friday–Saturday. Cards: AE, MC, V. Beer and wine only. Street parking.

San Francisco: Richmond District
MANDALAY
Burmese

$

Few restaurants serving Burmese food are to be found in Rangoon's steamy streets. As with so many Southeast Asian countries, Burma's restaurant culture, even in its capital city, is overwhelmingly Chinese, while the food of the indigenous people is available primarily in street stalls. Thus, San Franciscans are fortunate to have the opportunity to eat at the attractive, comfortable Mandalay restaurant, where the owners, former residents of Rangoon, offer a menu of traditional native dishes as well as a selection of Chinese plates. Stick to the former to experience a cuisine that has artfully drawn upon the foods of its neighbors to create truly exotic fare. Begin with the black pepper soup, a blend of paper-thin slices of green squash, threads of black fungus, pieces of catfish, bean thread noodles, whole garlic cloves, and plenty of ground black pepper. Another good beginning is mohinga, which, along with panthe kaukswe, a chicken curry with noodles, are the best-known dishes of Burma. Essentially mohinga is a fish chowder containing thin rice noodles and a bouquet of exotic spices. It is topped with roasted lentils and served with lemon wedges, fish sauce, and dried chilies, for diners to add to taste. A number of salads are offered, including the very special lap pat dok, a mixture of tea leaves, peanuts, roasted lentils, ground shrimp, fried garlic shreds, chili pepper, sesame seeds, and a hearty dose of fermented shrimp paste. Chin mong jaw, described on the menu as sour vegetable and prawns, is a delight: The unique green leafy vegetable, grown from seed imported from Burma, is tossed with the shellfish in a very hot, very sour sauce. There are also several curries, some of which reflect the influence of India, and a variety of satays, accompanied with complex, unusual dipping sauces. The Mandalay staff is courteous and anxious to help you in your selection of dishes. The surroundings are a peaceful atmosphere of blond wood, attractive wall hangings, and Buddhist artifacts.

MANDALAY, 4348 California Street (near 6th Avenue), San Francisco. Telephone: (415) 386-3895. Lunch: 11:30–3 Tuesday–Sunday. Dinner: 5–10 Tuesday–Sunday. Cards: MC, V. Reservations recommended. Beer and wine only. Street parking.

San Francisco: Ghirardelli Square
THE MANDARIN
Chinese (Mandarin) $$$

Mandarin cooking refers not to a specific region of China, but encompasses the finest foods from all areas as they were served to the emperors in Peking. At the Mandarin restaurant Madame Cecilia Chiang first introduced the total spectrum of Chinese haute cuisine to Californians. In addition to the subtle intricacies of the better-known Cantonese tradition, there are the peppery hot dishes of Szechwan and Hunan, the delicate seafood of Shanghai, the firepots and barbecues of the Mongols. The setting befits a Mandarin, too. An exposed-beam ceiling emulates ancient temple architecture. There are family paintings from Shanghai, Chinese rugs, Taiwanese tiles, and a glimpse of the Bay through narrow windows. Even though the Mandarin has been called the finest Chinese restaurant in America, Madame Chiang constantly strives to improve it by adding new dishes to the menu, such as a zesty combination of tangerine peel with chicken or beef. And many of the house specialties are not on the menu at all: minced squab wrapped in lettuce leaves, for example, or scallops or beef with citron, or five-spice shrimp, or an exotic edible basket woven from egg noodles and filled with seafood. If you have difficulty getting information on these dishes from your waiter, as

MANDARIN SWEET AND SOUR FISH
Whole fresh rock cod, baked in a special
delicate sweet and sour sauce or preserved ingredients

PRAWNS À LA SZECHWAN
A traditional Western Chinese dish: tender young prawns in a
spicy, flavorful, hot, red sauce

SMOKED TEA DUCK
Our incomparable version of Peking Duck, smoked in special ovens
over burning tea leaves; crispy skin, haunting flavor

CHUNGKING BEEF
An unusual dish from the West of China. Spicy hot!

MU SHUI PORK
Slices of pork lightly sautéed with eggs and mushrooms.
This is especially delicious rolled in paper-thin pancakes
with duck sauce and slivered scallions

MANDARIN CRAB
(In Season) Sautéed in the shell, with a pungent sauce of
Chinese rice wine and crushed, fresh ginger

RED-COOKED EGGPLANT
Combined with pork in a delicious wine sauce

SPINACH MANDARIN
Fresh spinach leaves and silvery noodles combined in a
light chicken sauce

ASPARAGUS À LA SHANGTUNG
(In Season) Crisply sautéed with a whisper of sesame flavor
Served cold

MANDARIN GLAZED APPLES
(OR BANANAS)
Apples or bananas dipped in batter, glazed with candy syrup and
then plunged into ice water at your table to
crystallize the candied coating

Cecilia Chiang

sometimes happens, ask for Madame Chiang or her managers Mr. Chien and Mr. Wong to assist you in ordering. In fact, the best plan for dining here is to call a day or so ahead and ask one of them to plan a banquet for you. This way you can sample some of the dishes that require 24 hours' notice, like Mandarin duck, beggar's chicken baked in clay, shark's fin soup, and the Mongolian firepot.

THE MANDARIN, Ghirardelli Square, San Francisco. Telephone: (415) 673-8812. Hours: noon–11 daily except Christmas and Thanksgiving. Cards: AE, CB, DC, MC, V. Reservations suggested. Full bar service. One hour free parking in Ghirardelli Square garage. Private banquet facilities: 30–50.

San Francisco: Downtown
MASA'S
French $$$

San Franciscans love to argue about restaurants, but few would dispute Masa's premier position among the city's French establishments. The restaurant's founder, Masa Kobayashi, was one of the great culinary geniuses of this century and after his untimely death in 1984, his fans wondered if anyone could possibly take his place in the kitchen. Well, Bill Galloway, Masa's assistant for several years, not only has carried on the master's tradition flawlessly, but, in the opinion of most critics, has even surpassed his mentor. The verdict is in that this nearly perfect restaurant is better than ever. Galloway, like Masa, has the eye of an artist, creating exquisite arrangements on the plate that are as beautiful to look at as they are to eat. He still prepares some of Masa's signature dishes, such as sweetbreads piped with salmon mousse and garnished with julienned cucumber, surrounded by a crayfish sauce accented

CARTE DE LA SAISON

petit filet cru d'agneau garni aux pointes d'asperges 9.25
lean raw lamb marinated in herbal vinagrette with asparagus

boudin de trois poissons, beurre blanc 10.75
sausage of lobster, scallop and shrimp with fresh herbs

huîtres chaudes, beurre vermouth au caviar noir 10.25
bluepoint oysters poached, sauce vermouth garnished with sevruga caviar

potage du chef

homard du maine grillé, sauce beurre blanc vert et quenelles de crevettes 35.00
grilled maine lobster with herbal beurre blanc and shrimp quenelles

aiguillettes de saumon king au caviar rouge, sauce ciboulettes 26.25
king salmon filets garnished with salmon roe, sauce of seasonal herbs

médaillons de poussin aux trois farces 27.75
breast of poussin with three stuffings, sauce supreme

escalopes de veau sautées forestières 28.50
sautéed veal medallions with garnish of wild mushrooms

poitrines de cailles farcies au riz sauvage 28.50
baby quail stuffed with wild rice garnished with puree of red peppers

sauté de ris de veau aux écrevisses de sacramento 28.75
sweet breads sautéed served with crayfish sauce

noisettes d'agneau grillées au poivre vert, sauce civet 32.00
grilled filet of lamb with green peppercorns, sauce zinfandel

mignon de boeuf avec la mousse de foie gras, coulis de truffes 31.00
filet mignon with goose liver mousse and black truffles

salade de la maison 9.25   ***salade mélangée*** 7.95

l'assiette de fromage 12.00
cheese plate

85

with a single crayfish tail. But he has also introduced some creations that are 100 percent his own like roasted partridge presented on a bed of braised savoy cabbage, garnished with fresh chives and marjoram and thinly sliced potatoes Anna. The atmosphere is understated elegance with pale lavendar walls, etched mirrors, colorful tableware, and an abundance of flowers. And the service matches the food in its perfection. You pay dearly, of course, for all of this: $55 for the four-course prix-fixe menu, which Galloway writes anew each day after he has surveyed the market for the best produce, seafood, and so forth. The encyclopedic wine list catalogs over 400 bottlings, ranging from seldom-encountered gems from California's boutique wineries, such as Hafner's Alexander Valley Chardonnay priced at $22, to collectors' vintages like a 1945 Chateau Lafite-Rothschild at $895!

MASA'S, Vintage Court Hotel, 648 Bush Street, San Francisco. Telephone: (415) 989-7154. Hours: 6–9:30 Tuesday–Saturday. Cards: MC, V. Reservations must be made three weeks in advance. Full bar service. Valet parking.

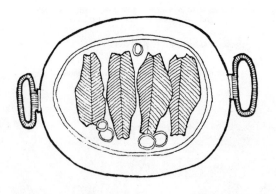

The Carnegie Delicatessen it is not. Nary a knish nor a matzo ball will you encounter. At first glance, the take-out section of Max's Opera Cafe *looks* like a deli with luscious lox, barbecued, roasted, and smoked chickens, chopped liver—even bottles of New York seltzer in the spritzer. But when have you ever been in a deli of such elegance, with a full bar and sidewalk service? Undoubtedly, the best corned beef and pastrami in town, but the rye is marbled. If this all seems schizophrenic, don't despair; just accept the fact that San Francisco will undoubtedly enter the twenty-first century maintaining innocence regarding real hard-core deli food—probably the only claim for hard-core innocence the city can make. Traditional sandwiches of rare roast beef, honey-glazed smoked ham, kosher-style salami and beef brisket are meals in themselves with appropriate side salads and garnishes. The Greek tomato salad of spinach, anchovies, calamata olives, feta cheese, red onions, and baby eggplants has a slightly sweet dressing which provides a good foil for the anchovies. The salad sampler is a good choice and includes an excellent chicken salad. Braised brisket and hickory-smoked ribs are outstanding dinner choices. The desserts are extravaganzas. The apple cobbler is served in its baking dish and piled with ice cream, and the New York cheesecake is a faithful rendition for purists, while the more adventuresome will enjoy Kahlúa and Dutch apple versions. Max's sundae sauces are made in New York and used lavishly here. Grand Marnier mousse-cake and black magic chocolate cake are specialties, as is the dessert sampler: a seven-layer cookie with several ice creams, butterscotch and nuts. Chocolate egg cream completes the nostalgia. In the evening the waiters gather to sing show biz tunes around a piano. Max's is a lot of fun and a happy blend of New York brass and California glamour.

MAX'S OPERA CAFE, 601 Van Ness Avenue, San Francisco. Telephone: (415) 771-7300. Hours: 11:15 am–midnight, Monday–Thursday, to 1 am Friday, 11:30-11:30 Sunday. Cards: AE, DC, MC, V. Reservations not accepted. Full bar service. Parking in building.

San Francisco: Mission District
MANORA'S THAI RESTAURANT
Thai $

When Passarin Prassl opened the small, attractive Manora's early in 1985, word spread quickly that a first-rate Thai chef was at work in the Mission. Within a fortnight, in-the-know diners were lined up outside. The queues are still forming, as early as six o'clock even on weeknights, and there is a good reason why. These savvy diners are awaiting the opportunity to try chef Prassl's many outstanding specialties, like her appetizer of poh-pier-sod, a round of rice paper encasing generous measures of crab meat, shrimp, Chinese sausage, ground pork, black fungus, and bean curd and dressed with a sweet-and-vinegary sauce; or her version of the classic tod mun, a quartet of large, beautiful deep-fried fish-and-green-bean cakes served with a condiment of cucumber and peanut. The popular Thai dish of pork with garlic and pepper receives royal treatment here, the large thin fillets of tenderloin perfectly cooked and served atop a bed of featherlight deep-fried Chinese broccoli leaves. Good, too, is the hor muk, a dish in which fish fillets and prawns are layered with basil leaves, topped with a red coconut curry sauce, and steamed; the result is a kind of fish mousse, deliciously permeated with the flavor of the fresh herb. The panaeng-sam-ros mates deep-fried beef, chicken, and pork with a dipping sauce based on coconut milk, chilies, and lemon grass; and the gai yang, chicken marinated in garlic, coriander, and Thai spices before grilling, is as good as barbecued chicken ever gets.

MANORA'S THAI RESTAURANT, 3226 Mission Street (near 28th Street), San Francisco. Telephone: (415) 550-0856. Lunch: 11:30–2:30 Monday–Friday. Dinner: 5–10 daily. Cards: MC, V. Reservations not accepted. Beer and wine only. Street parking.

San Francisco: North Beach
MAYKADEH
Persian $

To most diners, North Beach means Italian restaurants. That's also what it meant to Tehrani and Mahmood Khoussousi; so in 1985 they opened an Italian restaurant on the lower reaches of Telegraph Hill. The neighborhood competition for pasta eaters proved too fierce, however. In response, they completely revamped the menu and the following spring opened the elegant Maykadeh, which serves the traditional dishes of Iran. The moment you are seated, a waiter delivers warm pita bread, a block of feta cheese, and an array of raw vegetables—scallions, watercress sprigs, tomato, yellow onion quarters. From the list of ten entrées, some of which are daily specials, try ghorme sabzee, a pleasantly sour combination of lamb shanks, limes, small red beans, and half a dozen greens; joojeh kabab, chicken breast meat marinated in saffron-scented homemade yogurt and grilled over mesquite; khoresht bademjam, a subtly spiced mixture of eggplant and lamb shanks; or kabab koobideh, skewers of spiced ground meat and lamb. All of the entrées are accompanied with a great mound of fluffy buttered rice, over which you can sprinkle some sumak, the mild spice of crushed berries that sits in a small bowl on each table. If you are a yogurt lover, be sure to order a bowl of mast-o-musir, which combines the healthful food with minced shallots, or mast-o-khiar, which combines it with cucumber. A large Iranian clientele attests to the authenticity of Maydadeh's dishes. The big surprise here is the prices: You can dine for less than $10 in an ambience and with a caliber of food service that would normally assure a check three times that amount.

MAYKADEH, 470 Green Street, San Francisco. Telephone: (415) 362-8286. Hours: noon–10 Tuesday–Thursday and Sunday, noon–midnight Friday–Saturday. Cards: MC, V. Reservations accepted. Wine and beer only. Street parking and in nearby Vallejo Street lot.

San Francisco: Japantown
MIFUNE
Japanese $

Travelers through the scenic region that surrounds Osaka on the Japanese island of Honshu are served with stylish efficiency by the famous Kintetsu Railway. In San Francisco, the Kintetsu corporation is mainly known as owner of the Japan Center, in the west wing of which stands the Kintetsu restaurant mall—a charming row of traditional eateries modeled precisely on the lining malls of urban Japanese train stations. At the heart of the mall is Mifune, a branch of a Japan-based chain that dishes up some of the best udon (wheat) and soba (buckwheat) noodles on this side of the Pacific. Both of these noodles may be had hot in dashi (bonito-flavored broth), topped with any of 22 menu selections ranging from seaweed or fish cake to elaborate combinations such as the chicken, shrimp, tempura, and egg that make up an order of nabeyaki udon. Mifune patrons may also choose from six cold preparations, with the noodles arriving on a bamboo tray accompanied with a dipping sauce. And for children, there is the "Shinkansen," a tableware facsimile of Japan's celebrated bullet train with its roof sculpted for holding udon and tempura. Mifune's front window is lined with Japanese-style plastic models of many of the menu items, so you can more easily make your selection. A large waterwheel decorates another front window, and the interior is done in tasteful blue-and-white fabric and natural wood furniture. The beautiful ceramic noodle bowls and teacups used here can be purchased at the register, plus you can even take home packages of freshly made soba and udon for a future meal.

MIFUNE, 1737 Post Street, Japan Center West Building, First Floor, San Francisco. Telephone: (415) 922-0337. Hours: 11 am–9 pm daily. Cards: AE, MC, V. No reservations. Beer and wine only.Parking in nearby garage.

San Francisco: Japantown
MITOYA
Japanese $

Mitoya, located in Japantown, provides San Francisco with a taste of the Ginza. It is a transplanted example of the nightlife fare found in the entertainment districts of Tokyo and every other major Japanese city. The diversions are pure kitsch; the food is pure heaven. In effect, this corner of the Japan Center is really two establishments, one of which makes a peculiar metamorphosis come evening. Until 5:00, the large, comfortable seating area on the west side serves as the Sunshine coffeehouse; when the sun sets, it becomes an eccentric "pub," with entertainment supplied by the patrons themselves, who mount the room's stage and croon their favorite Japanese songs into a microphone while a tape plays back-up music. There are even hostesses, both Japanese and non-Japanese, who join male drinkers for conversation—and nothing more. Snacks are available in the pub, but the real eating is done in the room to the east, Mitoya itself, where the culinary style called robata-yaki reigns. Diners sit at a low counter, with their feet dangling into a well below. Before them is spread a sumptuous array of fresh fish, meats, and vegetables. One need only order from the multipage menu or point at a desired selection, and the robata-yaki master moves into action—grilling the item over an open fire, then saucing and garnishing it. The portions are small, but modestly priced; the idea is to try a wide variety of dishes. Among the best choices are the simply cooked eggplant with a splash of soy, chunks of beef heart or chicken on a skewer, the amazingly tender cuttlefish, a pleasantly salty mackerel, and large terra cotta–colored clams. But not everything is grilled. Mitoya also serves a superb cold bean curd buried under a mound of bonito flakes, a respectable range of tempura preparations, and a few sashimi and sushi plates. Always look to the specials blackboard, and study the menu carefully. There are some truly exotic dishes to be found here.

MITOYA RESTAURANT, 1855 Post Street, Japan Center West Building, Second Floor, San Francisco. Telephone: (415) 563-2156. Hours: 6 pm–2 am Sunday–Thursday, 6 pm–2:30 am Friday–Saturday. Cards: AE, MC, V. Reservations advised. Full bar service. Parking in nearby garage.

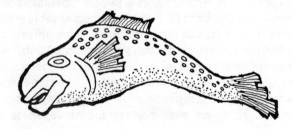

San Francisco: Civic Center
MODESTO LANZONE'S
Italian $$$

Those who remember Modesto as the genial maître d' at
Vanessi's several decades ago are not surprised that he
has become one of the city's most highly respected
restaurateurs. Since opening his own place in Ghirardelli
Square in the early 1970s (now called Lanzone and Son,
q.v.) he has made continuous efforts to introduce San
Franciscans to traditional Italian dishes that are rarely
encountered in this country. The pansoti, a ricotta-
stuffed pasta with a walnut sauce, is a good example.
"People thought I invented it," Modesto confesses,
"but the recipe is hundreds of years old." Modesto's
newer restaurant in the Opera Plaza showcases his
extraordinary collection of contemporary American art.
Hundreds of paintings and sculptures—on a par with
those at the nearby Museum of Modern Art—are
displayed in the otherwise stark dining areas. The works
are constantly changed and moved around, but one that
stays in place in the foyer is a bust of Modesto himself
on a pedestal; San Franciscans will immediately recognize
it as the work of sculptor Robert Arneson, whose
controversial bust of George Moscone made headlines
before it was removed from Moscone Center. The
Opera Plaza menu contains some regional Italian fare
not found elsewhere. One way to start a dinner here is
with a selection from the antipasto cart that is rolled to
your table, but heed this warning: You might be
tempted by the waiter to "try a little plate with a sample
of everything on the cart"; this tasting, though interesting,
costs $9 per person. If you choose only one item, the bill
will be only about a third as much. The appetizers
change nightly, but a sure winner is the pesto tart made
with garlic, basil, ricotta, and pine nuts in a flaky crust.
Among the entrées, a favorite is rabbit sautéed with
pine nuts, capers, and strips of red and green bell

peppers. Three or four fresh seafood specials are usually offered each evening as well. Since it's located only a block from the Performing Arts Center, Modesto's is geared to pretheater dining. Just tell your waiter that you're attending the opera, symphony, or whatever and you'll be out well before curtain time. But do take a few minutes to wander around the other dining rooms to admire the fantastic art collection.

MODESTO LANZONE'S, Opera Plaza, 601 Van Ness Avenue, San Francisco. Telephone: (415) 928-0400. Hours: 11:30–midnight Monday–Friday, 5–midnight Saturday. Cards: AE, CB, DC, MC, V. Reservations advised. Full bar service. Non-validated parking in Opera Plaza garage.

San Francisco: Marina
MULHERN'S
American $$

Mulhern's is perhaps the quintessential San Francisco bar-restaurant. Although it exudes a clublike atmosphere and its regulars are composed of a clientele with a goodly amount of discretionary income, the ambience is warm, friendly and not a bit aloof. The place retains the patina of old San Francisco and has not become yuppified. The front room contains a bar and several tables behind brass railings on a slightly raised level, many with a view of the corner fireplace. Walls are enlivened with colorful show-biz posters and the room suggests intimate dining and imbibing. In contrast, the rear room with its skylights and white walls splashed with posters has an airiness and sparkle that hints at al-fresco dining. A good beginning from the carefully planned menu is Kennebeck potato skins with sour cream and chives or an excellent Cobb salad. The Cajun-style andouille sausage sandwich with sautéed

MULHERN'S

3653 BUCHANAN STREET, SAN FRANCISCO, CALIFORNIA 94123 **346-5549**

Appetizers, Soups and Salads

SOUP OF THE DAY......................3.00　CHEESE NACHOS......................4.50
KENNEBECK POTATO SKINS *With Sour Cream and Chives*....................................3.95
HOUSE SALAD *Garnished with Watercress, Cucumber and Tomato*....................................3.50
　　With Roquefort........................**4.25**　　With Norwegian Shrimp......................4.95
PASTA SALAD *Fusili and Vegetables with Sweet Garlic Dressing*....................................6.50
COBB SALAD *Lettuce Topped with Chicken, Bacon,*
　Bleu Cheese, Shredded Egg and Tomato with Tangy Dressing....................................7.95
CHICKEN SALAD *Breast of Chicken, Vegetables, with Dijon Mayonnaise Dressing*....................6.95
SEAFOOD SALAD *Fresh Poached Fish and Shellfish with Greens*....................................7.95

Grill

14 OZ. DRY AGED NEW YORK STEAK....................................14.95
LAMB CHOPS MARINADE — WASHINGTON STATE....................................14.95
PORK CHOPS *With Sage and Cream Sauce*....................................11.25
SELECTION OF FRESH FISH....................................See Chalkboard　A.Q.

Sauté

SICILIAN CHICKEN *Spicy Chicken Breast with Cherry Peppers*....................................9.75
CALF'S LIVER *(WHEN AVAILABLE) With Pancetta and Onion Sauce*....................................10.95
PROSCIUTTO AND MORTADELLA TORTELLINI *With Fresh Tomato and Pancetta*............8.75
LINGUINI WITH OYSTERS *In a Fresh Tomato and Cream Sauce*....................................8.95
PASTA SPECIAL....................................See Chalkboard　A.Q.
FRESH PETRALE *(WHEN AVAILABLE) Sautéed in Lemon Butter*....................................9.95
CHICKEN BREAST *Sautéed, Served in Lemon and "Creme Fraiche"*....................................9.50

peppers and onions served on french bread with marinara sauce is outstanding. Dry-aged New York steak, calf's liver with pancetta and onion sauce, or linguini with oysters in a fresh tomato and cream sauce are all dependable dinner choices. Fish is always fresh, with petrale featured whenever available. In addition to the regular menu, five or six daily specials are served, such as hearty potato-leek soup, calamari, meatloaf and mashed potatoes, and other satisfying pub fare. Brunch ranges far beyond egg dishes, although they are well represented. Huevos rancheros with marinated skirt steak and a California taco salad are both welcome changes for brunch. Desserts are prepared daily on the premises and include double chocolate brownie with ice cream, and fresh fruit cobbler. Mulhern's is an understated, sophisticated, very San Francisco spot on a quiet side street off hectic Lombard, little more than a block from the Marina Green and Fort Mason attractions.

MULHERN'S, 3653 Buchanan Street, San Francisco. Telephone: (415) 346-5549. Lunch: 11:30–3, Monday–Saturday. Dinner: 5:30–11 Monday–Saturday, 5:30–10 Sunday. Brunch: 11:30–4 Saturday, 10–4 Sunday. Cards: AE, MC, V. Reservations accepted. Full bar service. Street parking.

San Francisco: Richmond District
NARAI
Thai/Chinese (Chao Chow)   **$**

Expertly prepared exotic food, moderate prices, a comfortable setting, an attentive staff—only rarely does one find all of these qualities under a single restaurant's roof. Narai meets such tough standards with aplomb, as every meal raises hopes for a repeat visit. Two culinary traditions are featured, the fiery food of Thailand and the seafood-oriented cuisine of south China's Chao Chow population. (Why this combination? Within Thailand live a large number of ethnic Chinese, many of them immigrants or their descendants from the area around Swatow in south China, home of Chao Chow food. These same immigrants make up a sizable portion of the restaurant owners of Thailand. Also, do not be confused by the use of Chiu Chow rather than Chao Chow. The former is merely the Cantonese phonetic form for the latter.) The menu, extensive on its own, is considerably expanded by the seasonal specials posted each evening. It is safe to say that almost anything ordered here will be not only good, but memorable. For example, there is the fish lung and black mushroom soup; don't let the name put you off, for this is a bowl of exceptional flavors and textures. The squid salad, a harmony of Thai spices, and the silver noodle salad are both to be recommended, and a plate of the Chao Chow–style "duck simmered in seasoning soy sauce," served with a mixture of garlic and vinegar for dipping, is unlike any other preparation of this fowl you've had. The pomfret (or pompano) is treated well here; order it with Narai's sauce, lemon sauce, or a brown sauce with slivers of black mushroom and pork. There are clay pots of mixed seafood, sea cucumber, and duck feet, and, on the specials board, large green New Zealand mussels in a lemon-grass-scented broth. The Thai noodle dishes are fine creations, the flavors perfectly balanced, plus there are curries, roasted quail, satays, and more. For dessert try the seasonally available durian (that sharp-odored fruit of Southeast Asia) and sweet rice, or a taro root concoction that will challenge the most self-assured possessor of a sweet tooth.

NARAI RESTAURANT, 2229 Clement Street (between 23rd and 24th avenues), San Francisco. Telephone: (415) 751-6363. Hours: 11–10 Tuesday–Sunday. Cards: AE, MC, V. Reservations advised. Beer and wine only. Street parking.

San Francisco: Mission District
NICARAGUA RESTAURANT
Nicaraguan $

The Nicaragua serves such a broad range of consistently good food at such reasonable prices, future visits to the Mission District will draw you to it like a magnet. Start with a flavorful dish of ceviche, chunks of white fish suitably vinegared and mixed with pieces of white onion and flecks of green chili. Tamale lovers swear by the two versions served here: the featherlight yoltamal is pure cornmeal, while the nacatamal is filled with perfectly seasoned shredded beef. Vigoron, a very popular Nicara-guan dish that nestles chicharrones (crispy pork skin) atop a bed of steamed yucca, is complemented by a side dish of fried cheese or bananas. Order a bowl of "crema"—sour cream—for slathering on the bananas. Baho, a platter of boiled beef, yucca, and banana; deschilachada, a mixture of shredded beef, onions,

peppers, and tomatoes; and lengua en salsa, sliced tongue smothered in a vegetable-based sauce are all very good. Two grilled thin-cut beef steaks, the classic carne asada and encebollado style (with onions); indio viejo con arroz y maduro (shredded beef with rice and fried bananas); and whole deep-fried red snapper are also recommended. Soups include mondongo (tripe), cangrejo (crab), and albondigas (meatballs), all available in two sizes. Imported and domestic beers, plus a whole line of traditional Nicaraguan drinks—pozol (hominy and milk), cacao (cocoa beans and milk), tamarinda—make up the beverage list. The simply furnished dining room, the walls covered with travel posters, is kept lively by a jukebox filled with Latin beats. This is a family-run place, with friendly service and a wait for your meal that reflects care in the kitchen.

NICARAGUA RESTAURANT, 3015 Mission Street, San Francisco. Telephone: (415) 550-9283. Hours: 11–10 Sunday–Thursday, until midnight Friday–Saturday. No cards. Reservations accepted. Beer and wine only. Street parking.

San Francisco: Cow Hollow
NORTH INDIA RESTAURANT
Indian $$

Small and cozy, this new place just off Lombard Street is less formal and less expensive than the city's other northern Indian restaurants. And the food is much hotter. "That's because we grind all our spices fresh daily and cook the dishes to order," says Punjabi owner-chef Parvesh Sahi. There's no doubting his word either, because the entire kitchen with its mesquite-fueled tandoor oven can be viewed behind a glass enclosure. The menu is quite simple and divided into two basic categories: Tandoori dinners offer a choice of chicken, lamb, prawns, or seekh kabab (a piquant sausage of minced meat) that have been marinated in spices and roasted in the clay oven. Curry dinners provide even more variety. In the murgh masala, chicken is treated to a hot dark sauce, while in the murgh makhani, chicken is first roasted in the tandoor, then sauced with a creamy butter and tomato combination. Curried lamb is cooked with onions, yogurt, and tomatoes, while in another version, fresh spinach is added. Prawns round out the list of curries and, as with all the other dishes, the individual preparation of each portion allows the flavor of the principal ingredients to shine through the sauces. All the dinners are amply accompanied with crispy breads from the tandoor, an assortment of curried vegetables, rice pilaf, sweet fruit chutney, and spicy peppers. Even so, it's hard to pass by the appetizers: samosas (deep-fried puffs of pastry stuffed with vegetables), shammi kabab (lamb ground with lentils), pakodas (vegetable fritters) and papadums (toasted lentil wafers). The best strategy here is to order an assorted platter of all. Waiters dressed in embroidered Indian vests provide excellent service. They do indeed care, because most are members of Sahi's family.

NORTH INDIA RESTAURANT, 3131 Webster, San Francisco. Telephone: (415) 931-1556. Hours: 5–10:30 Sunday–Thursday, 5–11 Friday–Saturday. Cards: AE, CB, DC, MC, V. Reservations recommended. Beer and wine only. Free city parking lot behind restaurant. Private banquet facilities: 20–50.

San Francisco: Richmond District
OCEAN RESTAURANT
Chinese (Cantonese)   **$**

"Good enough, but not as good as Chinatown." A few years ago, that was how most Chinese in San Francisco summed up the Asian restaurants of Clement Street. Today, thanks in no small part to the Ocean, culinary opinion is changing. The Richmond District has gradually emerged as a full-fledged, middle-class Chinatown in its own right, and has spawned a food establishment equal to the demanding Cantonese taste. The Ocean restaurants—there are two on Clement separated by five blocks and distinguished by the addition of the word "new" in the name of the most recent branch—stand at the pinnacle of that establishment, attracting a fervent clientele of Chinese and non-Chinese alike. As the name implies, seafood is the chief attraction here, and it is prepared with the simplicity and concern for freshness that characterize genuine south China cuisine at its best. A perfect example is the steamed whole catfish, selected live from a large tank at the rear of the restaurant and prepared in a delicious bath of soy, peanut oil, black beans, scallions, and just a touch of hot pepper. Another Ocean specialty is dry-fried prawns, lightly dusted in a salt-pepper mixture, then flash-cooked with slivers of fresh red pepper. Sacramento Delta frogs cooked in garlic and oil; lobster or Dungeness crab stir fried with ginger and scallions; black-bean-and-onion-topped steamed oysters; and eel with garlic, hot pepper, and ginger are all to be recommended. As with any good Chinese restaurant, your ability to extract information from the waiter about the specialties that day will make the difference between an acceptable meal and an exceptional one here. Both the Ocean and the New Ocean have the now-to-be-expected Formica-and-linoleum interior that marks many good Chinese eateries; the "New" branch is smaller and therefore a bit quieter.

OCEAN RESTAURANT, 726 Clement Street (between Eighth and Ninth avenues), San Francisco. Telephone: (415) 221-3351. Hours: 11:30–9:30 daily. NEW OCEAN RESTAURANT, 239 Clement (between Third and Fourth avenues), San Francisco. Telephone: (415) 668-1688. Lunch: 11:30–2:30. Dinner: 5–1 Sunday–Thursday, 5–3 Friday–Saturday. Cards: AE, MC, V. Reservations for six or more only. Beer and wine only. Valet parking at New Ocean, or street parking.

San Francisco: Pier 39
OLD SWISS HOUSE
Swiss/French $$

Here is an oasis of tranquility in the midst of the three-ring-circus hoopla of Pier 39. Old Swiss House exudes the charm of the motherland with pretty young waitresses dressed like Heidi. Seated on Alpine chairs and looking through picture windows, one would expect to see Lake Zurich instead of a magnificent view of San Francisco Bay. It is also surprising to find a family operation among the waterfront's mostly commercial establishments. Owner Roger Braun is the chef here, and his wife Marianne runs the dining room with an admirable blend of charm and efficiency. In keeping with the restaurant's name and atmosphere, a few Swiss dishes are offered, such as bündnerteller (an appetizer made with air-dried beef and prosciutto) and gschnätzlets (a main course of minced veal with cream sauce, accompanied with rösti potatoes). Wienerschnitzel reminds you that part of Switzerland is German, but most of the cooking is done with a French accent in the classic style: rack of lamb Provençale, duckling à l'orange flambéed at table, filet mignon topped with an artichoke bottom and sauce béarnaise, fillet of sole with crab legs in wine sauce. The

102

Brauns have obviously resisted the nouvelle band-wagon and stuck to their traditional ways, which in Switzerland also means a lot of food. All entrées are accompanied with two vegetables, potatoes, and rice.

OLD SWISS HOUSE, Pier 39, San Francisco. Telephone: (415) 434-0432. Lunch: 1:30–4 daily. Dinner: 5–10 Sunday–Thursday, 5–11 Friday–Saturday. Cards: AE, CB, DC, MC, V. Reservations advised. Full bar service. Validated parking in Pier 39 garage after 6 pm.

Entrées

All Entrées below include Bread and Butter, two Vegetables, and Potatoes or Rice.

Fresh Scallops "Queen Victoria" · Sautéed in Dry Sherry and Herbs, garnished with Baby Clams. **12.00**

Poached King Salmon · (Fresh in season) with Sauce Hollandaise, Boiled Potatoes. **12.00**

Filet of Sole Marguery · Poached Sole with Crab Legs in a White Wine Sauce, served with Rice. **11.50**

Sautéed Prawns "Portugaise" · Sautéed in White Wine with fresh Tomatoes and Green Onions and served with Rice. **12.50**

Roasted Chicken · Served with a Salad Elisabeth and Potatoes. **9.75**

Chicken Sauté A L'Indienne · Boneless Chicken Breast in Curry Sauce garnished with Fruits and served with Rice. **10.50**

Wienerschnitzel · Freshly breaded Veal Cutlet, pan fried in Butter and served with Potatoes. **10.50**

Veal Cordon Bleu · Homemade Veal Cutlets stuffed with Ham and Cheese and pan fried in Butter. Served with Potatoes. **12.00**

House Specialties

All Entrées below include Dinner Salad with House Dressing, two Vegetables, and Potatoes, Rice or Noodles.

"Gschnätzlets mit Rösti" · Thinly sliced pieces of Veal in a Cream Sauce with Mushrooms. Served with Rösti Potatoes. **13.75**

Milkfed Veal Steak "Morelle" · Pan fried in Butter and topped with a Cognac flavored Morelle Sauce with Noodles. **16.00**

Trois Filets "Old Swiss House" · Beef, Veal and Pork Tenderloins, each with a different garnish and Potatoes. **16.00**

Tournedos "Helder" · Filet Mignon wrapped in Bacon, topped with an Artichoke Bottom and Sauce Bearnaise. Served with Potatoes. **16.00**

Entrecôte "Café de Paris" · Grilled New York Steak with special Herb Butter, served with Potatoes. **15.50**

T-Bone Steak · 18 oz. grilled Steak, topped with Herb Butter. Served with Potatoes. **19.00**

PACIFIC HEIGHTS BAR & GRILL
Seafood $$

Here is a fish lovers' paradise and if your passion is raw oysters you might never get beyond the small shellfish bar in the front of the restaurant. Rarely is such a selection seen in this or any other city: usually a dozen types of half-shell offerings, ranging from mild bluepoints and Chesapeakes to perky mollusks from the Gulf to the tangy Olympias and Pacific oysters from the West Coast. If you do venture through the large and usually crowded bar to the pretty little dining room on the side, you will be well rewarded. You can also enjoy the oysters as an appetizer here, mixing your selections however you wish. And for entrées there's a choice of six or seven fresh catches grilled over mesquite and served with a topping to match your fancy: perhaps a shallot-scented sauce noisette, or lemon-herb butter, or a zesty salsa verde. If you want some fancier cooking, daily specials might include the likes of Chilean sea bass, shrimp and mussels braised with garlic tomatoes and white wine; or a rich jambalaya resplendent with prawns, scallops, mussells, andouille sausage, and a crayfish perched on top. You don't like fish? Well, a dry-aged steak sauced with wild mushrooms is sure to please.

PACIFIC HEIGHTS BAR & GRILL, 2001 Fillmore, San Francisco. Telephone: (415) 567-3337. Hours: 11–3, 5–10 daily. Sunday brunch: 11–3. Oyster bar: 11:30–midnight. Cards: AE, MC, V. Reservations advised. Full bar. Valet parking after 5:30.

San Francisco: Downtown
PADANG
Indonesian

$

Firman Symasu and his family (Minangkabaus from the Indonesian island of Sumatra) opened the Padang in June, 1984. The restaurant's name is taken from the city, halfway up the western coast of the island, that marks the urban center of the tribe's homeland. In Indonesia, Sumatrans are considered the best chefs, and the Padang goes a long way in substantiating that belief. The best dishes here are ikan panggang, a pompano that has been rubbed with oil and spices and then grilled to perfection; the satays served with thick peanut sauces; beef kalio minang, meat chunks cooked in an exotic mixture of coconut milk, lemon grass, onion, garlic, and spices; and dendeng, a dry beef curry coated with a thick, spicy red sauce. If you are interested in trying a whole gamut of Indonesian preparations, select the rijsttafel, a "banquet" of six classic dishes of the cuisine. Orders come with two great mounds of steamed white rice and a pungent-hot chili condiment, or sambal. There is a lunch menu that features, among many other items, mie bakso, a noodle dish of Chinese origin, and kari ayam, a simple chicken curry. The dining room walls are hung with native artifacts, and a small ledge along one of them holds foot-high dolls dressed in the traditional garb of Indonesia's many tribes. Mr. Symasu is on hand to answer any question you might have about the dishes, while his wife and sister keep the kitchen turning out their country's native dishes.

PADANG, 700 Post Street, San Francisco. Telephone: (415) 775-6708. Hours: 12–3, 5–11 Monday–Saturday. Cards: MC, V. Beer and wine only. Street parking.

San Francisco: Cow Hollow
PASAND MADRAS
East Indian $

San Francisco does have a number of East Indian
restaurants, but they are, for the most part, relatively
expensive establishments with decor to match the cost,
and menus that feature the dishes of north India. There
is no strong tradition here of the good, modestly priced
Indian eatery one finds in New York or London, and so
exploring this complex exotic cuisine must, out of
financial necessity, be relegated to special evenings out.
Fortunately, there is Pasand Madras, a restaurant that
specializes in the dishes of south India and offers them
at very reasonable prices. But the existence of only a
single good "everyday Indian restaurant" is not the only
incongruity in this story. First, the people that operate
Pasand Madras are not from Madras at all, but rather
from the state directly north, Andhra Pradesh. ("No one
has ever heard of our state, so we decided to use the
name Madras.") Second, the restaurant is located in a
space that once housed an eatery designed around a
vintner motif: Dozens of French wine labels are trapped
beneath the clear plastic top of the good-size bar, and
great oak casks protrude from the walls. Third, jazz
groups play here nightly, which is certainly not an
Indian art form, but is probably sound business judg-
ment in this highly competitive night-life area. The food,
though, is the real story, and Pasand Madras offers good
value for the money: crispy puris and rich, pliable
chapatis; the grandly long, crêpelike masala dosa, filled
with a spicy vegetable mixture; a variety of biriani
dishes; wonderful lamb curry and chicken korma; bowls
of coconut-scented yogurt and mango and mint chutneys;
crunchy onion pakoras and delicious potato-and-pea-
filled samosas; and much more. For those who are
struck with indecision when faced with the large array of
appetizing-sounding choices, there are special dinners

(both vegetarian and nonvegetarian) that are good samplings of what this kitchen can do. Pasand Madras has a very popular branch in Berkeley where prices are even more modest than the Union Street location, and the live music flows from a sitar rather than a trumpet.

PASAND MADRAS, 1875 Union Street, San Francisco. Telephone: (415) 922-4498. Hours: 11:30–10 daily. Live jazz every evening until about 1 am. Cards: AE, CB, DC, MC, V. Reservations recommended. Full bar service. Street parking. Private banquet facilities: 50.

San Francisco: Downtown
PIERRE
French $$$

So you want to impress an important client or conduct some high-level negotiations in strictest confidence? This very sophisticated salon in the luxurious Meridien Hotel a block away from Moscone Center is the perfect spot. Unlike most downtown luncheon rendezvous, the tables are spaced far apart, the atmosphere is ultraserene, and the service is attentive but unobtrusive, so you can concentrate on the business at hand without worrying about the wineglasses being filled. The decor is in restful shades of gray, punctuated by mirrors and a large mural of a French palace. The noted French chef Alain Chapel of Meaunais designed Pierre's original menu and, as consultant to the restaurant, he returns periodically to check out the kitchen—not that it needs it. Under the expert direction of food and beverage manager Jean-Pierre Moullé and chef Sebastian Urbain, the Pierre these days is serving some of the finest Gallic food in town. Luncheons are priced from $13 to $20 and include a first course with a choice ranging from light salads to duck terrine to a vegetable flan with fresh scallops. The menu changes seasonally. Among the ten or so luncheon entrées you might find veal chops with a sweet pepper coulis and spinach fettuccine, sea bass laved with a creamy white wine sauce studded with mussels, or a chicken liver and mushroom omelet with a rich port sauce. Dinner is à la carte, with appetizers like a sweetbread salad with avocado and citrus fruit, or a ragout of oysters and spinach in champagne sauce. At least a dozen entrées are offered ($16 to $24), such as breast of squab in puff pastry with a tarragon sauce, fricassee of sole and scallops in a saffron broth, or grilled sirloin with shallots and coriander served with sautéed artichoke bottoms. It is difficult to resist the dessert cart here laden with pastries, fruit tarts, or a bittersweet chocolate torte. From time to time Pierre features dinners prepared by guest chefs from two- and three-star French restaurants. Ask to be placed on the mailing list for more information.

PIERRE, Meridien Hotel, 15 Third Street, San Francisco. Telephone: (415) 974-6400. Lunch: 11:30–2:30 Monday–Friday. Dinner: 6–10 Monday–Saturday. Cards: AE, CD, DC, MC, V. Reservations recommended. Full bar service. Valet parking.

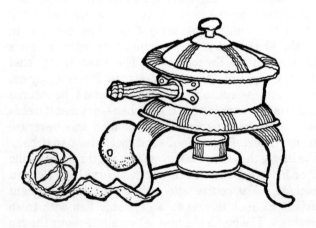

UNE FRICASSEE DE FILETS DE SOLE ET NOIX DE ST. JACQUES
A LA NAGE DE SAFRAN $16.00
Fricassee of fresh sole and scallops in a saffron broth

ROUELLES DE HOMARD DU MAINE POELEES, DES POMMES DE TERRE
GENRE MAXIME, UN BEURRE DE CORAIL $23.50
Sautéed Maine lobster medaillons in a coral butter served with potatoes Maxime

MEDAILLONS DE LOTTE POELES, UN BEURRE D'HUITRES A LA CIBOULETTE
ET UNE MATIGNON DE LEGUMES L'ACCOMPAGNE $18.00
Sautéed medaillons of fresh angler in an oyster chive butter,
served with a vegetable garni

SUPREME DE BAR A LA FONDUE DE TOMATE AUX HERBES
ET AUX PETITS POIS GOURMANDS $18.00
Filet of sea bass with a fondue of tomatoes, herbs and snow peas

POITRINE DE PIGEON AU VINAIGRE D'ESTRAGON, SA FEUILLANTINE
ET SON ETUVEE DE JEUNES CAROTTES AU CERFEUIL $17.00
Breast of squab in a delicate puff pastry, served with a
tarragon sauce and carrots braised with chervil

GRAS DE CUISSE ET MAGRET DE CANARD AU ZESTE D'ORANGE ET
POIVRE VERT SON DARPHIN DE NAVETS ET COURGETTES $17.50
Duck breast and thigh in a green pepper orange sauce,
with a zucchini and turnip gratin

UN SUPREME DE FAISAN A LA COMPOTE DE POIREAUX TRUFFEE,
SA CUISSE ROTIE DE JEUNES LAITUES BRAISEES $18.50
Roast breast and leg of pheasant with a compote of leeks,
truffles and braised lettuce

COTE DE VEAU A LA CREME D'ENDIVES ET OLIVES NICOISES,
DES PATES FRAICHES $19.50
Veal cutlet in an endive and nicoise olive cream sauce,
served with fresh homemade pasta

L'ENTRECOTE AUX BULBES D'ECHALOTES ET GRAINES DE CORIANDRE, UNE FRICASSEE
DE FONDS D'ARTICHAUTS,DES POMMES DE TERRE NOUVELLES AUX AMANDES $20.00
Grilled sirloin steak with shallots and coriander served with sautéed artichoke bottoms
and new potatoes with almonds.

FILET MIGNON EN COCOTTE, UNE SAUCE AU FOIE GRAS ET JUS DE TRUFFES,
SA FRICASSEE DES SOUS-BOIS $21.00
Filet Mignon with foie gras and truffle juice
served with sautéed wild mushrooms

UN CARRE D'AGNEAU POUR DEUX AU THYM FRAIS,
DES GOUSSES D'AIL CONFITES $42.00
Rack of lamb for two, roasted with fresh thyme and
served with a garlic confit

LES FROMAGES DE CALIFORNIE $5.50
California cheeses

109

PING YUEN
Chinese American $

Chinese cooks are among the best-kept secrets of San Francisco's European restaurants. Quick to grasp the most esoteric details of foreign cuisines, they can be found hard at work in dozens of the city's best eateries. But when the Chinese themselves want a European meal, they venture no farther than Chinatown and the Ping Yuen Bakery & Restaurant on lower Jackson (not to be confused with Ping Yuen on Stockton). Over the years, this establishment has acquired the status of a venerable institution, attracting huge throngs to its longtime quarters on Grant until a rent-bidding war with the bank presently located there forced a move. The popularity of Ping Yuen is no mystery: Where else can less than $5 buy wiener schnitzel, potatoes, fresh-baked rolls, and buttered vegetables? Or veal piccata, stuffed veal breast, roast lamb, or braised beef brisket? The mixed grill, at little more, includes beef steak, pork chops, calf's liver, sausage, and bacon. Add just a few dimes to these or to any of Ping Yuen's other generously portioned Western offerings, such as the beautifully rare roast beef, and the meal will be preceded by homemade soup and followed with ice cream and coffee. Now, the vegetable of the day may be that deservedly disdained medley of carrots, peas, and beans one remembers from one's nongourmet past, but at these prices it can be endured. For a mid-afternoon pick-me-up, look to the array of just-baked pies and cakes along the wall behind the long soda counter—the strawberry cream, apple, and custard pies here have been favorite Chinatown snacks and desserts for a generation. You can even special-order your Thanksgiving pumpkin pie at Ping Yuen. Rumor has it that the Chinese food is pretty good, too.

PING YUEN BAKERY & RESTAURANT, 650 Jackson Street, San Francisco. Telephone: (415) 986-6830. Hours: 7 am–7 pm daily. No cards. Reservations recommended. No alcoholic beverages. Street parking.

San Francisco: Cow Hollow
PREGO
Italian   **$$**

One of the most upscale Italian menus in town keeps the crowds pouring into this lively Union Street café. Although some 50 dishes are offered, they fall into three basic categories—pasta, pizza, and grilled foods—plus an enticing selection of antipasti. The latter include a number of salads, buffalo mozzarella with tomatoes, carpaccio, and a cold artichoke stuffed with artichoke hearts and bread. The pasta, made in house, comes in over a dozen imaginative varieties. The tortelloni, for example, is stuffed with ricotta and chard and the agnolotti crescents contain a filling of lobster, prosciutto, and ricotta. Gnocchi lovers are tempted with three sauces, pesto, gorgonzola, and pomodoro. And there is even a pasta for dieters: whole-wheat fettuccine sauced with fresh tomatoes, lemon, and herbs, but no oil or butter. The nine types of pizza have the usual good stuff in their fillings—mozzarella, tomatoes, pepperoni, mushrooms—but there are also versions with artichokes, eggplant, prosciutto, and even prawns. One also is made with the rich Italian bread, focaccia, drenched with basil-infused olive oil, onions, and sun-dried tomatoes. To top off your meal there are some rich desserts and gelati, too.

PREGO, 2000 Union Street, San Francisco. Telephone: (415) 563-3305. Hours: 11:30–midnight daily. Cards: AE, MC, V. Reservations advised. Full bar service. Parking on street or in nearby garages.

PRINCE NEVILLE
Jamaican   **$–$$**

The moment you see Neville Wright, a grandly sized fellow outfitted in white leather toque and apron, you just know he is a master at the stove. And your intuition proves accurate, for Prince Neville's is a Jamaican restaurant of the first order. The goat curry, a classic of the cuisine, is a memorable creation of complex seasonings and beautifully tender, lean meat. The rich, fragrant oxtail stew arrives in such a generous portion, one barely has room for the accompanying steamed fresh vegetables and Carib "pilaf" of pigeon peas and rice. There is a selection of West Indian vegetarian specialties, including one with ackee, an essentially indescribable tropical fruit. Some of the finest salt cod (saltfish to the Jamaicans) dishes in town are to be found here. For example, the Prince combines small pieces of boned cod with cabbage, tomato, onion, and carrot in a sauté that will immediately convert any salt-cod middle-of-the-roader into a shameless promoter. Another pairs the cod with callaloo, a leafy vegetable of the chef's island home. Soup comes with all the dinners, but the accompaniments vary with the entrées; excellent fried plaintains and torpedo-shaped corn dumplings are among the possibilities. Beer lovers should try the Jamaican Red Stripe, a good brew, or the ginger, bottled by Neville himself. The soft background music is reggae; if you like the beat, pick up a cassette at Wright's boutique of Jamaican goods, located at the rear of the dining room.

PRINCE NEVILLE'S, 424 Haight Street, San Francisco. Telephone: (415) 861-9433. Hours: 5–10 Wednesday–Saturday, 4–9 Sunday. No cards. Reservations not accepted. Beer and wine only. Street parking.

San Francisco: Tenderloin District
RACHA CAFE
Thai $

If there is one area in which food-conscious San Franciscans will concede superiority to Los Angeles, it is in the realm of Thai restaurants. Up north we just don't have the quantity, though we can boast a degree of quality, as the small, unpretentious Racha Cafe successfully illustrates. The two laap dishes, one made with beef, the other with pork, are highly flavored combinations of minced meat strong on lime, chili, onion, and mint. One of these, or the squid salad dressed with garlic, lime, chili, lemon grass, and fish sauce, is a good first course. Pork with garlic, the medallions arranged on a plate garnished with sliced tomatoes, and the chestnut-colored duck, served with a dipping sauce of vinegar and garlic, are both delicious. Curries are generous and tasty, the pork in a peanutty sauce atop a bed of deep-green spinach is satisfying, and the simply fried fish is a classic. Jars of condiments—fresh green chili pepper slices, dried red chili pepper flakes, ground peanuts, fish sauce—are set out for seasoning individual servings; beware, for those chilies are indeed as powerful as they look. The only real disappointments here have been some of the noodle dishes, which are generally too saucy. A counter near the kitchen is good for single diners or for those in a hurry; space at the limited number of tables is always hotly contested. And the good food and moderate prices are sure to keep it that way.

RACHA CAFE, 807 Ellis Street, San Francisco. Telephone: (415) 885-0725. Hours: 11 am–9 pm Monday–Saturday, closed Sunday. No cards. Beer and wine only. No reservations. Street parking.

RESTAURANT 101
French **$$$**

Unlike most downtown restaurants, 101 has a light and airy ambience. Its enormous windows look out on a plaza, where umbrella-shaded tables are set up for lunch or cocktails on sunny days. The artfully arranged dishes are the work of Fred Halpert, a young chef who trained with Alain Chapel and Roger Vergé in France, then went on to make a name for himself at Mangia in Los Angeles. Though Halpert changes the menu daily, he obviously favors certain ingredients, which appear frequently in different guises. Angel hair pasta is often present, sometimes sauced with prosciutto or pancetta and vegetables, at other times combined with fruits de mer or perhaps scallops and sun-dried tomatoes. Quail is another perennial favorite, grilled with vegetables (such as corn, onions, and garlic) at lunchtime and composed in a salad at dinner. Chicken is most always present, grilled or sautéed, with sauces ranging from

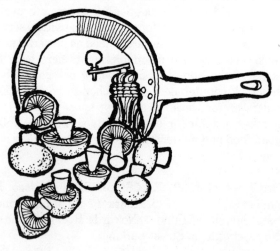

garlic, rosemary, and olive oil to white wine and soy. Chutney is Halpert's condiment of choice with pork tenderloin, which might be sauced with port wine or curry. Cabernet, combined with bone marrow, is often used to sauce the aged New York sirloin that usually appears on the dinner menu and is sometimes paired with a sauce of pommery mustard. And, at both lunch and dinner, there is always a selection of several fresh fish, grilled, poached, or baked. Exotic fruits are featured in 101's desserts. Look for such combinations as chocolate mousse with a compote of kumquats and lime, or a little almond cake with kiwi and vanilla sabayon.

RESTAURANT 101, 101 California Street, San Francisco. Telephone: (415) 788-4101. Lunch: 11:30–2:30 Monday–Friday. Dinner: 6:15–10 Tuesday–Saturday. Cards: AE, CB, DC, MC, V. Reservations advised. Full bar service. Valet parking at night. Private banquet facilities: 8–14.

San Francisco: South of Market
RINGS
California Cuisine $$

Even though chef and co-owner Julie Ring has recently arrived from Chicago (where she cooked professionally for ten years), her culinary style can best be described as Californian. The emphasis is on fresh local seafood and produce, prepared with a variety of ethnic nuances. The menu changes daily, but usually a shellfish appetizer is included, such as mussels aswim in a heavenly broth flecked with bits of red potatoes and tomatoes, or mariscos mexicanos—clams, cockles, and scallops scented with jalapeño and cilantro. One pasta is also offered and in this department Ring often gets quite creative; perhaps it will be a ravioli stuffed with chicken liver mousse and sauced with sage-seasoned brown butter.

Entrées emphasize grilled fish with sauces varying from wasabi-ginger butter to saffron-sorrel cream; a grilled meat or chicken dish is featured as well. Desserts are divine, especially the mud pie and unusual pastries, such as apple pie with a white-chocolate crust and strawberry sauce. From the exterior, Rings could pass for yet another Folsom Street auto parts shop, but inside it's lovely and springlike, with the walls painted in shades of salmon, pink, and mauve and a lavender wainscoting that serves as a backing for the wooden benches that line the narrow room; in the rear is a space for outdoor dining. The decor looks like it was done on a thoughtful shoestring: paper covers on the tables and fresh flowers in restaurant-supply parfait glasses. As the South of Market area booms, so does Rings's popularity, causing some hang-ups in service, especially at lunchtime.

RINGS, 1131 Folsom Street, San Francisco. Telephone: (415) 621-2111. Lunch: 11:30–3 Monday–Friday. Dinner: 6–10 Tuesday–Thursday, 6–10:30 Friday–Saturday. Cards: MC, V. Wine and beer only. Street parking.

San Francisco: Marina
RISTORANTE PARMA
Italian

$$

Here is one of those warm, wonderfully honest trattorias that are becoming harder and harder to find, with excellent food at modest prices. The place is not about to win a design award, but it's pleasant, with mirrors set in brick walls, Italian travel posters here and there, and tables crammed together down each side of the long narrow room. But the food—aah. Start by sharing an antipasto plate, almost a meal in itself, with about a dozen items including melon and prosciutto, a vinaigrette of mixed seafood including shrimp and calamari, olives, marinated mushrooms and artichoke hearts, a beef sausage especially made for the restaurant, zucchini rounds and carrot spears toasted in salt to a golden brown—delicious. Along with traditional pastas, Parma offers some unusual combinations such as fettuccine with bacon, onions, and tomato sauce, and pennine with mushrooms, sausage and vodka! It's called pennine Romanoff. If you're here on a weekend, don't miss the gnocchi: plump little dumplings of spinach swimming in a nutmeg-scented cream sauce. The veal also is excellent— superbly tender and rendered in ten different ways. The chef's specialties are scaloppine with eggplant and cheese, and a veal roll stuffed with spinach, cheese, mushrooms, and prosciutto, served with a delicate tomato sauce. Entrées are accompanied with pan-fried potatoes and al dente vegetables. And when the check comes, it's a pleasant surprise: Dinner for two with a shared antipasto and pasta, plus entrée, will run about $35 without wine.

RISTORANTE PARMA, 3314 Steiner, San Francisco. Telephone: (415) 567-0500. Hours: 5–10:30 Tuesday– Sunday. Cards: MC, V. Reservations advised. Wine only. Street parking.

San Francisco: Tenderloin District
SAI'S RESTAURANT
Vietnamese $

Tens of thousands of Vietnamese refugees have settled in San Francisco in recent years. Their numbers have most notably transformed the Tenderloin, where Vietnamese-run food and dry-goods stores and restaurants have displaced shuttered storefronts and the businesses that serviced the longtime neighborhood population of down-at-the-heels city dwellers. Among the most popular of these recent establishments is Sai's, which more often than not is crowded with young Vietnamese enjoying rock and roll music recorded in their native language. This is not the place for a quiet dinner amidst charming surroundings, nor is it the spot to bring even a slightly finicky friend, for decor and general order and hygiene fail the most modest expectations. But this is a kitchen where authentic Vietnamese food is prepared and served to an appreciative native clientele at very reasonable prices. Good first courses are banh xeo, the Hue-style yellow "pancake" filled with shrimp, pork, and bean sprouts; goi cuon, dry rice-paper cylinders of pork, shrimp, and vegetables; or banh cuon, fresh rice-paper "packets" of minced mushroom and meat served with thin slices of Vietnamese-style pork pâté, pieces of deep-fried "cake" studded with mung beans, fresh mint leaves, and french-fried shallots. Chicken curry can be ordered with rice sticks, steamed rice, or french bread. The lamb stew, various grilled pork dishes, and chao long, a thick rice porridge with mixed meats and a healthy crown of shallots, are all delicious. The menu section devoted to special dinners includes a grill-your-own pork or beef selection, an elaborate hot and sour soup with catfish, and a combination fire pot that is superb; powdery gray coals keep a vessel of extremely flavorful broth loaded with shrimp, crab, fish cake, pork stomach, and napa cabbage perking at your table.

Finish with Vietnamese-style drip coffee or one of the traditional "dessert drinks," such as che dau xanh, a coconut and green bean mixture. The Sai Cam Huyhn family, formerly of Saigon, operate this place and a recently opened second restaurant, on Kearny Street in Chinatown.

SAI'S RESTAURANT, 491 Ellis Street, San Francisco. Telephone: (415) 928-5188. Hours: 10–9 Tuesday–Sunday. No cards. Beer and wine only. Street parking.

San Francisco: Financial District
SAM'S GRILL
Seafood $$

The outside of Sam's looks like a scruffy corner bar. Inside, by 11:30 every weekday morning you'll find brokers, bankers, and business people waiting five deep at the bar for a table. No reservations are accepted, even though you'll note a few regular customers being whisked away to private booths that they most likely inherited from their grandfathers. Sam's is a San Francisco institution, the epitome of no-frills, no-nonsense dining. Only old-fashioned coat hooks decorate the walls, and there is nothing but starched white cloths on the tables to interfere with the serious business of eating. Black-tied waiters serve with utmost efficiency some of the finest and freshest seafood available from both the East and West coasts. Boned rex sole or sand dabs aswim in a sea of butter are classics, as is the steamed Alaskan cod.

Olympia oysters appear in season, along with eastern scallops, Dungeness crab, Little Neck clams, or broiled swordfish. Most often only a plain boiled potato will garnish your plate, but an à la carte order of creamed spinach rounds off a meal nicely. Sam's wine list offers a small, but discriminating selection, from California's boutique wineries. Crowded as Sam's is at lunchtime, it's a very quiet place for dinner, most likely due to the financial district location and the early closing hour.

SAM'S GRILL, 374 Bust Street, San Francisco. Telephone: (415) 421-0594. Hours: 11–8:30 Monday–Friday. Cards: MC, V. Reservations accepted only for parties of six or more. Full bar service. Parking in downtown garages. Private banquet facilities: 17.

San Francisco: Japantown and Richmond District
SAN WANG
Northern Chinese $

For years, being seated quickly at the modest-sized San Wang restaurant on Post Street was nearly impossible. The doorway was always jammed with northern Chinese who missed their native dishes, Koreans who longed for the same fare they had enjoyed in Seoul's many Chinese restaurants, and the rest of us who were smug about our discovery of an accomplished northern kitchen in our south China stronghold. When San Wang opened a second large branch out on Clement Street a year ago, we long-patient diners breathed a sigh of relief. But now, alas, both locations are crowded with loyalists enjoying such classic fare as cold plates of aromatic beef and jellyfish, fish in wine sauce, pot stickers, eggplant in garlic sauce, braised whole fish in bean sauce, and pulled noodles, the extraordinary northern "pasta" that is formed without the aid of a knife: a pulled-noodle master magically "twists" the dough into beautiful long strands. San Wang's plum-sauce version, a treasure trove of shrimp and sea cucumber in a dark, rich mildly piquant blend, cloaks these artworks admirably. The unusually named "sautéed pork with two pieces of skin" is outstanding: Individual hillocks of cold pork, squid, shrimp, cloud ear, jellyfish, and other ingredients surround a mountain of hot stir-fried pork and shredded mung bean sheets; at table, the hot and cold foods are tossed together in a mustardy sauce. San Wang is also justly famed for its stir-fried clams flecked with chilies, and even for some classic Cantonese dishes, such as fresh lobster or crab with ginger and scallions. The Wang brothers, who hail from north China's Hebei Province, have carried to the newer branch a Post Street tradition savored by their Korean patrons: a bowl of fiery kim chee at every table.

SAN WANG No. 1, 1682 Post Street, San Francisco. Telephone: (415) 982-0471. SAN WANG No. 2, 2239 Clement Street, San Francisco. Telephone: (415) 221-1870. Hours: 11:30–10 daily. Cards: MC, V. Reservations recommended. Full bar service at Clement Street location, beer and wine only at Post Street. Street parking or in nearby lots.

San Francisco: Potrero Hill
S. ASIMAKOPOULOS CAFE
Greek $

At peak hours people stand elbow to elbow waiting for a seat at the long counter or one of the bare-topped tables crammed against the wall. No one seems to mind the discomfort, however, for this tiny café turns out one of the most extensive Greek menus this city has seen, the quality of the food is excellent, and the price is very reasonable. Gather up a party of four so you can share a platter of mezethakia (a selection of appetizers that is too much for two). There's a row of plump phyllo dough envelopes, each with a different filling—spanakopitta (spinach and cheese), kreatopitta (spicy meat), tiropitta (tangy cheese) and kotopitta (chicken)—plus rows of keftethes (piquant little meatballs) and locanico (sausage spiced with orange). A generous mound of hummus (garbanzo bean and sesame purée) and lots of hot pita bread complete the platter. Be forewarned to come here hungry because the dinners are bountiful and include Greek lemon soup or a large salad topped with tomatoes, onions, olives, and feta; entrées are embellished with roast potatoes or pilaf and fresh vegetables that are blessedly not overcooked. Lamb appears in ten dishes on the printed menu ranging from simple charcoal-broiled chops fused with garlic, lemon, and oregano to long-simmering stews to slices of roast lamb with artichoke hearts and egg-lemon sauce. Fresh local snapper is the favored seafood here, either baked with a mélange of vegetables or sautéed with garlic and kalamata olives. Several chicken dishes are also offered, as well as squid sautéed in butter and garlic. If the full dinner is too much food after the mezethakia, consider the souvlakia, skewers of juicy marinated lamb, pork, or chicken served on hot pita bread with sliced tomatoes, bermuda onions, just-fried potatoes with bits of their skin intact, and a cup of lettuce filled with tzajiki—a refreshing sauce of homemade yogurt, garlic and cucumbers. The house coffee—a blend of Antigua and dark french roast—is a wonderful finale with honey-drenched Greek pastries.

S. ASIMAKOPOULOS CAFE, 288 Connecticut at 18th, San Francisco. Telephone: (415) 552-8789. Hours: 11:30–10 Monday–Friday, 5–10 Saturday. Cards: MC, V. Reservations not accepted. Wine and beer only. Street parking.

San Francisco: Richmond District
SHIMO
Japanese $$

With so many Japanese restaurants opening in San Francisco, lovers of sushi, tempura, yosenabe feel almost drowned in choices. A menu posted in the window, a peek at the decor, a whiff of the cooking fragrances are all elements of the selection process. One of the most telling signs, however, is the Japan Central Bank (JCB) sticker, a sure indication that the establishment caters to visitors from Japan. Shimo has that red-and-blue credit-card decal affixed to its window, and every other "good-restaurant indicator" is in evidence as well. The small interior, with its blond wood, blue highlights, wall hangings, and busy sushi bar, is overseen by a friendly staff outfitted in traditional costume. There are two menus, one for sushi and one for hot fare, but these choices are expanded by a specials board at the rear of the room and a query to the person serving you. And there are *wonderful* surprises to be had: silken raw shrimp tails resting on pads of sushi rice, followed by the golden-egg-filled shrimp bodies, with madly twisted "antennae" intact, prepared tempura style. All of the sushi is generous and exquisite; the unagi (eel), uni (sea urchin), hamachi (yellowtail), and maguro (tuna) are illustrative of Shimo's commitment to high quality. An order of the grilled fish brings a mackerel with crispy skin and rich, flavorful flesh—true kitchen artistry. The yosenabe is heavy with fish cake, noodles, chicken, vegetables, seafood, all afloat in a remarkable broth. Green tea ice cream is a cool, refreshing finish to a meal at Shimo, where even visitors from Japan will find the food "just like home"—and they can charge it on JCB.

SHIMO, 2339 Clement Street (between 24th and 25th avenues), San Francisco. Telephone: (415) 752-4422. Hours: 5:30–midnight Tuesday–Sunday. Cards: DC, JCB, MC, V. Reservations recommended. Beer and wine only. Street parking. Private banquet facilities: 8–10.

San Francisco: Jackson Square Area
SQUARE ONE
International   **$$–$$$**

When Square One opened in 1984, it was an instant hit and no one was even slightly surprised. Owner-chef Joyce Goldstein brought to her upscale trattoria some 20 years of experience as a cooking teacher and more recently as head chef for the Café at Chez Panisse. While some might think of Square One as trendy, Goldstein's cooking has solid roots in the culinary traditions of the Mediterranean area, which she has researched in depth during her many trips to Europe. Take, for example, fennel and orange salad. "There's nothing new about that," she admits. "I found it mentioned in a 16th-century menu from the Veneto." She also avoids the clichés of California cuisine in her ambitious menu, which is changed completely each day. She usually offers nine entrées, robust dishes inspired by a potpourri of ethnic cuisines. A given day might bring a choice of several hearty pastas; a grilled flank steak with a Korean marinade redolent with ginger, garlic, and chilies; a Portuguese-style ragout of clams, chorizo, and prosciutto; sautéed prawns and scallops in a hot citrus-based sauce from Yucatán; to name a few. Among the half dozen or so salads and light entrées, you might find a provençal soup of chick-peas spiked with cloves and coriander, a lavish medley of five Middle Eastern salads, or an elegant pairing of radicchio and endive with pears, gorgonzola, and walnuts. The dessert list is also extensive and includes such enticing goodies as a puff pastry tart with blood oranges and caramel-rum pastry cream. The Wednesday menu, however, is a different story altogether. Goldstein reserves that day for her on-going exploration of the cooking of a particular cuisine, which changes every four to six months and no recipe is ever repeated. She has covered Italy, France, North Africa, and the Middle East and at this writing is back to Italy, region by region, which might go on as long as ten months, she guesses. Square One is a comfortable restaurant with large windows looking out to the greenery of the Golden Gateway commons and a restful, contemporary decor that does not intrude upon what appears on the plate.

SQUARE ONE, 190 Pacific Avenue at Front, San Francisco. Telephone: (415) 788-1110. Lunch: 11:30–2:30 Monday–Friday. Dinner: 5:30–10 Monday–Thursday, 5:30–10:30 Friday–Saturday, 5–9:30 Sunday. Cards: AE, MC, V. Reservations advised. Full bar service. Parking at nearby garage during day, street parking at night.

San Francisco: Civic Center
STARS
California Cuisine $$$

Jeremiah Tower needs no introduction to the foodies of this world. As chef, he helped make Chez Panisse a must stop on the international culinary circuit. After a relatively quiet stint at Ventana Inn in Big Sur, he created media blitzes when he took over the kitchens of several supertrendy Bay Area grills. Thus when he opened Stars in 1984, it was a welcome surprise to find a rather traditional, comfortable ambience in the large dining room with its dark wooden pillars and turn-of-the-century posters and lighting fixtures. Tower's menu, though, does offer the grilled meats and seafood and the unusual sauces punctuated with garlic, ginger, and chili peppers that have become his signature. But the repertoire at Stars is much broader than that: curries and pizzas, ragouts and sautés frequently appear. He will come up with some very unorthodox combinations like steak tartare garnished with radicchio, grilled mushrooms, and cèpe mayonnaise. And at the same time offer an item as pure as premium oysters on the half shell with a classic sauce mignonette. Desserts are provocative, such as the rich black walnut and fig tart with champagne sabayon. Stars has been a phenomenal success; within a year of opening it showed the highest gross of any independent San Francisco restaurant.

STARS, 150 Redwood (between Van Ness and Polk), San Francisco. Telephone: (415) 861-7827. Hours: 11 am–2 am Monday–Friday, 4 pm–2 am Saturday–Sunday. Cards: AE, MC, V. Reservations advised. Full bar service. Parking at nearby lots.

DINNER MENU

JEREMIAH'S SELECTIONS: GRECO DI TUFO, MASTROBERARDINO 1983 15.00

VINOT, ANGELO GAJA (NEBBIOLO "NUOVO") 1985 15.00

TONIGHT'S DESSERT SOUFFLE: TOASTED ALMOND with maraschino creme anglaise
(please order in advance)   5.50

APPETIZERS

SIX OYSTERS ON THE HALF SHELL WITH SAUCE MIGNONETTE 6.75
FOUR OYSTERS ON THE HALF SHELL WITH SMOKED SALMON,
   BITTER GREENS & A LEMON-PEPPER CREAM 8.50
COLUMBIA RIVER STURGEON PAILLARD WITH GARLIC, GINGER,
   SESAME & SCALLIONS 7.25
GRILLED SNAILS & ARTICHOKES WITH RADICCHIO, PASTA SALAD &
   ROAST GARLIC AIOLI 7.50
WARM PASTA SALAD WITH SMOKED TROUT, SHIITAKE MUSHROOMS,
   HERBS & FONTINA CHEESE 7.50
STARS GRAVLAX WITH GRILLED HERB BRIOCHE 8.00
WARM CABBAGE SALAD WITH GOAT CHEESE, ROASTED HAZELNUTS & PANCETTA.. 7.50

SALADS & SOUP

MIXED GREEN SALAD WITH VINAIGRETTE 4.75
MIXED GREEN SALAD WITH BLUE CHEESE VINAIGRETTE 5.25
STAR FARM GARDEN SALAD WITH FIELD GREENS, HERBS &
   SMOKED STURGEON BUTTER TOASTS 6.25
AVOCADO & PEPPERED MANGO SALAD WITH BELGIAN ENDIVE,
   WATERCRESS & ACITO BALSAMIC VINAIGRETTE 7.50
SPICY LENTIL & EGGPLANT SOUP WITH A RED BELL PEPPER CREAM 5.00

GRILLS & MAIN COURSES

RISOTTO WITH GULF COAST PRAWNS, SUNDRIED TOMATOES, GARLIC & HERBS 15.50
SAUTEED CHICKEN BREAST WITH FRIED POLENTA, SWISS CHARD,
   PEARL ONIONS & A NICOISE OLIVE-SAGE HOLLANDAISE 15.50
POACHED HALIBUT WITH BUTTERED FENNEL PUREE, RADICCHIO &
   A CEPE BEARNAISE 16.50
BRAISED SWEETBREADS WITH SHIITAKE MUSHROOMS, ARTICHOKES,
   BACON & AN ANCHO CHILI SAUCE 16.50
GRILLED LOUISIANA REDFISH FILET WITH ROASTED SWEET PEPPERS,
   LEEKS & A CILANTRO-GINGER CREAM 16.50
GRILLED DOUBLE PORK CHOP WITH JAPANESE EGGPLANT, TOMATOES,
   POACHED GARLIC & A ROSEMARY BUTTER SAUCE 17.50
GRILLED FILET OF BEEF WITH FRIED POTATOES, MUSHROOM DUXELLES &
   A GREEN PEPPERCORN BUTTER 21.00

SEE OUR DESSERT MENU FOR TODAY'S DESSERT SELECTIONS.

PEERLESS COFFEE .... 1.60 ICED RUSSIAN CARAVAN TEA 1.00
TEAS .... 1.00 EVIAN WATER 1.25

MINIMUM FOOD CHARGE $5.00 NO PERSONAL CHECKS
AMERICAN EXPRESS, MASTERCARD & VISA ACCEPTED
SALES TAX WILL BE ADDED

STARS is available for private functions, Saturday & Sunday days

If any restaurant can be said to wear a happy smile and give a warm embrace, it is Stoyanof's. Justifiable pride and joy exude from the kitchen. Little attempt is made to proclaim its Greek cuisine by decor. A basic storefront building has been transformed into a most inviting room where white walls, polished wood floors, and blue table tops welcome with a clean and uncluttered look. Outdoor garden seating is available on fine days and is equally pleasant. By day, food is served cafeteria style and at 5 pm dinner begins and full restaurant service prevails. The surprises at Stoyanof's appear not in the originality of the menu, but in the consistently high quality of the ingredients and the careful preparation of simple, traditional dishes. Everything, from the filo dough encasing the spanakopita and cheese börek to the last scrumptious dessert crumb, is made from scratch on the premises, often within view. At lunch a good selection is a half portion of Greek salad and a pair of savory pastries, one with a three-cheese filling and the other a meat filling, both partially encased in a flaky buttery dough, but left open-faced. A summer meal could be made from an array of appetizers and either a Macedonian salad of diced potatoes and vegetables or a fresh red snapper salad, both bound with delicious homemade mayonnaise. Especially good is caciki, a blend of cucumbers and yogurt, olive oil, garlic, and fresh dill. Both a beef and a meatless moussaka are made daily. Chicken Kokinisto from a family recipe is deceptively simple, but outstanding: half a chicken baked with fresh tomatoes, green peppers, and herbs. Both lamb and beef shish kebab are offered, as well as boned leg of lamb. Swordfish lovers will enjoy marinated chunks of that firm fish charbroiled on the grill. The seasonings are unmistakably Greek-Macedonian, but never overstated nor oily. Desserts command a special menu. Stoyanof's can be enjoyed all day from a snack of coffee and baklava or apple strudel to a complete evening dinner. A good place to remember after a visit to the De Young Museum or any of the Golden Gate Park attractions.

STOYANOF'S CAFE AND RESTAURANT, 1240 Ninth Avenue, San Francisco. Telephone: (415) 664-3664. Lunch: 10–5 Tuesday–Sunday. Dinner: 5–9 Tuesday–Thursday, 5–10 Friday–Saturday. Cards: AE, MC, V, dinner only. Reservations accepted only for parties of five or more. Wine and beer only. Street parking.

San Francisco: Financial District
TADICH GRILL
Seafood $$

Tadich's roots go back to the Gold Rush, when a group of Yugoslavian immigrants set up a wharfside tent to dispense coffee to arriving forty-niners. The coffee tent became a coffeehouse and eventually turned into one of San Francisco's finest seafood restaurants. Owners have changed over the years, but they have always been of Yugoslav origin, like the Buich family, who have owned it since 1929 with scions Steve and Bob in charge today. Tadich has changed locations a number of times, too, but at the present site the atmosphere of a 19th-century men's lunchroom has been re-created. It's not difficult to spot at lunchtime, for there's usually a lengthy line of financial-district workers outside patiently waiting for a seat at the long lunch counter or a table in one of the intimate walnut booths. The menu usually offers some 20 types of local or imported fish and shellfish, prepared in a variety of ways including simply broiled or pan-fried as well as complex dishes like Newburg or cioppino. If standing in line for lunch doesn't appeal to you, try Tadich at dinnertime when the daytime clientele has returned to Pacific Heights or suburbia and tables are more readily available.

TADICH GRILL, 240 California Street, San Francisco. Telephone: (415) 391-2373. Hours: 11–9 Monday–Friday. No cards. Reservations not accepted. Full bar service. Parking in nearby garages; street parking at night.

SEAFOOD

Subject to season, weather and fishing conditions

CHARCOAL BROILED

Served with Long Branch Potatoes, Butter Parsley and Tartar Sauce

Rex Sole or Sanddabs	9.50
Filet of Petrale Sole	12.25
Pacific Red Snapper	9.50
Halibut Steak	11.95
Salmon Steak or Filet	13.95
Swordfish Steak	14.75
Boneless Rainbow Trout	9.25

POACHED

Served with Boiled Potatoes and Vegetables

Smoked Alaskan Cod with Butter Sauce	9.95
Salmon with Chopped Egg Sauce	14.25

GRILLED (PAN—FRIED)

Served with Long Branch Potatoes and Butter Sauce

Rex Sole or Sanddabs	9.50
Boneless Rainbow Trout, Meunière Sauce	9.25
Hangtown Fry (Oysters, Bacon, Eggs)	9.95
Calamari Steak (Squid), Bordelaise Sauce	9.75
Pacific Red Snapper with Sauteed Crab or Bay Shrimp	11.50
Filet of English Sole, Tartar Sauce	8.95
Filet of Petrale Sole, Tartar Sauce	12.25

SAUTÉ

In White Wine and Mushrooms with Rice and Vegetable

Scallops	12.75
Jumbo Prawns	13.95
Crab Legs	14.95
Seafood Sauté (Scallops, Prawns and Crab Legs)	14.95

DEEP—FRIED

Served with Long Branch Potatoes and Tartar Sauce

Pacific Oysters with Bacon	10.75
Calamari (Squid)	8.25
Scallops	10.75
Jumbo Prawns	12.25
Crab Legs	14.25
Seafood Plate (Oysters, Scallops, Prawns & Calamari)	13.95

130

San Francisco: Western Addition
THEP PHANOM
Thai
$

Every neighborhood looks forward to the opening of a modestly priced restaurant serving good food—a relaxing place to eat when the day has been hectic and you can't face the stove. Within a week of hanging out a menu in early 1986, the Western Addition's Thep Phanom had a packed house. And with good reason. This handsomely decorated establishment, operated by a family whose members have worked in such well-known Thai kitchens as Khan Toke and Racha, does justice to the complex cuisine of Thailand. For starters there is yum plamuk, a beautifully presented squid salad highly flavored with lemon grass and chili, or the larb gai of finely minced chicken and fresh mint. The seafood-rich po-tak brings squid, clams, crab claws, and prawns in a tart, spicy-hot broth, while kaeng ped, served in a lovely blue-and-white bowl, combines boneless roast duck in a rich curry sparked with fresh Asian basil leaves. In addition, there is moo kra tiem, slices of tender pork marinated in garlic and pepper and then fried to a succulent finish, or squid stuffed with seasoned pork and topped with bamboo shoots in a fiery sauce. During the late spring through summer, look for pad pak boong, a favorite leafy vegetable of Southeast Asians (commonly called water spinach or long green) that Thep Phanom's chef prepares with minced garlic and bean sauce. The list could go on. Suffice it to say that many of Thep Phanom's customers see the attractive restaurant and its charming staff as a welcome addition to the neighborhood.

THEP PHANOM, 400 Waller Street (corner of Fillmore), San Francisco. Telephone: (415) 431-2526. Lunch: 11:30–2:30 Monday–Friday. Dinner: 5–10 daily. No cards. Reservations advised. Beer and wine only. Street parking.

Daly City
TITO REY OF THE ISLANDS
Filipino $

Philippines natives Ray Bautista and Larry Cruz are crusaders. They want Americans to learn about Filipino food. To this end, they have opened a restaurant in Washington, D.C., and another is planned for Los Angeles. Fortunately for those of us in the Bay Area, our education can begin at their self-described "upscale" restaurant-nightclub in Daly City, Tito Rey of the Islands. The large menu combines the national favorites of the island nation with many regional specialties. The appetizer list alone numbers 13 entries, with everything from stuffed eggplant slices and fried frog legs to crispy squid tentacles with a vinegar and garlic sauce. Tito Rey's adobo, the national dish, is a memorable version, the chunks of braised pork and chicken in a perfectly balanced tart vinegar sauce. The sour broth soups are delicious, especially the milkfish (bangus, to the Filipinos) one that combines the fish with long beans, eggplant,

onion, and tamarind, the source of the tartness. Laing Mayon Volcano, a dish named for the great cone on Bicol peninsula, is extraordinary. Taro leaves are stewed in coconut milk and spices to produce what looks very much like an eastern rendition of the creamed spinach of the West. You can also sample Luzon-style paella or puchero, essentially boiled beef ribs, both drawn from the kitchens of the islands' former Spanish rulers; crispy skin roast pork, a favorite food at Filipino festivals; juicy deep-fried shortribs with a spicy sauce; and four kinds of lumpia (spring rolls). One piece of advice: try for a table in the front dining area, if you want to skip the crooners and combos that perform in the rear room.

TITO REY OF THE ISLANDS, No. 3 St. Francis Square (off Highway 280 and St. Francis Boulevard), Daly City. Telephone: (415) 756-2870. Cards: AE, MC, V. Hours: 11–midnight Tuesday–Thursday, 11 am–2 am Friday–Saturday, 11:30 am–11 pm Sunday. Reservations recommended on Friday and Saturday. Full bar service. Parking lot. Private banquet facilities: 50.

San Francisco: Richmond District
TON KIANG
Chinese (Hakka) $

Chin Boon Wong's old friends in Rangoon know of his success as a restaurateur in America. That finely constructed network that binds the overseas Chinese keeps the flow of information constant, and the restaurant empire of this Burmese-born entrepreneur is worthy of comment. Wong opened Ton Kiang on Broadway in Chinatown in the late 1970s; it was the first place to serve Hakka food in the city, and among the earliest in the country. A few years later he opened two more branches, this time in the Richmond, the city's "second

Chinatown." Early in 1986, he sold the Broadway location in order to concentrate on his Richmond kitchens. At either one you can sample expertly prepared Hakka cuisine, a south China cooking style noted for its delicate seasoning and light, clear sauces. The "wine flavored" dishes, which feature shrimp, pork, chicken, beef, or tripe, are unusual and delicious, the unique flavoring the result of fermented rice kernels and pickled mustard greens. The stuffed bean curd, braised or steamed, boasts bulging pockets of expertly seasoned pork. Fish balls and beef balls, either stir-fried with tender greens or in soup, are finely textured, full-flavored spheres. Salt-baked chicken, the premier dish of this cuisine, is so succulent and pleasantly salty that it compels any diner to recognize the superiority of simplicity in food preparations. Other fine dishes include pork with pungent preserved mustard greens, and a full line of clay-pot dishes. Two special dinners for four to six persons, one featuring seafood and the other a representative selection of Hakka dishes, are recommended. Which location serves a better meal? Ton Kiang No. 2 is the favorite right now.

TON KIANG No. 2, 5827 Geary Boulevard (between 22nd and 23rd avenues), San Francisco. Telephone: (415) 387-8273. TON KIANG No. 3, 3148 Geary Boulevard, San Francisco. Telephone: (415) 752-4440. Hours at both locations: 11–10 Monday–Thursday, 11–10:30 Friday–Sunday. Cards: MC, V. Reservations advised for parties of six or more. Beer and wine only. Parking lot at No. 3; street parking at No. 2.

TRADER VIC'S
International   **$$$**

In this, the mother restaurant of the far-flung Trader Vic's empire, you will find the usual rooms filled with Polynesian artifacts, fishnets, carved tikis, and gawking tourists. And you'll find the same encyclopedic menu that roves the globe from Cantonese to Continental dishes and features exotic drinks with wild names. But the San Francisco branch is unique: Besides being headquarters of the chain, it shelters the Captain's Cabin, which many San Franciscans regard as their own exclusive club. This is a simply furnished room with a slightly nautical motif and tables spaced close to each other so you're assured you will overhear all the latest gossip. A lot of people come here because it is a status ploy to get a reservation in this sanctuary of the rich and famous—and the closer your table to the door, the higher your status. But many San Franciscans come here simply because the food and service is sure to be excellent. And you won't find them eating Chinese food or sipping a "suffering bastard." Those in the know are likely to order fresh salmon mousseline or Indonesian rack of lamb. Those really in the know are likely to refuse to navigate the vast menu and leave the ordering to the captain. Instead they concentrate on the wine list, one of the most superb collections of California bottlings in the city. A reservation in the Cabin isn't easy to come by, but if you lunch late or dine early you might be lucky enough to get a seat for one of the best people-watching shows in town.

TRADER VIC'S, 20 Cosmo Place, San Francisco. Telephone: (415) 776-2332. Hours: 11:30–2 Monday–Friday, 5–midnight daily. Cards: AE, CB, DC, MC, V. Reservations advised. Full bar service. Valet parking. Private banquet facilities: 15–200.

WASHINGTON SQUARE BAR & GRILL
Italian $$

Since its opening, this boisterous bar and grill facing
Washington Square has been a hangout for San Francisco's
literati, as well as for advertising and PR people. They
come here because owners Ed Moose (an ex-newspaper-
man) and Sam Deitsch (a fugitive from New York's
advertising world) make them feel at home. And they
come here because the drinks are ample and the food is
good. Although Moose and Deitsch started with the
intent of serving just "good saloon food," the menu early
on became "North Beach Italian," emphasizing pastas,
veal dishes, and local rex and petrale sole, as well as
calamari and the indigenous North Beach dish known as
Joe's Special—a mélange of eggs, ground beef, and
spinach. Daily specials run the gamut from fettuccine
primavera to calamari stuffed with Cajun barbecued
pork and rice. If you're lucky, you'll dine here on a day
when the entrée is served with puntette, an unusual and
delicious rice-sized pasta steeped in butter, onions, and
broth. A nice way to end a meal here is with a plate of
asiago cheese and fresh fruit, plus a cup of Graffeo's
coffee. The WSB&G swings from mid-morning through
the dinner hours, when a jazz pianist adds to the
liveliness. He is joined by one or more other musicians
at 9:30 for a jam session that goes on to the wee hours.

WASHINGTON SQUARE BAR & GRILL, 1707 Powell
Street, San Francisco. Telephone: (415) 982-8123. Lunch:
11:30–3 Monday–Saturday. Dinner: 6–11 Monday–
Thursday, 6–11:30 Friday–Saturday, 5:30–11 Sunday.
Sunday brunch: 10–3. Cards: AE, MC, V. Reservations
advised. Full bar service. Validated parking at nearby
garages.

Today's Soup

Boston Clam Chowder 2.75

Pasta

Spaghettini with Meat Sauce	7.95
Spaghettini with Tomato Sauce	7.95
Penne Arrabbiata (Hot Pepper Sauce)	8.95
Spaghettini Pescatore (Spicy Calamari)	9.50
Cheese Ravioli, Tomato or Meat Sauce	8.95
Tortellini alla Panna (Cream)	8.95
Fettuccine Alfredo	7.95
Fettuccine Bardelli (Mushrooms, Tomato, Cream)	8.95

(Small order any pasta above: 5.95)

Salads & Vegetables

California Field Salad, Vinaigrette	3.95
California Field Salad with Anchovies	4.95
California Field Salad with Montrachet Goat Cheese	4.95
Small Seasonal Greens Salad	2.75

(Extra for Roquefort or Goat Cheese 1.00)

Vine Ripened Tomatoes, Basil Dressing	4.95
Vine Ripened Tomatoes, Sweet Onion & Anchovies, Basil Dressing	5.95
Fisherman's Salad of Calamari & Scallops, Vinaigrette	
Appetizer size: 5.95 — Entrée size:	9.25
Salad Niçoise	9.25
Salad of Bay Shrimp, Egg, Red Pepper, Field Greens, Basil Dressing	9.95
Shrimp Louis	9.95
Today's Fresh Vegetables	2.25

Veal & Chicken

Scaloppine Piccata, with Capers	12.95
Scaloppine with Mushrooms, Marsala	12.95
Scaloppine & Mushrooms, Silvio	12.95
Veal Rib Eye Cutlet Milanese	12.95
Eastern Veal Rib Chop	15.95
Chicken Parmigiana	9.95
Grilled Chicken Breast	9.95

Grill

The WSB&G Hamburger Sandwich	6.75
The WSB&G Hamburger, Melted Cheese	6.95
New York Cut Steak Sandwich	13.95
New York Cut Steak with Café de Paris Butter	16.95

137

San Francisco: Chinatown
YUET LEE
Chinese (Cantonese)

$

If seductive smells and the absence of pretension be the marks of a good restaurant, Yuet Lee fits the description. Until a few years ago there were but ten tables in this favorite spot of fanciers of Hong Kong–style seafood, and one frequently saw the line of prospective patrons snake into the street. The eviction of a tobacconist next door permitted an expansion that doubled the size of the dining room. The kitchen, though, remains the same long narrow space, blocked from the diners by a modest partition, and the crowds continue to be formidable. This restaurant knows full well that no self-respecting Chinese would ever consider dining on water life long from the deep, and the double-decker tanks filled with live crabs, lobsters, hardheads, and catfish just inside the door ensure there is no need to worry about such an eventuality. And indeed, seafood is special here—stir-fried clams in black bean sauce, steamed whole hardhead or rock cod, double squid, stir-fried lobster, prawns in the shell, catfish steamed or in a clay pot. But every dish is good, including the large array of nonseafood items: steamed pork, pork kidney with kew choy, dumplings and noodles in soup, thick rice soups, a selection of clay pots, crispy deep-fried intestines served with plum sauce, roast duck. Ask for the soy-based dipping sauce thick with hot peppers if it is not automatically delivered to your table. Yuet Lee not only promises good food, but also a setting that is strong on authentic atmosphere: decorative mirrors covered with Chinese calligraphy reveal the best dishes to those who can decipher them, and flames lap at the edges of the partition as the cooks expertly maneuver their woks.

YUET LEE, 1300 Stockton Street (corner of Broadway), San Francisco. Telephone: (415) 982-6020. Hours: 11 am–3 am Wednesday–Monday. No cards. No alcoholic beverages. Street parking.

San Francisco: Richmond District
WOODEN CHARCOAL BARBECUE
Korean $

The back streets of Seoul are home to scores of small, smoke-filled restaurants where Korea's famous barbecue dishes are the specialty. Until recently, San Franciscans had to be satisfied with Korean restaurant fare grilled over gas jets. But the real thing hit the city for the first time with the 1984 opening of the simply named Wooden Charcoal Barbecue. A sturdy-armed carrier hauls a brazier filled with glowing charcoal to your table, followed by plates of marinated beef ribs or beef or pork strips. The accompaniments include a mild-flavored broth, steamed rice, and half a dozen varieties of kim chee, the various condiments of brined vegetables or seafood that range from cooling to fiery hot. On the nonbarbecue side of the menu, try yuk hwe, the Korean version of steak tartare; hong au hwe, raw skate and vegetables in a mouth-searing sauce; a casserole of kingfish, tripe, or bean cake; or a crock of cold noodles with meats and vegetables. An elaborate dinner for four that includes not only the barbecue items, but also tempura, cold noodles, dumplings, and tiny fish- and vegetable-filled omelets is available for those who take their Korean food experiences seriously.

WOODEN CHARCOAL BARBECUE, 4609 Geary Boulevard, San Francisco. Telephone: (415) 751-6336. Hours: 11–11 daily. Cards: MC, V. Reservations accepted. Wine and beer only. Street parking.

ZOLA'S
French $$

Catherine Pantsios is an art major turned chef who brings to her tiny café seven years of eclectic experience that includes training with French, Italian, and Japanese chefs. Her French training is evident in her menu, which changes every six weeks or so, and is based upon regional French cooking with her own creative touches. Her art background unquestionably affects the stunning presentation of her work. An appetizer that usually stays on the menu is crépinettes, spicy little sausages garnished artistically with strings of wilted greens. Another unusual hors d'oeuvre is a turnover of chèvre and roasted garlic. Catherine seems to favor saffron with shellfish, using it to spike a creamy sauce for mussels and a tomato broth for a stew of mixed shellfish. Breast of duck (cooked a perfect pink) is sometimes served with wild mushrooms and a surprisingly light-textured polenta. Cassoulet is another house favorite, with a combination of beans, lamb, homemade sausage, and duck confit. Desserts are sumptuous here, featuring pastries and ice cream made in house. One of the best is a flourless chocolate cake, made with egg whites like a soufflé and almost as light and airy. The small dining room has a high beamed ceiling and stark white walls. In the center spotlights shine on a table with a massive flower arrangement and an array of pastries. It's obvious that the food is the star of the show here.

ZOLA'S, 1722 Sacramento Street, San Francisco. Telephone: (415) 775-3311. Hours: 6–11 Tuesday–Sunday. Cards: AE, CB, DC, MC, V. Reservations advised. Beer and wine only. Validated parking at lot across the street.

San Francisco: Civic Center
ZUNI CAFE GRILL
California Cuisine   **$$**

Zuni is like a piece of New Mexico set right down on Market Street. The whitewashed walls, skylights, and multicolored woven upholstery give the dining room, on two levels, a bright, sun-baked feeling—like the Southwest landscape. When Zuni opened several years ago, it was a daytime place, where the only hot service was coffees and soups. Now there are three menus—weekday, Sunday brunch, and evening—and an imaginative, always experimenting kitchen that regularly keeps new dishes appearing. The "cold seafood bar" offers several kinds of raw oysters, from bluepoint to Portuguese, served with either shallot sauce or a fresh salsa. The rich and finely accented sweet potato soup seasoned with chili, fresh coriander, and lime, or a plate of linguine with a smooth, creamy gorgonzola and walnut sauce makes a good first course. The salads combine crisp greens—spinach, watercress, arugula, lettuces—with top-quality reggiano parmesan or Sonoma-made goat cheese. Among the light entrées, which are particularly suited for ordering before or after a performance at the nearby Performing Arts Center, are carpaccio, paper-thin slices

of raw beef served with parmesan and olive oil; a lean hamburger cooked to order with jack cheese, salsa, and very good french fries; and a half a poussin accompanied with grilled radicchio. For a more substantial entrée, there is rib eye steak or fresh sausage with polenta. Do not ignore the daily specials; some of the best dishes can be found on this board. Pecan torte with crème anglaise, and house-made ices and ice creams are delicious finishes. A whole array of wines, aperitifs, beers, coffees, even six bottled waters are available to accompany your meal. The Sunday brunch menu may include an omelet filled with goat cheese, anchovies, and garlic, fresh sausage with scrambled eggs, and pancakes combined with fresh fruit. A wood rack filled with newspapers and magazines stands near the kitchen area, a holdover from the days when Zuni was principally a place to grab a light afternoon snack and while away the time with good reading or conversation. Now time here will more likely be spent exploring some of the most creatively assembled dishes in the city. Menus here undergo constant revision, so be prepared to see favorite dishes go—and equally good ones debut.

ZUNI CAFE GRILL, 1658 Market Street, San Francisco. Telephone: (415) 552-2540. Hours: 11:30–11 Tuesday–Friday, 6–11 Saturday, 11–10 Sunday. Reservations recommended. Full bar service. Street parking.

San Francisco
THE AMERICAN BARBECUE SCENE

The barbecue tradition is relatively new in San Francisco. In fact, Leon McHenry claims that he was the first in the city to offer sit-down service for barbecue at **Leon's Bar-BQ,** which started as a funky little six-table café on Sloat Boulevard in the mid-1970s and later expanded to a larger branch on Fillmore. Leon's accompanies its oak-smoked ribs, links, brisket, and chicken with, among other things, freshly baked corn muffins and crunchy pecan pie. Leon's sauce is hot enough for the average palate, but the asbestos-mouth bunch head for the **Firehouse Bar-B-Que,** where Carl English, a firefighter by profession, has developed one-, two-, and three-alarm sauces; the latter is so hot you feel like calling the SFFD to extinguish the flames in your mouth. Take-out is big here, but there are tables on the premises as well. Texas-style barbecue came to San Francisco with the opening of **Bull's Texas Café,** which is decorated with Lone Star memorabilia—neon signs, longhorn heads, cowboy hats, cactus and even a Houston Yellow Cab sign. The ribs, links, and brisket are cooked over green oak in pits especially built for the restaurant in Mesquite, Texas. Bull's also makes a mean chili, with brisket simmered in beer, accompanied with a tray of condiments—chilies, salsa, onions, and the like—so you can adjust the hotness to your own taste. For barbecue, see also separate listings for Hog Heaven and MacArthur Park.

BULL'S TEXAS CAFE, 25 Van Ness Avenue (Civic Center Area). Telephone: (415) 864-4288. FIREHOUSE BAR-B-QUE, 501 Clement (Richmond District). Telephone: (415) 221-7427. LEON'S BAR-BQ, 2800 Sloat Boulevard (Sunset District). Telephone: (415) 681-3071. 1913 Fillmore (Lower Pacific Heights). Telephone: (415) 922-2436.

San Francisco
THE ASIAN NOODLE SCENE
Chinese/Vietnamese/Japanese/Thai

San Francisco is in the enviable position of having an abundance of restaurants that feature Asian noodle dishes, along with rice plates and other complementary fare—good sources of satisfying meals at midday and midnight. These are usually simply decorated places, spots to grab a quick and filling meal for a modest price. And don't believe for a moment that plain appointments or a small dining area means that there is little menu choice. You will discover that the dishes are many—that these compact kitchens are capable of great variety. What follows is not a comprehensive list, for there are dozens of these eating spots in Chinatown alone. Rather the choices reflect a cross section based on location, style of service, operating hours—and personal taste.

The 1983 opening of the **Silver Restaurant** could not have gone unnoticed. The long-standing building that housed it underwent a most dramatic remodeling: It was completely sheathed in silver-colored metal. The interior contains a "delicatessen" of barbecued and soy-cooked meats and poultry and a limited kitchen area at the front; the remainder of the room is done in brick, with multipaned windows that "look out onto" photo murals of Hong Kong. The Silver has two menus, one a standard Cantonese dinner menu and the other a comprehensive noodle and rice compendium. This latter listing offers 108 dishes, including noodles in soup with everything from roast duck to beef organs. There are also braised noodles, chow mein, chow fun (stir-fried rice noodles), steamed soft rice noodles— noodle rounds encasing a choice of chicken, shrimp, beef, or barbecued pork—plates of roast duck and/or pork, soy chicken, green vegetables with or without meats, rice plates or bowls with a choice of more than 20 toppings, and over 30 varieties of rice soup, or porridge, that favorite morning and late-night repast of the Chinese. Indeed, you can enjoy a bowl of rice soup or a plate of noodles at any point on the time spectrum, for the Silver is open 24 hours.

There are three smaller, more modest places in Chinatown that are longtime favorites of the Chinese community. At **Junmae Guey,** you must squeeze by the crowds of shoppers stopped at the front counter for take-out fare: crispy-skin pork or suckling pig, roast duck, curried cuttlefish, barbecued duck livers, salt-roasted chicken, braised cellophane noodles. Stir-fried noodles or noodles and won tons in soup are recommended here, as are the generous rice plates. This is a daytime place; by 6:30 the last of the barbecued pork has been sold and the door is locked.

At **Hon's Wun Tun House,** you can see steam rising from the cooking pots through the large front windows before you enter. This is the place for bowls of dumplings and noodles in broth, topped with everything from pigs' feet to beef tendon. There are only a few noodle plates, so concentrate on the soups. Hon's is short on decor but long on simple, honest food. A seat here is hard to come by at noon or midnight.

In the Tenderloin, there are half a dozen small restaurants that specialize in pho, the beef and noodle soup that is a classic of northern Vietnam. The **Pacific Restaurant,** at Larkin and Eddy, is always packed with locals enjoying outsized bowls of star-anise-scented broth loaded with thin rice noodles and hearty portions of beef. With the soup arrives a dish heaped with beans sprouts, onion slices, coriander sprigs, chilies and lemon wedges, to be added according to the diner's taste. Pho, and its southern Vietnam equivalent hu tieu, a shrimp, pork, and crab noodle soup, can also be sampled at Vietnamese restaurants in the Richmond District and Chinatown.

Downtown workers can explore the wonders of Asian noodles at two popular South of Market eateries. One is the always-jammed **B & M Mei Sing,** which must be the lunchtime haunt of every Chinese office worker in the neighborhood. And with good reason: Prices are very reasonable and you can request almost any topping—from fish balls to black-bean-sauce chicken—with your plate of noodles. The line snakes out the door at high noon, so go after 1:00 pm or before 11:30 am to avoid a wait.

Linda's, only about a block from B & M Mei Sing, offers a variety of Thai noodle dishes, in broth and stir fried. The fish ball with spinach soup is thick with rice noodles and spiced with a fiery chili paste. There is a marvelous silver noodle salad with shrimp and pork, and a very good version of the national noodle dish of Thailand, pad thai, a fish-sauce-scented mixture of rice noodles, egg, shrimp, and green onions. Bowls of condiments—ground peanuts, chilies, chili-soy sauce—are available for spicing according to taste. Also to be recommended here is the steamed chicken with garlic rice and the chicken with mint. The soup noodles are available at the noon hour, but to try the more complex preparations, such as pad thai, come after 1:00 pm when the lunch crowd has thinned, or in the early evening.

About two years ago, the Japan Center gained a new noodle shop that looks as if it was transported directly from Tokyo. Done in pleasant shades of green, the tiny **Ramen House** features delicious, house-made ramen served in a variety of ways: miso, cha shu (pork), shoyu (soy), shio (fish cake, squid, pork, and vegetables), and hiyashi (prepared as a salad). These Chinese-inspired Japanese noodles, cooked here to a delightfully chewy finish, are especially good lunch and late-night fare, and Ramen House's late hours reflect that.

But this new noodle house faces stiff competition from longtime Japan Center resident, **Sapporo-ya.** House-made ramen is the specialty here as well, served in outsized ceramic bowls with a variety of additions such as miso, barbecued pork, and/or soy. The doors are open until 2:00 am, making this even more of a night-owl spot. Also, Sapporo-ya serves a number of other types of dishes, so that a group of persons can satisfy varying appetites and tastes. To make your choice between these competitors, watch their front windows: Each has someone hard at work making the noodles, by machine at Sapporo-ya, completely by hand at Ramen House.

Of course, almost every Chinese restaurant has its share of noodle dishes on the menu, and most Thai and Japanese eateries serve them as well. This is just a sample of some of the best. Look to the entry for Mifune for good Japanese noodles, and to the one for Yuet Lee for Chinese fare. And remember, in San Francisco, an Asian restaurant paradise, wonderful noodles are always just around the corner.

B & M MEI SING, 62 Second Street (between Mission and Market, Downtown). Telephone: (415) 777-9530. HON'S WUN TUN, 648 Kearny Street (Chinatown). Telephone: (415) 433-3966. JUNMAE GUEY, 122 Stockton Street (Chinatown). Telephone: (415) 433-3981. LINDA'S, 512 Mission Street (Downtown). Telephone: (415) 546-7376. PACIFIC RESTAURANT, 601 Larkin Street (Tenderloin). Telephone: (415) 673-7604. RAMEN HOUSE, 22 Peace Plaza, Japan Center East Building, Second Floor (Japantown). Telephone: (415) 921-4961. SAPPORO-YA, 1581 Webster Street, Japan Center West Building, Second Floor (Japantown). Telephone: (415) 563-7400. SILVER RESTAURANT, 737 Washington Street (Chinatown). Telephone: (415) 433-8888.

San Francisco:
THE BEST BURGERS

Many San Franciscans swear that **Bills Place** on Clement is the city's premier burger palace. The beef for the one-third pound patties is ground fresh daily and there are over 30 combinations of embellishments to choose from. Other pluses are an old-fashioned soda fountain and tables set in one of the prettiest Japanese gardens in the city.

But there are others who staunchly defend **Hamburger Mary's** right to the title of burger queen. Also weighing in at one-third pound, Mary's patties come on nine-grain bread and the cheeseburger is made with raw-milk cheddar on *both* sides of the meat. Mary's wildly mixed Soma clientele (gays and straights, yuppies and aging hippies, and even wide-eyed tourists) provides one of the best people-watching shows in town.

On the other side of town, the swinging young professionals who patronize **Perry's** and **Balboa Café** are split on the best-burger verdict. Both places serve half-pound patties of ground chuck; Perry's serves its hamburgers on poppyseed egg rolls, while the Balboa version arrives on crunchy French rolls.

BALBOA CAFE, 3199 Fillmore (Cow Hollow). Telephone: (415) 921-3944. BILL'S PLACE, 2315 Clement (Richmond District). Telephone: (415) 221-5262. HAMBURGER MARY'S, 1582 Folsom Street (South of Market Area). Telephone: (415) 626-5767. PERRY'S, 1944 Union Street (Cow Hollow). Telephone: (415) 922-9022.

San Francisco:
BREAKFAST, BRUNCH, LUNCH, AND TEA

The following places are particularly pleasant for daytime dining, but some do serve dinners as well.

For breakfast a top choice is **Doidge's Kitchen** on Union, which serves that meal all day and features honey-cured bacon with no preservatives.

Eichelbaum & Co. on California also starts the day early with a small breakfast menu. Lunchtime at this small café offers a choice of Oriental chicken salad, pâté-charcuterie plates, quiche and green salad, or perhaps a focaccia sandwich. And the weekend brunch is marvelous, featuring a 10-layer crêpe called crepaz. The dinner menu here changes weekly and the take-out counter does a booming business at all hours. Pastries are terrific: Key lime pie, fresh fruit tarts, chocolate truffle cake are but a few.

The **Tuba Garden,** housed in an old Victorian building on outer Sacramento, has one of the loveliest garden dining areas in the city. The place is open only for lunch and weekend brunches, which include (besides the ubiquitous egg dishes) wonderful homemade cheese blintzes served with fresh fruit, and a baked crab diablo au gratin.

Golden Gate Park is a manmade wonder and so is a museum café not dedicated to soggy tuna and egg-salad sandwiches or coffee in Styrofoam cups. The **Cafe de Young** is a secret that should be shared. The food is first class. Outside in the semiformal garden, the dining area is one of the city's little jewels.

The **Waters Upton Tea Room,** another of the city's little gems, is mostly staffed by attentive volunteers to benefit the Student League of San Francisco. This well-appointed room, looking out to a tree-lined street, is by no means a ladies' enclave, but a favorite luncheon and afternoon-break spot for doctors from three nearby hospitals. The specialty of the French-trained chef is the "motorloaf," a nutty, whole-grained loaf filled with six different and individually wrapped finger sandwiches. Soups are especially good, as are pâtés. At teatime look for the delicious house-made scones, Lady Baltimore cake, and crumpets with Devonshire cream. Over two dozen varieties of tea are offered, each pot covered with a cozy.

After dark, **The Oasis** is one of Soma's hottest night clubs, but during the day alfresco lunches (and weekend brunches) are served at umbrella-topped tables around a pool. The food is California-style, featuring unusual salads and sandwiches, as well as mesquite-grilled poultry and seafood.

Perched on the water with a fabulous bay view, the multilevel dining room at the **Waterfront** is always crowded with seafood lovers for lunch or dinner. But weekends bring out the brunch bunch for strawberries and cream, eggs Benedict and pots of steaming coffee.

CAFE DE YOUNG, Eighth Avenue and Kennedy Drive (Golden Gate Park). Telephone: (415) 752-0116. DOIDGE'S KITCHEN, 2217 Union Street (Cow Hollow). Telephone: (415) 921-2149. EICHELBAUM & CO., 2417 California (Lower Pacific Heights). Telephone: (415) 929-9030. OASIS CAFE, Eleventh Street and Folsom (South of Market Area). Telephone: (415) 621-0264. TUBA GARDEN, 3634 Sacramento Street (Presidio Heights). Telephone: (415) 921-8822. WATERFRONT RESTAURANT, Pier 7 (Embarcadero). Telephone: (415) 391-2693. WATERS UPTON TEA ROOM, 2103 O'Farrell Street (Western Addition). Telephone: (415) 929-1485.

North Beach is home to some of the city's most popular coffeehouses, and rightfully so. Despite what is definitely a steadily disappearing Italian population, this area remains a reflection of the European life style—a neighborhood of Italian delicatessens, bookstores, and gift shops, where Italy winning soccer's World Cup can still bring crowds into the street.

But it is not only soccer that generates excitement among Italians; an aria can bring them to their feet as well, and at **Caffé Puccini,** a light-filled comfortable room, the jukebox is programmed with enough of the work of the establishment's namesake to keep you humming through their very good sandwiches. Try prosciutto on focaccetta, a crunchy flat roll that is split in half, and cap it off with a slice of the almond torta and an espresso that does the tradition of fine Italian coffee proud.

Café Europa, which is more appropriately described as a "European" coffeehouse rather than a strictly Italian one, offers a number of cold-meats plates, salads, sandwiches, and a dessert case that is particularly irresistible to chocolate lovers. The tables are on two small floors, both with large windows that look out onto Columbus Avenue. You can easily while away an afternoon here, watching the street activity and munching on french bread and cheese chased with a glass of red wine.

Farther down Columbus stands the brightly painted **Mario's Bohemian Cigar Store,** a place that is long on authentic neighborhood feeling. A football game is installed at the rear of the cafe, and dozens of photographs of loyal customers are tacked up above the bar. French bread rolls layered with cold cuts, and wedges of Italian-style cheesecake are the best things to eat here. Plus, Mario's serves one of the finest espressos in town.

Before departing North Beach, the Italian ice cream controversy must be addressed. Walking these streets, one wonders if the ice cream business has lost its good sense: It almost seems as if a purveyor of this frozen dessert occupies every other storefront. Needless to say, this has produced great arguments and unwavering loyalties among ice cream afficionados. Given this climate, it is only correct that this book put in its two cents' worth: **Gino Gelateria** serves the closest thing to true *Italian* ice cream to be found in North Beach. This is a light, bright establishment, the back room of which is filled with ice cream machinery imported from Italy. The front of the shop has several tables and an array of ice creams and ices: chestnut, zabaglione, white and dark chocolate, coffee, hazelnut, lemon, raspberry, currant, and more. There are also coffees, sandwiches, and pastries, and a few tables, protected with the familiar red, green, and white Cinzano umbrellas, right outside.

At **Fettuccine Bros.,** the sunny Russian Hill salumeria-café founded by Bob Battaglia and Don Woodall, you can enjoy first-rate fettuccine alla marinara, crunchy french rolls and sweet butter, and a glass of Italian wine for the price of a salad course at many less-accomplished restaurants. Fettuccine Bros. was originally a take-out shop that sold fresh pasta, homemade sauces, and delicatessen items. But customers kept asking Battaglia and Woodall when they were going to start *serving* pasta, so they added the café area. Now they offer lunch every day except Sunday, and dinner on Friday, Saturday, and Sunday. In addition to the fine marinara sauce, there is a light tomato sauce with walnuts and herbs, a garlicky pesto, and a creamy Alfredo, among others.

When well-known cooking teacher Carlo Middione opened his combination delicatessen-trattoria a few years ago, the local culinary community took notice. In quick order, **Vivande's** popularity as a place both to eat and to shop was assured. The surroundings immediately entice the customer: Just inside the door are cold cases with meats, salads, cheese, and in-house creations such as pizza rustica, terrines, and eggplant "sandwiches" of mortadella. Across from the prepared foods are the tables, and at the rear of the shop is a simple counter for diners near the large, beautifully equipped kitchen. The menu changes daily, but always includes pasta and salad choices, plus simple entrées like roast chicken. The most serious complaints about Vivande have centered on its seasoning; some find it to be done with too light a hand. This is a good choice for a light meal— and a great place to take out the fixings for a party or for an easy, delicious dinner when you don't want to face a stove.

The 1980s have seen a new style of café take root in San Francisco. With the arrival of thousands of refugees from Southeast Asia has come the Vietnamese sandwich shop, an establishment that specializes in assembling baguettes filled with pork-liver pâté, ham, or headcheese, charcuterie items adapted from the kitchen of Vietnam's one-time French rulers. A strong dose of coffee, brewed right at the table in a traditional Vietnamese drip pot, is the usual accompaniment to these "submarines." The same little shops also often serve simple noodle soups and rice-paper-wrapped rolls of pork, shrimp, and/or vegetables. In Chinatown, you can find these hearty sandwiches at the **Little Paris Coffee Shop** and the **Vietnam Restaurant** on Broadway, as well as other cafés in the neighborhood. The Tenderloin boasts at least a dozen places to stop for a Vietnamese sandwich, including the **Larkin Coffee Shop** and the **Café Tai.**

CAFE EUROPA, 362 Columbus Avenue (North Beach).
Telephone: (415) 986-8177. CAFE TAI, 410 Ellis
Street (Tenderloin). Telephone: (415) 771-0208. CAFFE
PUCCINI, 411 Columbus Avenue (North Beach). Tele-
phone: (415) 989-7034. FETTUCCINE BROS., 2100
Larkin Street (Russian Hill). Telephone: (415) 441-
2281. LARKIN COFFEE SHOP, 668 Larkin Street
(Tenderloin). Telephone: (415) 441-0435. LITTLE
PARIS COFFEE SHOP, 939 Stockton Street (China-
town). Telephone: (415) 982-6111. MARIO'S BO-
HEMIAN CIGAR STORE, 566 Columbus (North Beach).
Telephone: (415) 362-0536. VIETNAM RESTAU-
RANT, 620 Broadway (North Beach). Telephone: (415)
788-7304. VIVANDE PORTA VIA, 2125 Fillmore
(Lower Pacific Heights). Telephone: (415) 346-4430.

San Francisco: North Beach
THE CITY'S LONGTIME TRATTORIAS
Italian

Out-of-towners and San Franciscans alike remember
the city as the place to search out small family-style
restaurants in that long-established preserve of Italian
life, North Beach. But times have changed. The neighborhood's residential makeup is now more Asian than
southern European, and the overall restaurant picture
is more upscale than homey Italian. But amidst the
constantly altered storefronts, their "hand-changing"
most often the result of escalating rents, a few favorite
eateries—the kind of places visitors and locals wax
nostalgic about—remain.

And before the letters that announce overcooked
vegetables, bland minestrone, and doughy raviolis start
coming in, a qualification must be made. Great food is
not promised at the following restaurants. Rather, this
is a chance to find some San Francisco tradition, honest
old-country ambience, and simply prepared food at
reasonable prices. These are the places that made

North Beach the neighborhood people headed for when they craved home-style Italian food.

Long waits and large portions mark **The U.S. Restaurant** and the wait is immediately apparent as you approach the Columbus Street location, for the line forms outside the door. Here your entrée may be accompanied with as many as three vegetables, and more often than not, they will be overcooked. Despite this, loyalists keep returning for deep-fried calamari, spaghetti with pesto, a serving of tripe in tomato sauce that would suffice for two hearty eaters, osso buco, baccala, hearty hamburgers, plus great breakfasts of eggs, thick-cut fried potatoes, and sausage.

Columbus Restaurant has been a North Beach fixture since 1927, the place that everyone swore by for deep-fried calamari for Friday lunch. Recently the Columbus underwent a modest renovation—a new deep green awning and a logo in the colors of the Italian flag, a brightening of the small interior—but the menu remains much the same: a place for boiled beef, sweetbreads, pastas, veal dishes, daily specials, and, of course, the famed calamari. A counter seat keeps you abreast of the kitchen routine.

When locals talk of a family-style restaurant in North Beach, what they traditionally mean is a place that serves a complete dinner for a set price, generally minestrone, pasta, a choice of entrée with vegetable, salad, ice cream or cheese, and coffee. A handful of these eateries, all with varying degrees of kitchen success, remain in the neighborhood, each with its admirers and detractors. **The Green Valley** opened in 1906 and much old neighborhood charm remains. **Golden Spike** and **Capp's Corner,** even without the backup of so many years, are also solid institutions. Capp's boasts a neighborhood bar peopled with enough interesting true San Francisco types to keep onlookers relaxed and amused through any wait for a table, while Golden Spike's bar is delightfully homey, with a level of clutter and a measure of staff charm that makes it irresistible. As for the food at these spots: Some swear by the lamb chops at the Green Valley; Capp's can pull off a decent dish of osso buco; and Golden Spike is respected for the particularly hearty portion.

For those evenings when a desire for relaxation amidst true San Francisco tradition is combined with an undemanding attitude toward dinner fare, the North Beach trattorias are good destinations.

CAPP'S CORNER, 1600 Powell Street. Telephone: (415) 989-2589. COLUMBUS RESTAURANT, 611 Broadway. Telephone: (415) 781-2939. GOLDEN SPIKE, 527 Columbus Avenue. Telephone: (415) 986-9747. GREEN VALLEY, 510 Green Street. Telephone: (415) 788-9384. U.S. RESTAURANT, 431 Columbus Avenue. Telephone: (415) 362-6251.

San Francisco
THE DIM SUM SCENE
Chinese

The Cantonese must be thanked for the invention of dim sum, one of the most civilized and enjoyable of all eating experiences. Literally translated, dim sum means "touching the heart" or "little hearts," but this dining ritual of south China is best described as the partaking of small portions of foods at midday.

A dim sum restaurant is a maze of tables with a troop of waitresses moving trays or carts laden with foods through the labyrinth. Most of these establishments open sometime between 7:00 and 10:00 in the morning, and close around 3:00 or 4:00. During these hours, all manner of delicacies are presented, with the most complete selection usually appearing during the noon hour. Chefs at the larger dim sum houses have a great repertoire of dishes, and vary the choices daily; on any single day, between 25 and 40 individual preparations will vie for the attention of patrons.

These myriad choices are all so tempting, you will find yourself wanting to try everything that is brought past your table. Usually, each waitress carries only between two and four of the many offerings of the day, and what is available will vary as the day progresses. There are steamed wheat dumplings stuffed with minced shrimp, pork and shrimp, or beef; rice flour rolls filled with a variety of meats; snow-white buns with a center of barbecued pork; diamonds of steamed turnip cake; deep-fried taro balls; steamed spareribs in black bean sauce; braised duck and chicken feet; tripe with scallions and ginger; pieces of succulent chicken enclosed in foil; glutinous rice encased in a leaf packet; dumpling triangles of minced pork and mushrooms; bell-pepper boats of minced shrimp; custard tarts; coconut balls; and more.

You need not even be confined only to what appears on the constantly circulating trays. A large variety of noodle dishes can be ordered from the person who brings you tea and a place setting when you are first seated. You may even ask for a favorite item that you do not see on the passing trays.

In some of the restaurants, the empty plates are left to pile up on the table. At the end of the meal, the plates are counted (the various sizes have different values) and the bill toted up accordingly. You will discover that you have enjoyed a very exotic lunch for a modest price.

A few hints to make your dim sum outing more enjoyable: When you arrive at the restaurant, immediately let the person at the door know the size of your party. If there is a line, you will be given a number. Wait for it to be called, listening carefully, for the numbers are amplified in both Cantonese and English. Going midday on a Saturday or Sunday will mean enduring a long wait; for the Chinese, a dim sum lunch is a customary weekend outing. Also, go as early as possible to eliminate some of the waiting time and to be assured of the greatest variety and the freshest food. And a tip on the ordering of tea: Ask for a measure of chrysanthemum to be added to your pot of black tea. The flowers improve the digestion and thus increase the pleasure of the meal. A filling dim sum lunch will run $5 to $7 per person.

For a number of years, San Francisco's Chinatown has had two very large, Hong Kong–style dim sum restaurants, **Asia Garden** and **Hong Kong Tea House.** These restaurants offer a large number of choices each day, and most dim sum aficionados respect both kitchens. It must be understood, however, that some preparations are more expertly handled by one kitchen than another. For example, loyalty may go to the shrimp dumplings at Hong Kong Teahouse over those at Asia Garden. And all kitchens do have off days. Almost as large is the **Canton Tea House,** with its noodle dishes especially recommended.

Two additional "large-scale" dim sum houses opened in Chinatown in the last few years, both owned by Asian-based companies. **Ocean City,** located in a garish structure on Broadway that also houses a movie theater showing films of the Far East, spreads its dim sum service over two stories. **Miriwa,** though confined to only one floor, is no less extravagant in its array of dumplings and other offerings. Both restaurants have one big draw for those beating the pavement in search of authentic dim sum: mobile gas griddles that waitresses roll up to tableside for cooking such items as gin law bak go (fried turnip "pudding") and minced shrimp nestled in bell pepper boats.

The long-established **Tung Fong,** very small by Hong Kong standards, is the haunt of many serious dim sum diners. In fact, there are substantial numbers that consider its overall quality far superior to that of the larger houses. And it must be agreed that high-quality food is the trademark here, especially the shrimp dumplings, spareribs in black bean sauce, and turnip cake. The Singapore-style rice-stick noodles and the beef chow fun make good additions to your table.

Another old Chinatown resident, **Yank Sing,** is gone from its original Broadway location, but the two branches it spawned in other areas of the city remain. Both attract a clientele different from the Chinatown crowd. The downtown branch, near the foot of Market Street, is where office workers congregate. Here the menu is limited and dishes more expensive than at many Chinatown dim sum establishments. The other location is in the Embarcadero Center area, where prices, again, are higher and the appointments considerably more upscale. The secret about this branch is that you can visit it on weekends when prices are lowered because there is no Financial District crowd to patronize it.

Nearby, in Embaracadero Four, is **Harbor Village.** With its linen tablecloths, high-class furnishings, and city view, this Hong Kong restaurant-chain member is shamelessly bidding for the expense-account crowd. Prices are about 50 percent higher than those of the competition, but there are some extraordinary delicacies to try here, such as the "magical" soup dumplings of thin dough encasing a flavorful liquid flecked with seafood and vegetables and the thinly sliced stuffed pig trotter.

Clement Street in the Richmond District is an area thick with Asian restaurants. Three large, Hong Kong-style eateries, all with a sizable dim sum trade, opened here in the 1980s. The **Ming Palace** marks a new high in interior design for Chinese dim sum spots. A two-story dining area, with the first story open to the ceiling of the second, mezzanine fashion, has as its most prominent design element an imposing central fountain. This is no conventional fountain, however. The spray of water alters its pattern in closely paced, regular intervals in harmony with a series of continually changing colored lights. If you are seated too near the fountain, this elaborate display becomes serious competition for conversation. But the dim sum here is good enough to overcome the mesmerizing effects of the interior decor.

Next door to the Ming Palace looms the stainless-steel-sheathed **King of China,** complete with photographs of the various dim sum offerings lining the upper walls of the first floor. Seating on this lower level is spartan in comparison with what awaits you upstairs. Almost the moment this place opened, the city's Chinese residents were filling its tables. And you can't ask for a better endorsement of a dim sum restaurant than that.

The Fook, just a few blocks away, is also large, but the quality of its dim sum is less consistent than that of its neighbors. There will be a wait at any of these places, however. All three also serve a Cantonese dinner menu, and The Fook, unlike many Clement Street Chinese restaurants, is open until midnight.

Long before any of these grand dim sum palaces opened on Clement, there was the small, modest **Clement Restaurant.** It has a limited number of items, but the quality is good, and the wait for a table need not be as time-consuming as at the more elaborate establishments.

For something a little different, sample Shanghai-style dim sum, weekends only, at **Fountain Court,** also located on Clement. The menu features, among other things, a variety of small steamed dumplings and buns filled with delicately seasoned mixtures of ground pork, crab meat, or shrimp; hot soybean milk; sesame-seed pastries, and some half-dozen noodle dishes.

If all this talk of long waits has put you off, you can avoid the lines and still enjoy a dim sum lunch. Take-out counters are found in most of the places described here.

ASIA GARDEN, 772 Pacific Avenue (Chinatown). Telephone: (415) 398-5112. CANTON TEA HOUSE, 1108 Stockton Street (Chinatown). Telephone: (415) 982-1030. CLEMENT RESTAURANT, 621 Clement Street (Richmond District). Telephone: (415) 752-9520. THE FOOK, 332 Clement Street (Richmond District). Telephone: (415) 668-8070. FOUNTAIN COURT, 354 Clement Street (Richmond District). Telephone: (415) 668-1100. HARBOR VILLAGE, Embarcadero Four (Financial District). Telephone: (415) 781-8833. HONG KONG TEAHOUSE, 835 Pacific Avenue (Chinatown). Telephone: (415) 391-6365. KING OF CHINA, 939 Clement Street (Richmond District). Telephone: (415) 668-2618. MING PALACE, 933 Clement Street (Richmond District). Telephone: (415) 668-3988. MIRIWA, 728 Pacific (Chinatown). Telephone: (415) 989-9888. OCEAN CITY, 644 Broadway (Chinatown). Telephone: (415) 382-2328. TUNG FONG RESTAURANT, 808 Pacific Avenue (Chinatown). Telephone: (415) 362-7115. YANK SING, 53 Stevenson (Downtown). Telephone: (415) 495-4510. YANK SING, 427 Battery Street (Financial District). Telephone: (415) 362-1460.

San Francisco
THE MOROCCAN SCENE

A time-honored ritual of dining prevails in the city's Moroccan restaurants. You are seated on pillows or hassocks at low tables and the meal begins with the ancient hand-washing ceremony of scented water poured from a large brass pitcher. This is important because no knives or forks are provided; you eat with your fingers in the North African tradition. The menus are similar, too. Five-course banquets start with soup, most often a spicy, lentil-based harrira, drunk from the bowl. Next come platters of diced vegetables to be scooped up with Moroccan bread and then that marvelous dish, bastilla—

layers of paper-thin pastry, dusted with powdered sugar, encase slivers of chicken, almonds, and hard-cooked eggs. There follows a choice of entrées, with lamb and chicken predominating in couscous or kabobs or stews with various combinations of honey, nuts, fruits, or vegetables. (Consider ordering a different entrée for everyone in your party and sharing). Then the grand finale: banana fritters or pastries and mint tea.

Marrakech Palace is the oldest of the city's Moroccan establishments, the most elaborately decorated, and the most expensive ($17.50 to $19.50 for the banquets). With its downtown location, it is also the most accessible to out-of-towners. **Mamounia** was opened, far out on Balboa Street near the ocean, in the early 1970s by Mehdi Ziani, former chef at Marrakech. The complete dinners here are priced from $15.50 to $17.50. Also in the Richmond District, but a little closer to downtown, is **El Mansour,** where the dinners range from $13.75 to $15.75, clearly a bargain considering the amount of food you receive.

EL MANSOUR, 3123 Clement (Richmond District). Telephone: (415) 751-2312. MAMOUNIA, 4411 Balboa (Richmond District). Telephone: (415) 752-6566. MARRAKECH PALACE, 419 O'Farrell (Downtown). Telephone: (415) 776-6717.

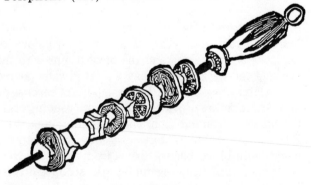

San Francisco
OYSTER BARS

Once upon a time, not too long ago, about the only half-shell oysters served in San Francisco restaurants were the midget-sized Olympias from Puget Sound and "bluepoints," a term used loosely to refer to any oyster from the East Coast. The large, briny Pacific oyster (originally imported from Japan) was considered déclassé. Recently, a new wave of oyster grower has started cultivating West Coast oysters for half-shell connoisseurs and throughout the Bay Area, upscale oyster bars have opened to provide samplings of many varieties from both coasts. Among the Pacific oysters commonly found in these places are complexly flavored Hog Island Sweetwaters from nearby Tomales Bay, cucumbery sweet little Kumamotos from Humboldt Bay, small pungent Golden Mantles from British Columbia, tangy mollusks from Willapa Bay, and the larger, salty Portuguese from the Pacific Northwest. When available, you will also find native Olympias, coppery-tasting French Belons from American waters, and an assortment of eastern oysters that often includes the popular Chincoteaques from Chesapeake Bay and the Apalachicolas from Florida's Gulf Coast. The selections at the following seafood bars range from three to a dozen different types of oyster and you may mix the varieties to your liking.

BENTLEY'S OYSTER BAR, Galleria Park Hotel, Sutter and Kearny (Downtown). Telephone: (415) 989-6895. KIMBALL'S, 300 Grove (Civic Center). Telephone: (415) 861-5555. PACIFIC HEIGHTS BAR & GRILL, 201 Fillmore (Lower Pacific Heights). Telephone: (415) 567-3337. PJ'S OYSTER BED, 2229 Van Ness (Van Ness). Telephone: (415) 885-1155. 737 Irving (Sunset District). Telephone: (415) 566-7775.

San Francisco: Mission District
THE PUPUSA SCENE
Salvadoran $

In Salvadoran restaurants, one name always tops the list of *comidas típicas*. It is the pupusa, a stuffed cornmeal round that is the hamburger of its homeland. Introduced to San Francisco by the venerable Coatepeque, the city's oldest extant Salvadoran establishment, this savory dish is fast becoming a Mission District standby.

You usually hear the pupusa before you eat it. A rhythmic pat-pat-pat comes from the restaurant kitchen, as the pupusa makers slap handfuls of yellow dough into perfect shape, almost magically filling them with cheese or meat. At Los Panchos, one of the very best places to try this wonderfully filling food, there is a "con loroco" variation, which incorporates a minced green herb into the dough. The rounds are quickly grilled, and delivered with a shredded cabbage mixture; the customer slits open the pupusa and adds "salad" to taste.

In most restaurants, you can order your pupusas with beans and rice or fried platanos on the side, a grand meal for about half the cost of a record album. Following is a list of selected pupusa stops.

COATEPEQUE RESTAURANT, 2240 Mission Street. Telephone: (415) 863-5234. EL AMANECER, 1183 Potrero Avenue. Telephone: (415) 282-2110. EL TAZUMAL, 3522 20th Street. Telephone: (415) 550-0935. EL TREBOL, 3324 24th Street. Telephone: (415) 285-6298. LOS PANCHOS, 3206 Mission. Telephone: (415) 285-1033.

San Francisco
THE SUSHI SCENE
Japanese

Not so many years ago, the sushi bar was a rare institution on the San Francisco restaurant landscape. Today, it is almost commonplace, with many longtime Japanese dinner houses having added sushi bars to "keep up with the times." Of course, any food specialty, from chocolate chip cookies and Italian ice cream to sushi, can suffer from a popularity too quickly attained. With sushi, the result is many mediocre restaurant experiences where quality has been abandoned for fashion. Fortunately for San Franciscans, there are also many reliable—and varied—choices for exploring the very special "rites of raw fish." The places that follow reflect both of these considerations, and because of the broad scope of the sushi scene here, this writer's taste as well.

First, a brief discourse on "sushi etiquette." Once you are seated at the bar, a waitress will bring a hot towel for freshening up. From her order a drink—sake, beer, tea—and, if you wish one, a bowl of soup. All sushi orders, however, whould be directed to the sushi chef, who will also keep you supplied with gari, the thinly sliced pickled ginger eaten between sushi "courses" to refresh the palate, and wasabi, the strong-flavored green paste that can be mixed with soy for dipping. You may either point to a fish in the case or read from the plastic menu on the counter. Sushi is ordered by the name of the fish served atop the rice. Request either one or two items at a time (sushi is served in pairs), letting the chef make suggestions if he seems so inclined. Use your chopsticks or fingers to hold the sushi, and dip it *fish down* into the soy sauce or the rice will become soggy and the "package" will fall apart. There are a number of sushi "forms" beyond the well-known rice oval topped with fish and the "makis," the seaweed-encased rice rolls, but you will easily discover these at the sushi counter. When you have eaten enough, the chef will tote up the bill and give it to the waitress, who will then present it to you. Now, on to where you can explore this true culinary art.

Kinokawa, near the gates to Chinatown, has a discriminating followint, and once you have tasted the rich maguro (tuna) folded into a seaweed coronet, the buttery hamachi (yellowtail) tapped onto a small rice oval, or the delicate—and costly—uni (sea urchin) tucked into a high-sided seaweed boat with a rice keel, you will be Kinokawa devotee, too. Also try the exceptional version of yamakake: grated mountain potato, bits of raw tuna, and raw quail egg whipped to a froth. For lunch, a small dining area to the left of the sushi bar offers a very good bento (box lunch) and assorted sashimi; the remainder of the restaurant is devoted to hibachi-style dining.

A pair of longtime dining establishments can be recommended only for their sushi bars: **Yamato** and **Nikko.** Their dining rooms, which offer the usual Japanese fare of tempura, sukiyaki, and the like, are formal, expensive, and generally disappointing, but the sushi operations are first-rate. At both restaurants, the fish is high quality and the chefs expert. Though the prices match these standards, the traditional Japanese surroundings and the commendable fare make these good stops for those with sufficient assets to handle the tab.

At the Japan Center, three very different sushi experiences are possible. First, there is the gimmicky **Iso Bune,** with its water-lane conveyor belt transporting "boats" of sushi past diners seated at the large oval counter. The color-coded plates designate prices; at the end of the meal, the plates are tallied and the bill presented. This "assembly-line" design is an import from Japan, where these fast-food emporiums are popular for quick snacks and meals at low prices. (The water-bound traffic is, however, unique.) Iso Bune, in contrast, is not inexpensive, and you may end up spending nearly as much here as at a traditional sushi bar—and for fish of somewhat lesser quality. This is, however, a one-of-a-kind sushi outing in San Francisco.

Upstairs in the center, across from the Kinokuniya bookstore, is **Kamesushi,** a bar of only a half-dozen stools, two small tables, and a single sushi master. Premier fish is combined with expert skill and moderate prices here. The service in this husband-and-wife-run establishment is friendly, and the ambience reminiscent of Japan.

Kitty-corner from Kamesushi is **Fuku-Sushi,** which doubles as both a sushi bar and a dinner house. Very good quality and high prices to match are the standards here, with attractive appointments that give the feeling of traditional Japanese dining. Just a few blocks away, up Fillmore Street, is **Osome,** an old-timer that has always juggled sushi service with standard dinner fare. This neighborhood institution went upscale a few years ago, abandoning its noodles and donburi offerings to concentrate on more elaborate—and expensive—dishes. Despite the change, Osome still houses one of the most popular sushi bars in town, and deservedly so.

One of the great sushi "shows" can be seen at **Kabuto,** in the Richmond District. Here the sushi master, one-time star at Kinokawa, entertains raw-fish fanatics with his swift movements, actions so quick that the motion of fish to rice is almost imperceptible. The fish is first-rate, and, for sushi and sashimi lovers, there is a special dinner that can be ordered in the dining room that adjoins the sushi bar. It includes chawan mushi, steamed egg custard with bits of seafood and vegetables; grilled oysters; sunomono; a beautiful array of raw fish served as sushi and sashimi; and dessert. If you are joined by those uninterested in sea fare, the dinner menu also offers the standard Japanese favorites—sukiyaki, teriyaki, tempura. Service is sometimes slow and on the haphazard side, but any disappointments, such as a bowl of tepid rice, are properly handled by the staff.

And finally, the eccentric side of San Francisco sushi. On your initial visit to **Nippon** (which won't be easy to find because there is no sign marking the restaurant), you assume that the kitchen is operating under some nonprofit status, since the low prices matched with fine fresh fish defy even the most soft-pedaled spirit of capitalism. For example, a nine-piece nigiri sushi is about $5, and this price is not based on serving the least expensive ingredients. Impossible, you say. But it isn't, and oftentimes when one orders this combination, a few extra sushi grace the assortment. Lobster and eel are priced so low here that to mention the figure would make you think Nippon was located in Oz. The menu is large, you can order anything you want, in any combination, including just one piece of sushi instead of the customary pair order required in most bars. The restaurant is small, and the walls are covered with notes from the staff explaining closings over the past months (such as we made too much money yesterday), messages from happy patrons, cutouts from magazines, samurai swords—all manner of memorabilia. This is a remarkable place that has been discovered by a small, but loyal, patronage who find the friendly surroundings and good value unbeatable, so always be prepared for a wait. To beat the crowds, try for lunch on a weekday.

Godzila Sushi (yes, one *L*) deserves a mention in the eccentric category for its new-wave format, Japanese style. From the digital display board that prints out reminders that tofu sushi is served, to music that threatens hearing loss, this is an experience. The menu is divided into four kinds of sushi: traditional, vegetarian, modern, and tofu. The traditional is just that—a pair of oval rice pads topped with your choice of fish or shellfish. The vegetarian and modern sections feature a variety of items encased in the center of a seaweed-wrapped rice cylinder. Alfalfa sprouts, mushrooms, and the like make up the vegetarian list, while the modern is, believe it or not, everything from roast beef, ham and cheese, and bacon and spinach, to New York pizza and Mexican. Tofu sushi is, as might be guessed, a cube of bean curd topped with fish or clam. The people who work here are as new wave as the surroundings, and hardly distinguishable from the customers. This is modern Japan at its pop-neon best—and at affordable prices.

Finally, there is **Wasabi Sushi,** another entry in the new wave's current sushi bar boom. It is the self-described "workshop" of Taki, a charming young Japanese who has fashioned his restaurant to match his artistic temperament. As of this writing, the wood tables and chairs are done in a wild, wonderful mixture of aquas, pinks, and greens, while sculpted light fixtures angle down from the ceiling and five-foot-high sculptures grace the front windows. But Taki says that he intends to change the decor of the room from time to time, to keep his customers coming to a continually changing creative environment. The sushi is as artistic as the surroundings: order a preset nigiri assortment, or make up your own mix from the à la carte nigiri and temaki choices listed on the menu. Either will produce a stunning assortment of carefully arranged vinegared rice and raw fish at very reasonable prices.

FUKU-SUSHI, 1581 Webster, Japan Center West Building, Second Floor (Japantown). Telephone: (415) 346-3030. GODZILA SUSHI, 1800 Divisadero Street (Upper Fillmore). Telephone: (415) 931-1773. ISO BUNE, 1737 Post Street, Japan Center West Building, First Floor (Japantown). Telephone: (415) 563-1030. KABUTO, 5116 Geary Boulevard (Richmond District). Telephone: (415) 752-5652. KAMESUSHI, Japan Center West Building (Japantown). No telephone listing. KINOKAWA, 347 Grant Avenue (Downtown). Telephone: (415) 956-6085. NIKKO SUKIYAKI RESTAURANT, 1450 Van Ness (at Pine Street). Telephone: (415) 474-7722. NIPPON, 314 Church Street (between 15th and 16th streets, Upper Market). No telephone listing. OSOME, 1946 Fillmore Street (Upper Fillmore). Telephone: (415) 346-2311. WASABI SUSHI, 553 Haight Street (near Steiner, Western Addition). No telephone listing. YAMATO SUKIYAKI HOUSE, 717 California Street (Downtown). Telephone: (415) 397-3456.

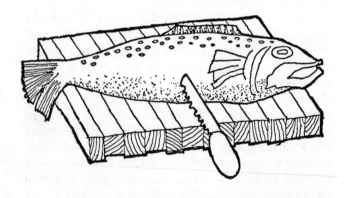

San Francisco: Mission District
THE TAQUERIA SCENE
Latin American

San Francisco's Mission District, with its low riders, salsa music, and pleated pants, is home to dozens of taquerías—purveyors of tacos and burritos. These are usually small, unpretentious establishments, each with a dedicated following. The boom in this type of establishment parallels the city's growing Central American population. Once these immigrants had enough pocket money to afford a simple meal out, taquerías seemed to appear on every corner to cater to the new clientele.

Of course, the Mission District has not cornered the taquería market, but the places that exist there are generally superior to those in other districts, where the food is often altered to meet the expectations of a largely non-Latino clientele.

The key to a taquería's success in this highly competitive neighborhood is its respect for the proper burrito and taco. The classic burrito is a huge soft flour tortilla enclosing moist rice, beans with bite, a meat of choice, and a fresh spicy-hot salsa. The taco is simpler: A pair of pliable corn tortillas holds only meat and salsa. Variations are permitted: The rice or beans may be omitted and the customer can choose to add the salsa at table. Beer or a fresh fruit drink is the perfect accompaniment, and perhaps a few vinegared chili peppers to top off the meal.

The choice of meat makes the taco or burrito distinct. Two taquerías, **San Jose** and **El Farolito,** excel at the "variety meats" versions—seso (brains), lengua (tongue), and cabeza (head)—absolutely delicious if you prefer these meats over more conventional beef and pork fillings. (San Jose also serves very good tortas—sandwiches—made with these same meats.) **La Cumbre,** a longtime taquería that underwent a remodeling several years ago, offers a good range of filling choices, and has kept patrons of the nearby Roxie movie house in

171

delicious hot food through many double bills. A bright outdoor mural marks **Taquería Tepatitlan,** where the carne asada (beef) and tongue burritos are favorites and the fruit and spiced milk drinks are irresistible. Tepatitlan is more comfortable than some of the other places mentioned, and additional dishes are available, such as menudo (hominy and tripe).

Now set out in search of your favorite burrito and taco joint; develop a loyalty like Mission District residents do. And be smug about the fact that Taco Bell will never make a dent in the true taquería landscape of San Francisco.

LA CUMBRE, 515 Valencia Street. Telephone: (415) 863-8025. TAQUERIA EL FAROLITO, 2779 Mission Street. Telephone: (415) 824-7877. TAQUERIA SAN JOSE No. 1, 2830 Mission Street. Telephone: (415) 558-8549. SAN JOSE No. 2, 2282 Mission Street. Telephone: (415) 558-8549. TAQUERIA TEPATITLAN, 2198 Folsom Street. Telephone: (415) 626-1499.

EAST BAY

AUGUSTA'S
Seafood/Pasta $$

Augusta's grills its fish over *gas*—not mesquite—and owner Bonnie Hughes is proud of it! In fact, she conducted a blind tasting among Bay Area food critics between gas-grilled versus mesquite-grilled fish and 75 percent of them preferred the gas-cooked version. However it is cooked, the seafood here is delicious and the selection changes daily, as do the sauces, which might include aioli, lemon-ginger butter, chive beurre blanc, or a piquant salsa fresca. Besides a selection of four or five grilled fish, there is usually a sautéed fish, a seafood stew, and several grilled meat and chicken dishes for nonpiscivorous types. Pasta shares the billing with seafood and it is all fresh fettuccine, made in-house and presented in a number of guises, from the classic Alfredo to robust toppings of sausage and clams. Augusta's list of appetizers has always held promise, but now tapas are also being offered in the late afternoon. A typical day's selection of nine or ten items might range from ragout of bacalao (salted cod) to eggplant salad to fried squid. You can make an entire meal of these little dishes, as they often do in Spain. The atmosphere of Augusta's resembles an art gallery filled with contemporary drawings and prints and that's no accident: For eight years Hughes was membership director at the San Francisco Museum of Modern Art. On a nice day, however, you might want to bypass the art and opt for a table in the pretty patio.

AUGUSTA'S, 2955 Telegraph Avenue, Berkeley. Telephone: (415) 548-3140. Lunch: 11:30–2:30 Tuesday–Friday. Tapas: 3–6 Tuesday–Saturday. Dinner: from 5:30 Tuesday–Sunday. Brunch: 10–2:30 Saturday–Sunday. Cards: MC, V. Reservations advised. Wine and beer only. Street parking.

East Bay: Oakland
BAY WOLF
Mediterranean/American $$

Bay Wolf's owner and executive chef Michael Wilde finds it difficult to put a label on his restaurant's cuisine. His culinary background is French (he studied with Roger Vergé) and many dishes reflect a Mediterranean heritage. But recently a trip to Louisiana sparked an interest in Cajun-Creole cooking and you will find dishes like pork paillards with corn cakes and spicy greens, or Cajun-style duck with "dirty rice." These might share the menu, which changes nightly, with sea bass with leeks, ginger, and white port or roast chicken stuffed with ricotta and herbs. Lately Bay Wolf has also been presenting a series of special Monday-night dinners featuring tapas and other Spanish foods prepared by Rick Hackett, a former assistant of Wilde who has just returned from two years in Spain. The restaurant is located in a homey turn-of-the-century residence on busy Piedmont Avenue. A garden in back provides fresh herbs for the kitchen and in front a deck is the setting on sunny days for luncheon, which offers simpler fare than the evening repasts. Bay Wolf prints its menus for the week in advance and a phone call will bring you information of forthcoming treats.

BAY WOLF, 3853 Piedmont Avenue, Oakland. Telephone: (415) 655-6004. Lunch: 11:30–2 Monday–Friday. Dinner: 6–9:30 Monday–Friday, 5:30–10 Saturday–Sunday. Cards: MC, V. Reservations advised. Beer and wine only. Street parking.

The immense popularity of this tiny cafe in a residential district above the Claremont Country Club is due to the imaginative cooking of owner Albert Katz. Although the menu constantly changes, its structure is consistent: Among the appetizers, a different pasta is offered each day; the luscious combinations might include smoked chicken with hedgehog mushrooms, golden bell peppers, and a black-chanterelle vinaigrette. Gorgonzola is a favorite salad component and is often combined with romaine, fruits, and nuts. Most of the entrées are grilled and the selection always includes four choices of fish, served with lively sauces. There's usually a pork choice, too, like grilled loin with a kumquat-and-honey glaze, as well as grilled lamb, perhaps sauced with balsamic vinegar, mint, and port. In addition, you'll most likely find an offering of veal sautéed with surprising combinations, such as lemon, blood oranges, asparagus, and crème fraîche. Desserts are special and always include a selection for chocoholics, perhaps chocolate soufflé cake with blood oranges. Brie cheesecake is a perennial favorite, as are the house-made ice creams and sorbets. Katz also deserves some sort of award for serving one of the best cups of coffee in the Bay Area at an unbelievably honest price: $1 for perfectly brewed french roast!

BROADWAY TERRACE CAFE, 5891 Broadway Terrace, Oakland. Telephone: (415) 652-4442. Dinner: 5:30–10:30 Tuesday–Saturday, 5–9:30 Sunday. No cards. Reservations required. Wine and beer only. Parking lot.

CAFE PASTORAL
California Cuisine   **$$**

When architect Hi-Suk Dong and his wife San-Ju, an artist, opened the tiny, 36-seat, Café Pastoral on Shattuck Avenue in 1982 neither had any prior restaurant experience. The café had virtually no publicity either, but word spread about San-Ju's innovative cooking and the place was always packed. Four years later, they moved around the corner to spacious two-story quarters on University and the crowds keep coming. The stark peach-colored walls are adorned only with a huge abstract painting by San-Ju and enormous windows face the street. The food at Café Pastoral is hard to categorize. (When asked what she would call it, San-Ju was stumped for an answer and settled for Californian only because it's a catch-all term.) Her methods are French, but her food also has a strong Asian accent from her Korean heritage in some of the seasonings. Steak tartare, for example, is concocted in the Korean fashion, using sliced raw beef dressed with soy and sesame oil. And salmon is garnished with napa cabbage, eggplant, and soy. Yet San-Ju can also express herself in a Mediterranean manner, to wit the house pasta: homemade fettuccine tossed with bacon, tomato, pine nuts, feta cheese, garlic, parmesan, and cream. The eye of an artist, and an Oriental one especially, is evident in the colorful and exquisite presentation of the dishes here.

CAFE PASTORAL, 2160 University Avenue, Berkeley. Telephone: (415) 540-7514. Lunch: 11:30–2:30 Tuesday–Friday. Dinner: 5:30–10 Tuesday–Thursday, 5:30–10:30 Friday–Saturday, 5–9:30 Sunday. No cards. Reservations advised. Wine and beer only. Street parking.

East Bay: Berkeley
CHEZ PANISSE
California Cuisine

$$–$$$

In the early 1970s, when Alice Waters and friends set up their kitchen in an old shingled house in North Berkeley, few people dreamed that a culinary revolution was brewing within their pots and pans. The cooking here from the beginning has been exceptionally creative and experimental, resulting in detractors as well as admirers, for the experiments do not always succeed and the guinea pig is the customer. Nevertheless the Waters's style, her insistence on the freshest of ingredients, her searches for unusual local produce and products such as Sonoma goat cheese, and her defiance of tradition have been widely copied locally and nationally, contributing to the new styles of Californian and American cooking. Many of Waters's early associates—Jeremiah Tower, Mark Miller, and Joyce Goldstein—have moved on to open their own highly successful restaurants. Today, the kitchen is in the very capable and creative hands of Italian-trained Paul Bertolli. Chez Panisse is actually two restaurants in the original locale. The downstairs dining room with its beautiful woodwork, and its open kitchen in the rear, operates as it always has with a five-course prix-fixe dinner (currently $45) that changes nightly and is rarely repeated. The menus are printed a week in advance so you can pick the night that best suits your tastebuds. A typical week (if there is such a thing here) is reproduced on the following page. The "other" restaurant at Chez Panisse is the newer upstairs café, which is preferred by most locals for its lighter food—and lighter prices. The atmosphere here is informal and especially pleasant at lunch when sun floods the dining room from the skylight. The café's menu also changes daily, but there is always a choice of several innovative pastas—perhaps infused with saffron and topped with mussels or tossed with gorgonzola, parmesan, and

:CHEZ:PANISSE:

Tuesday $45.00	Roast spring lamb with marinated artichokes, farm eggs, and olives, with aioli Ravioli with greens, ricotta, & Parmesan Sole baked with bread crumbs, garlic, & parsley Garden salad Blood orange zabaglione cake
Wednesday $45.00	Warm puff pastry with sweetbreads & artichokes Spring vegetable consommé Sautéed quail with four varieties of turnips and Chino Ranch greens Garden salad Frozen Meyer lemon soufflé or blood oranges in caramel syrup
Thursday $45.00	Stuffed artichokes and salt cod brandade with spring garlic Chino Ranch fennel, carrot, & spinach soup Roast leg of veal with Chino Ranch spring onions and snap peas Garden salad Crêpes with pistachio ice cream & warm chocolate sauce
Friday $45.00	Caviar & smoked fish Cheese puff pastries, parchment beef on toast, and albacore tuna vinaigrette Giant asparagus with Hollandaise sauce Seafood ravioli Charcoal-grilled spring lamb with straw potatoes and Chino Ranch spring vegetable ragoût Strawberry torte
Saturday $45.00	Crêpe cake with Smithfield ham & Gruyère cheese Fish soup with green garlic Mixed grill with pigeon, bacon, & duck sausages with garden lettuces & wild mushrooms Blood orange salad Vanilla ice cream & coffee granita in almond cookie cups

Corkage, $10.00.

cream—and notable pizzas from the oak-burning brick oven, such as the calzone (folded pizza) stuffed with goat cheese and prosciutto. There's also a selection of appetizers and salads, which may be ordered as small entrées. One of these plus one of the magnificent desserts—the likes of lemon-lime curd tart, almond torte with strawberries, and coffee-cognac mousse— can serve as a light meal at a very affordable price.

CHEZ PANISSE, 1517 Shattuck Avenue, Berkeley. Telephone: (415) 548-5525. Café telephone: (415) 548-5049. Prix-fixe dinner seatings at 6, 6:30, 8:30, and 9:15 Tuesday–Saturday; reservations required. Café hours: 11:30–4, 5–11:30 Monday–Saturday; reservations accepted for lunch only, if you call that day. Cards: AE, MC, V. Wine and beer only. Street parking.

East Bay: Berkeley
FOURTH STREET GRILL
Southwestern $$

Worry not that famed chef Mark Miller has left the Fourth Street Grill. The cooking here is better than ever. Miller's partner Susan Nelson (who helped Alice Waters get Chez Panisse started) has reworked the menu in a more southwestern direction and done a lot to brighten up this little café alongside the railroad tracks in west Berkeley. Bold paintings of chili peppers and desert scenes (even an Andy Warhol frog serigraph) emblazon the stark white walls, and pillows covered with bright Navajo prints are scattered around the banquettes. Among the new dishes that Nelson has introduced is a sensational, original creation of her own: queso frito (actually a fresh teleme), breaded with oregano-and-sage-spiked cornmeal, fried in butter, and served with tortilla chips. (Nelson calls this a "gourmet nacho.") Another fine appetizer is caldo michi, a delicate fish broth scented with cilantro and lime juice in which bits of fish and shellfish float. One thing that has not changed at Fourth Street is the terrific fresh seafood grilled over mesquite; the selection changes each night, with such choices as a marvelous amberjack tuna generously topped with a relish of sweet roasted peppers. In shellfish season, seafood stews are also offered. Other holdovers from the original menu include the fabulous house-made Yucatecan-style sausages: a mélange of pork and chicken spiced with green chilies and cilantro and served on a bed of black beans. Bobwhite quail marinated in lime juice, pork chops with a barbecue sauce, and dry-aged New York steak with black pepper butter are a few other favorites from the grilled meat choices. The café's side patio has also been spruced up with urns of fresh flowers and lunch is now served there on balmy days.

FOURTH STREET GRILL, 1820 Fourth Street, Berkeley. Telephone: (415) 549-0526. Lunch: 11:30–2:30 Monday–Friday. Dinner: 5:30–10 Monday–Thursday, 5:30–10:30 Friday, 5–10:30 Saturday, 5–9:30 Sunday. Cards: MC, V. Reservations accepted only for dinner Monday–Thursday. Wine and beer only. Street parking.

East Bay: El Cerrito
GOU BU LI
Northern Chinese $

Though chef David Sung has hidden his kitchen in a suburban shopping center, those who know fine northern Chinese cooking have made it their business to seek out this master. The eight-year-old Gou Bu Li is a showcase for Sung's talents, sharpened in a 30-year stint teaching cooking and running a restaurant in Taiwan. It is also a showcase for the complexities of China's northern cuisines. First, there is a tantalizing list of appetizers, including a platter of 10 boiled dumplings filled with meat and cabbage; a plate of shredded jellyfish with cucumber; Shanghai's famous smoked fish; "pies" filled with slivered beef, vegetables, and onions; and the unusual house "cakes," which are very much like Hunan onion cakes that have been fashioned into great waves. One of the house specials is Chinese chives with pork, a mountain of flat-bladed garlic chives stir-fried with fine slivers of tender pork and braised bean curd. A dish called dry-cooked string beans, a favorite of Szechwan Province, is expertly handled here; minced pork and preserved mustard and tiny dried shrimp set off the crunchy beans beautifully. Sung also serves another

Szechwan standby, ma po do fu, bean curd heavily laced with ground pork and red chili. In addition there are three sea cucumber dishes, a nod to Shandong cooking; more than two dozen pork dishes, including such esoterica as Shandong jar of pig's feet; and some very elaborate clay-pot dishes, even one that holds an entire fish. On weekends, Gou Bu Li features northern-style dim sum, with everything from sesame cakes and oil sticks to hot soybean milk.

GOU BU LI, Moeser Lane Shopping Center, 10684 San Pablo Avenue, El Cerrito. Telephone: (415) 525-5362. Hours: 11–9:30 Monday–Thursday, 11–10:30 Friday–Sunday. Cards: MC, V. Reservations accepted. Beer and wine only. Parking in shopping center.

East Bay: Oakland
LA CREME DE LA CREME
French/Californian $$

A little spruced-up Victorian cottage, on College near Broadway, shelters what was, until recently, one of the best-kept dining secrets in the Bay Area. David Nugent, a talented and self-taught cook, realized a 28-year-old dream when he opened the restaurant in 1984, with his wife Kathy acting as hostess. Nugent combines classic French concepts with California-style ingredients, such as a demi-glace sauce (reduced for three days), spiked with Dijon mustard and California chilies, as a topping for pork loin chops, served with red cabbage and pears. He is also particularly adept at pastries and you will usually find among the entrées on the weekly changing menu several flaky tarts with fillings like goat cheese and onions or duxelles and gruyère, as well as brioche stuffed with chèvre and berries. Each entrée at dinner is served with its own accompaniments to enhance the particular dish. For example, on a given evening, you might find poached salmon paired with asparagus pastry, eggplant gratin, and nutmeg-scented spinach; poussin stuffed with sage and onions, served with baked apple rings, gratin of potato purée, and sugar snap peas. Desserts are another area where Nugent excels and you will know he is a chocoholic when you taste his chocolate mousse ice cream or his flourless chocolate cake. But breakfast (served daily) even beats the dinners at La Crème de la Crème and is a bargain to boot with most dishes in the $6 range. At the morning meal, you can sample his glorious homemade breads, preserves, and herb-scented sausages. All sorts of eggs and omelets are found on the menu, along with French toast, griddle cakes, and his terrific cheese-filled tarts. And, as a bonus on a balmy day, you can bask in the sunlight of the little patio behind the restaurant.

LA CREME DE LA CREME, 5362 College Avenue, Oakland. Telephone: (415) 420-8822. Breakfast: 7:30–11 Monday–Friday, 8–2 Saturday–Sunday. Dinner: 6–9:30 Tuesday–Thursday, 6–10 Friday–Saturday, 6–9 Sunday. Cards: AE, DC. Wine and beer only. Reservations suggested. Street parking.

East Bay: Albany
LALIME'S
French $–$$

It's unusual to find both imagination and very reasonable prices in a Bay Area French restaurant, but that's just what Lalime's delivers. The owners are Lebanese of Armenian ancestry, but the food is contemporary French with input from California cuisine and Middle Eastern kitchens. Menus change weekly. On weeknights you order à la carte from a choice of three or four salads and soups, about eight main dishes priced a dollar or so more than a first-run movie ticket, and three desserts.

Friday and Saturday nights a prix-fixe menu, usually with six courses, is served, all for half the price asked at most other local restaurants of this caliber. Some of the superb creations you'll encounter here are a salad of roast leg of lamb slices atop tender watercress sprigs and cucumber rounds; a generous portion of sautéed sweetbreads served on a bed of braised leeks; chicken breast stuffed with an herby mushroom and cheese mixture, and then lightly doused with a garlicky sauce; a pale-green cream soup of sorrel and oyster; a salad of tender young greens, fresh mango spears, and nasturtium flowers; and desserts like kiwi and strawberry tart or baked apple half topped with a scoop of smooth, rich ice cream and drizzled with a caramel sauce. The wine list features boutique bottlings at reasonable prices, and the house bread, a fennel-seed-coated baguette from Semifreddi's on Colusa Avenue in Kensington, is addictive. On occasion a sauce may be a bit too sweet, or a tart crust a bit too browned, but the overall experience of dining at this small, comfortable restaurant, with its totally charming staff, is a truly memorable one.

LALIME'S, 1410 Solano Avenue, Albany. Telephone: (415) 527-9838. Hours: 5:30–10:30 Tuesday–Thursday, seatings for prix-fixe meal on Friday and Saturday nights at 6 and 9. No cards. Reservations required. Beer and wine only. Street parking.

Philip and Nancy Chu, ethnic Chinese who hail from Rangoon, are excellent hosts for a foray into the varied cuisines of Southeast Asia. The menu of their modest, comfortable restaurant in the heart of Oakland's Chinatown offers key selections from the culinary repertoires of Burma, Singapore, Malaysia, and Thailand, as well as a sizable list of Chinese dishes and some Indian curries. From Singapore's irresistible food stalls comes a pork satay with a peanut and curry sauce, and poached chicken with broth-flavored rice, a Singaporean variation on the popular main course of China's Hainan Island. There is a Malaysian chicken curry, a Burmese prawn curry and a chicken and noodle curry (the latter one the national dish of the country), and an Indian beef curry. On the "special delicacies" section of the menu is eight-treasure bean curd, a dish Philip Chu remembers fondly from his Rangoon days. Surprisingly, it contains no bean curd at all, but is instead deep-fried cubes of seasoned, thickened milk mixed with crab meat and shrimp and served with a tomato-chili dipping sauce. Another specialty of the house, which does not appear on the menu, is the 16-part Burmese ginger salad, a mosaic of ginger, powdered dried shrimp, roasted lentils and peanuts, lime slices, coriander, slivers of chili and onion, and eight other exotic ingredients. Another excellent off-the-menu item is a salad of fish cake and jellyfish tossed with a complex spice mixture. Admittedly, it is not often that a restaurant can manage such a polyglot menu, but the Nan Yang handles the challenge.

NAN YANG, 301 Eighth Street, Oakland. Telephone: (415) 465-6924. Hours: 10:30–9 Tuesday–Sunday. Cards: MC, V. Reservations accepted. Beer and wine only. Street parking.

RESTAURANT METROPOLE
French/Eclectic $$

French-born, classically trained Serge Bled migrated to
California in 1973 to become chef for a while at the just-
opened Metropol in Berkeley, but soon moved to San
Francisco as chef at Le Central, where he helped
popularize the bistro concept in the Bay Area. Nevertheless, he dreamed of owning his own place and in 1981
bought the Metropol, added an "e" to its name, and
developed a loyal clientele for his own style of cuisine,
based on classic French technique, yet influenced by
Oriental and American cooking. Vegetables are stir-
fried in a wok and he has borrowed a number of ideas
from the Old South. Chicken, for example, is stuffed
with andouille sausage and served with a creamy sauce
of peanut butter, sherry, and crayfish; gumbo is sometimes offered and Georgia pecan pie is a popular
dessert. Game is a house specialty and among the
several selections listed each night you might find boar
with lingonberry sauce or venison with orange-cranberry
sauce or partridge with a mousse of its liver in a
chocolate-flavored sauce or antelope cooked with pink
and green peppercorns. Seafood is also featured and
ranges from bouillabaisse to paella to grilled or baked

catches of the day. Located in a landmark brick building in downtown Berkeley, the Metropole exudes Old Country charm: a cheery fire in the entry, rich wood paneling and furnishings, handsome antiques, and classical music on most nights. Downstairs from the Metropole, Bled operates the Café-Bistro, which is patterned after a Left Bank jazz club. Live music is offered nightly along with sandwiches, French-style individual pizzas, and, in season, an oyster bar.

RESTAURANT METROPOLE, 2271 Shattuck Avenue, Berkeley. Telephone: (415) 848-3080. Restaurant hours: 11:30–10:30 daily. Café hours: 4–10:30 Sunday–Thursday, 4–midnight Saturday–Sunday. Cards: AE, V. Full bar service. Parking in nearby lots. Private banquet facilities: 15–50 lunch and weeknights only.

East Bay: Berkeley
SIAM CUISINE
Thai $

Although San Francisco now has a number of good Thai restaurants, there's a cult that swears by Berkeley's Siam Cuisine. Chai Aksomboon started wooing his fans several years ago at a tiny hole-in-the-wall on San Pablo, but when the lines for a seat at the counter lengthened, he moved into larger quarters on University, and recently remodeled them in contemporary style. Now the fan club has grown, so there is still a wait for a table. This time can be pleasant, however, if you grab a seat at the bar and while away the time with a beer and an order of deep-fried tofu or sweet potatoes with a piquant peanut dipping sauce. Once seated in the attra tively decorated dining room, start your meal with a refreshing soup of chicken and bamboo shoots in a coconut broth seasoned with lime juice and coriander, or with a salad, such as the one of lovely pink prawns doused in a nicely tart dressing and crowned with coriander, or the grilled beef on a bed of lettuce—again with coriander singing through a magical combination of seasonings. Include a curry in your dinner plans; the pork in a green chili pepper sauce, the medium-hot yellow curry of chicken simmered in turmeric-seasoned coconut milk, the thick, mild Muslim-style curry of beef, potato, and peanut, and the fillet of cod in a fiery red coconut blend are good choices, the latter appearing occasionally on the specials board. Highly recommended are the chili-laced seafood dishes—prawns, scallops, calamari, or combinations thereof—stir-fried with basil, garlic, onions, and bamboo shoots. One of the mild ginger dishes of chicken, pork, or calamari combined with onions and dried mushrooms provides a nice contrast to the hot food. At lunchtime, Siam Cuisine offers an incredible deal: a bowl of soup, a choice from half a dozen or so dishes (pork in green curry, fish curry and rice noodles, chicken curry), *and* an Anchor Steam beer for $4.95. In addition, you can stop by here for a Thai-style breakfast, including a wonderful clear rice soup.

SIAM CUISINE, 1181 University Avenue, Berkeley. Telephone: (415) 548-3278. Breakfast and lunch: 8–3 Monday–Saturday. Dinner: 5–11 Sunday–Thursday, until midnight Friday–Saturday. Cards: AE, MC, V. Reservations accepted only for parties of four or more. Beer and wine only. Street parking.

SKATES ON THE BAY
Seafood   **$$**

Advertised as an "American bar-brasserie-restaurant-sushi bar-bistro-café," Skates has something for everyone, including special dishes low in sodium and cholesterol. But the two chief reasons for coming here are the view and the seafood. Built on piers over the bay at the Berkeley waterfront, the restaurant has floor-to-ceiling glass windows that reveal a panoramic view of the bay, San Francisco, the Golden Gate, and Marin. Don't be confused by the vast, eclectic menu; concentrate instead on the "fresh" section, which lists the latest catches from western waters. You'll find Northwest shellfish, perhaps half-shell oysters from Quilcene or Willapa bays, or steamed Manila clams from Vancouver Island. You'll also find six or seven fish choices, such as California snapper, Washington sand sole, and Idaho rainbow trout, which are either baked or grilled over Hawaiian kiawe wood and sauced with herb-infused butters. On the regular menu, some of the best bets are the pastas (which are served both as entrées and as small portions with small prices); the garlicky pesto-stuffed agnolotti are divine. The house salad of romaine and onions with an anchovy vinaigrette is another fine starter and the luscious pastries from Skates bakery top off a pleasant, and reasonably priced, meal. Be forewarned, however. This is a high-volume operation with an equally high noise level; the seafood and the view keep it jampacked day and night. And there's one final reason for coming here: the fine selection of boutique California wines, imported beers and connoisseur's whiskeys.

SKATES ON THE BAY, 100 Seawall Drive, Berkeley. Telephone: (415) 549-1900. Hours: 11:15–12:30 daily. Sunday brunch: 10–3. Cards: AE, MC, V. Full bar service. Parking lot.

East Bay: Oakland
SORABOL
Korean

$–$$

Although a number of Korean restaurants have opened in recent years, Sorabol might well be the best, and it most certainly merits a drive across the bridge. It's a pretty place with wood paneling and a beamed ceiling to emulate a typical Korean courtyard; in the rear is an open kitchen. And the menu is varied and extensive (48 main-course dishes), combining the family recipes of owner Young Hong with those of her chef, who was formerly with the Chosun Hotel in Seoul. The complete dinners, priced from $8.95 for broiled herring to $18.50 for a mixed seafood casserole, start with soup—perhaps soy bean sprouts, or short-rib broth or shrimp. Next an appetizer of beandae-duk is served; this is a traditional fritter concocted of ground mung beans mixed with minced kim chee, beef, pork, onions, and garlic. An array of condiments accompany the entrée—hot kim chee, sun-dried shredded daikon, sprouts, and a chilled fresh vegetable. (The Koreans serve most of their vegetables cold due to the hotness of much of the rest of the food.) About half the entrées are broiled dishes—thinly sliced beef or pork, marinated pork ribs, chicken, salmon, rock cod, and exotics like eel, squid, and tripe. The sauces range from a mild, but very garlicky, sauce to a hot sauce that's a guaranteed mouth-searer. Casseroles and deep-fried and sautéed dishes are also offered. At the back of the menu is a listing of "dishes for the more adventurous palate," which include a number of à la carte noodle, dumpling, and casserole dishes; these appear to be the favorites of Sorabol's Oriental customers. If you would like an overview of Korean cooking, you might try the weekend buffet brunch, a spread of some 20 delicacies, many of which are not on the regular menu.

191

SORABOL, 372 Grand Avenue, Oakland. Telephone: (415) 839-2288. Hours: 11–9:30 daily, Sunday brunch 11–3. Cards: AE, CB, DC, MC, V. Full bar service. Free parking across the street at 375 Grand. Private banquet facilities: 30.

East Bay: Lafayette
TOURELLE
French $$–$$$

There was a time when serious diners in the East Bay did not venture beyond Berkeley's Shattuck Avenue. But the boundaries of the "gourmet ghetto" have extended eastward lately to Contra Costa County. Here in the heart of downtown Lafayette Annette Esser (former owner-chef of A la Carte in Berkeley) has opened the beguiling Tourelle. Once inside the towered, ivy-covered brick building, you would think you were in the countryside. A flower-filled courtyard, where a fountain splashes, separates two distinct dining rooms—a café and a formal restaurant—each with its own kitchen. Both are furnished with antiques and 18th- and 19th-century French paintings hang on the exposed brick walls. In the café, an open kitchen turns out moderately priced pastas and pizzas, mesquite-grilled seafood, and hearty country fare like homemade sausages and pâtés, cassoulets, and braised meats. Across the courtyard the restaurant serves à la carte lunches and prix-fixe dinners for $35. The dinner menu changes monthly, but typically you might find such elegant concoctions as oyster bisque with black caviar or cold smoked scallops with lemon crème fraîche among the half-dozen appetizers. After an intermezzo of, say, rhubarb ice, the entrée choices might include rabbit with three sauces (mustard, green peppercorn, and wild mushrooms), rack of lamb served with a watercress sauce and stuffed squash blossoms, or grilled fillet of beef paired with brie fettuccine. Dinner ends with a salad the likes of butter lettuce and nasturtiums; house-made pastries and desserts are à la carte.

TOURELLE CAFE & RESTAURANT, 3565 Mt. Diablo Boulevard, Lafayette. Telephone: (415) 284-3565. Café hours: 11–11 Monday–Saturday, brunch 10:30–2:30 Sunday. Restaurant hours: 11–3, 5–11 Monday–Saturday, brunch 10:30–2:30 Sunday. Cards: AE, DC, MC, V. Reservations accepted in restaurant only. Wine, beer, and brandies. Street parking.

Icy Three Caviar Soup made with American sturgeon caviar, salmon caviar and golden caviar in a chilled soup with creme fraiche, mint and cucumber.

Cream of Shiitake Mushroom Soup made with Lillet rouge.

Black Forrest Ham in an herb aspic and served with a sauce remoulade.

Peppered and Smoked Carpaccio with capers, red onions and virgin olive oil.

Sweetbread and wild Mushroom Ravioli with julienned Amador bacon.

Fresh Seafood Boudin sauced with fresh herb butter.

Tomato Basil Intermezzo

Smoked Prawns with Prawn Cream served with lemon fettucini.

Baby Pheasant braised with white wine, marjoram, ginger and horseradish.

Medallions of Veal sauteed with truffle oil and orange zest, deglazed with Armagnac and veal glace.

Boned Rabbit Roulade made with fresh basil, sliced and served with a shallot and red wine cream.

Broiled Beef Filet with roasted garlic puree and artichoke and potato gratin.

Baby Coho Salmon stuffed with scallop mousse and baked in parchment paper with tarragon butter and julienned vegetables.

Salad of Belgian Endive tossed with grapefruit dressing and mache.

$35.00

Our Own Special Blend Coffee or Decaffeinated Coffee	*1.00*
Espresso or Decaffeinated Espresso	*2.00*
Cappuccino	*2.50*
Assorted Teas	*1.00*
A Selection of our Freshly Made Pastries and Desserts	*3.00-6.00*

East Bay: Livermore
WENTE BROS. RESTAURANT
New American   **$$$**

This new restaurant at the Wente Bros. Sparkling Wine
Cellars blends the atmosphere of 19th-century California
with a cuisine that is on the cutting edge of the new
American style of cookery. The fourth generation of the
Wente winemaking family started making sparkling
wines in 1981 at the historic Cresta Blanca winery,
located in a sylvan glen on the edge of Livermore Valley.
Four years later, they built a restaurant on the site and
put the noted chef Robert Baird in charge of the
kitchen. Baird, who was raised in the South, trained at
London's Cordon Bleu, and has cooked in a number of
top California restaurants, combines classical style with
traditional American foods and California's agricultural
bounty. Local oysters, such as Hog Island Sweetwater,
are included among the appetizers along with house-
made sausage. Free-range chicken and Pacific Coast
seafood are grilled over Chardonnay vines. And the beef
is from the shorthorn cattle raised by the Wente family
for their own use. (The Wentes started raising cattle
during Prohibition when wine sales were restricted to
the sacramental trade.) Desserts, such as a heavenly
chocolate-mint sorbet, are divine. Wente's sparkling
wines, made according to the traditional *méthode cham-
penoise,* are of course featured here, but the family very
unchauvinistically offers an extensive selection of other
California table wines.

WENTE BROS. RESTAURANT, 5050 Arroyo Road,
Livermore. Telephone: (415) 447-3023. Lunch: 11:30–
3 Wednesday–Monday. Dinner: 5:30–10 Thursday–
Sunday. Cards: AE, MC, V. Wine only. Reservations
advised. Parking lot.

MARIN COUNTY

Marin County: San Rafael and Mill Valley
ADRIANA'S and GIRAMONTI
Italian $$

When Adriana and Nino Giramonti opened Giramonti Restaurant on Mill Valley's Shelter Bay in 1977, they encountered instant success. Soon after Adriana's Roman-style cooking with a light touch brought her fame as one of the Bay Area's leading chefs. As the restaurant prospered, it grew in size and somehow lost the aura of a family-run trattoria, and with it part of its early magic. Then in 1985, they opened a second place, Adriana's in San Rafael. The new restaurant lacks Giramonti's romantic ambience and view of Mount Tamalpais, but it has a lot of vitality and, from a serious eater's perspective, the view is even better: Adriana and ranks of cooks busily at work in the long open kitchen. (For the best view, take a seat at the counter.) The menus at both places are almost identical (though you get a little more for your money at Adriana's), with veal, pasta, and seafood among the specialties. Veal Adriana, swathed in a tangy, creamy Dijon-mustard sauce, is one of this talented chef's great dishes. But the outstanding choices are often found chalked on the blackboard: seafood,

pastas, and combinations thereof. The menu at Giramonti is à la carte; at Adriana's, soup (often a terrific minestrone) or a bountiful salad with a slice of fresh mozzarella are also included. In short, if your priority is atmosphere, you'll probably prefer Giramonti. But if your goal is simply good food, efficiently served in a lively trattoria, Adriana's is the place to go.

ADRIANA'S, 999 Anderson Drive, San Rafael. Telephone: (415) 454-8000. Lunch: 11:30–2 Tuesday–Friday. Dinner: 5–10 Tuesday–Saturday. Cards: AE, MC, V. Reservations advised. Wine and beer only. Parking lot.

GIRAMONTI, 6555 Redwood Highway, Mill Valley. Telephone: (415) 383-3000. Hours: 5–10 Tuesday–Sunday. Cards: AE, MC, V. Reservations advised. Wine and beer only. Parking lot.

Marin County: Mill Valley
THE CANTINA
Mexican $

Drop into the Cantina almost any night and you'll think that everyone in Marin County got a yen for Mexican food at the same time. It's a mob scene. You have to wait at least an hour for a table. And it's noisy—very noisy—especially later in the week when mariachis add to the din. But it's fun and the food is fresh and good, if not all that authentic. The place is also very pretty: The walls are adorned with brightly colored yarn pictures and straw baskets, and there are hanging plants, blond wood tables, and bentwood chairs upholstered in bold prints. There's also a deck that overlooks the woodsy foliage of a nursery next door. The inevitable wait here is made less painful by some large, dry, and potent margaritas. The large menu offers almost every popular Mexican dish: nachos, three kinds of quesadillas, carne asada, camarones, chile verde, chicken mole, flautas, and chimichangas, to name a few. Enchiladas come in seven versions, including a Cantina original stuffed with onions, cheese, beef, and black olives and covered with mild chili sauce and melted cheese. Then, of course, there are the usual *platos* of enchiladas paired with tacos, chiles rellenos, tamales, and tostadas, but a nice feature here is that they range from single-item *platillos* to combinations of two or three, depending on the size of your appetite and budget. Service is by friendly, if at times somewhat harrassed, young people dressed in Cantina T-shirts. And if you have trouble catching the eye of your waiter, the menu offers a friendly bit of advice: "Pretend that the help is hard of hearing. Feel free to wave, whistle, shout, etc. You might as well forget the polite stuff. We certainly will." That sums up the spirit of the Cantina.

THE CANTINA, Blithedale Plaza, 651 East Blithedale Avenue, Mill Valley. Telephone: (415) 381-1070. Hours: 11:30–2 am daily, Sunday brunch 11–3. Cards: MC, V. Reservations accepted only for parties of eight or more. Full bar service. Free parking in Blithedale Plaza lot.

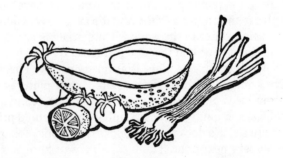

Daniel's is as perfect a little French bistro as you are likely to encounter this side of Paris—or paradise for that matter. The small room is artfully designed with mirrors creating an illusion of space, and polished brass railings partially curtaining off sections on one side of the room suggest privacy. Marble tabletops further establish the bistro atmosphere, as does a small counter in the rear which serves single diners and allows a view of chef-owner Claude Collomb engaging in his artistry. Dinner includes both soup and salad. Saddle of lamb en croûte dijonnaise, stuffed prawns Florentine, and veal preparations are especially popular. Veal piccata normande is served with a cream sauce prepared with Calvados and surrounded by gently simmered apple slices which have also made the acquaintance of the Calvados. Not one, but a macédoine of garden-fresh vegetables is served, as well as a delicate vegetable purée, which in winter is often butternut squash. Fresh grilled salmon can be accompanied on the plate with lightly steamed spinach and yellow and green squash, as well as delicate tortellini, a house specialty. Needless to say, oversize dinner plates are used. Mousse of chestnut Chantilly is a light and lovely dessert. Lunch is served every day but Saturday, and on Sunday a wide-ranging brunch menu is offered. The French love of fine food and conversation is catered to in this unpretentious and charming bistro.

DANIEL'S, 1131 Fourth Street, San Rafael. Telephone: (415) 457-5288. Lunch: 11:30–2:30 Monday–Friday. Dinner: 5:30–10 Tuesday–Saturday. Brunch: 10–3 Sunday. Cards: MC, V. Reservations accepted for dinner only. Wine and beer only. Street parking or city lot behind restaurant.

Marin County: Tiburon
GUAYMAS
Mexican $$

Sitting on the flower-edged deck, sipping a sangrita and munching "sweating tacos" (soft tortillas encasing shredded beef, steamed in banana leaves), you might imagine yourself in old Mexico—except for the view. Spread before you are the blue waters of the bay and beyond that glitter the high-rises of San Francisco. Guaymas was opened in 1986 by Spectrum Foods (Ciao, Prego, MacArthur Park) to showcase the authentic, regional foods of Mexico. Among the unusual concoctions are poached breast of chicken topped with snowy milk curds, elegantly presented on a bed of silky chili sauce. Fresh seafood from Mexican waters grilled over mesquite is also featured. And the pride of the house is the variety of tamales offered, ranging from tiny appetizer tomalitos to a sweet, fruit-filled version that they plan to serve at brunch in the future. Desserts, which are minimized at most Mexican restaurants, are important here: goodies like Mexican bread pudding, pecan cake with honey glaze, and "drunken bananas," soaked in rum and sitting on a puffy fritter. You'll find many surprises on the extensive menu. What you *won't* find is the typical Cal-Mex combination plate of tacos, enchiladas, and refried beans.

GUAYMAS, 5 Main Street, Tiburon. Telephone: (415) 435-6300. Hours: 11:30–10 Monday–Thursday, 11:30–11 Friday–Saturday, 10–10 Sunday. Cards: AE, MC, V. Reservations advised. Full bar service. Private banquet facilities: 25.

Marin County: Ross
LE COQUELICOT
French/California Cuisine

$$$

The atmosphere of this small restaurant in the village of Ross is romantic and understated, with bouquets of fresh flowers on tables that are candlelit at night, and al fresco dining under colorful umbrellas on the patio at lunchtime. The cooking of Swiss-born owner-chef Max Schacher is brilliant, and though he was trained in the classic French method, many of his innovative dishes are as refreshingly Californian as the poppy—which in French translates as le coquelicot. An abstract poppy appears in a stunning painting, one of several contemporary works that hang on the dining room's white walls. Le Coquelicot has both an à la carte and a prix fixe dinner menu. The latter offers four courses that change nightly, for $30. You start with an appetizer—perhaps baby zucchini stuffed with fish mousse, or a confit of rabbit garnished with red bell pepper and fennel, or a mousse of duck liver spiked with port and cognac. The second course might be poached salmon, or homemade tortellini stuffed with veal brain, or Max's herb-coated oysters Tahaa served with a creamy shallot and wine sauce. There is always a choice of two entrées: Duckling, stuffed quail, and roast rabbit are among the possibilities, or they might be as exotic as sea scallops sauced with red bell peppers and cilantro, or as traditional as New York steak with green peppercorns. A green salad and cheese completes the fixed dinner. On the à la carte side of the menu an excellent choice is the house salad composed of spinach, watercress, endive, and tomatoes, lavishly sprinkled with grated roquefort. Although this menu changes every four months, some typical entrées are chicken in a tangy vinegar sauce or prawns in a sauce that blends a multitude of seasonings—including saffron and Pernod—so skillfully that no single flavor predominates. All dishes are beautifully presented and garnished with touches like an artichoke bottom ablaze with strips of pimiento. Desserts are not to be missed, especially the chocolate decadence and the ultra-rich walnut pie. Le Coquelicot is most certainly worth a special trip across the Golden Gate Bridge.

LE COQUELICOT, 23 Ross Common, Ross. Telephone: (415) 461-4782. Hours: 11:30–2, 6–10 Tuesday–Friday; 6–10 Saturday. Cards: MC, V. Reservations advised. Wine and beer only. Street parking.

Marin Conty: Point Reyes Station
THE STATION HOUSE CAFE
American $$

The diversity of the wide-ranging menu at the Station House Café reflects the tastes of this multifaceted community in rural West Marin. Hearty country fare and city-slicker tastes comingle harmoniously. Breakfasts are carefully prepared: The eggs don't have to travel far, and the omelets are outstanding. Bolinas Bay Bakers provides a wide variety of breads, and the French toast is made from sourdough. Steamed milk with almond makes a cozy companion on a misty morning, and the house coffee is a marvelous blend known to seduce inveterate tea drinkers. A surprise in the country setting is excellent tempura—fresh local fish and garden vegetables lightly battered—served with brown rice pilaf and tamari sauce. Pan-fried oysters from nearby Johnson's Oyster Farm at Drake's Bay are served with one of the house specialties: cross-cut potatoes deep fried to order. Tomales Bay mussels are favorites, either steamed in white wine or served with fettuccine in a wine, butter, and garlic sauce. A popular light supper dish is chicken and sausage pot pie with small whole mushrooms.

Outstanding entrées include loin pork chops with gingered apples and shoestring yams, and orange-sauced chicken breast stuffed with dried apricots and walnuts. Chef Dennis Bold adjusts his menu seasonally and there are always daily specials. A pleasing autumn salad is warm cabbage with smoked turkey, apples, pumpkin seeds, and raisins. Needless to say, fish is always fresh and usually local. A basket of freshly baked popovers and cornbread is served at dinner. Vegetarians are well provided for with a vegetable-based soup, crêpes, spanikopita, quiche, and a Station House chef's salad. Desserts are homemade, and there is even a small three-stool fountain at the rear serving old-fashioned sundaes, sodas, malts, and shakes. From early morning through dinner or late supper there is thoughtful provision for every dining need. The Station House Café occupies a corner building across from the original 1875 railroad station.

THE STATION HOUSE CAFE, Main Street, Point Reyes Station. Telephone: (415) 663-1515. Hours: 8 am–9 pm Wednesday–Monday. Cards: MC, V. Reservations only for parties of six or more. Wine and beer only. Street parking.

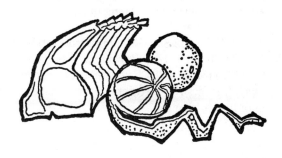

Marin County: San Geronimo
VALLEY INN
California Cuisine
$$

Way back in 1975—long before California cuisine became a food writer's buzz word—Bard Clow quietly began to devise dishes based on the state's bounty and its heritage. Even the site of his delightful country inn— a historic railroad structure in the beautiful San Geronimo Valley—is reminiscent of old California. The redwood-paneled dining rooms—one with a large fireplace—are charming and cozy, and on warm nights or sunny afternoons a spacious deck provides a sylvan al fresco setting. California produce, of course, is emphasized. Among the appetizers is a whole artichoke, served with mustard mayonnaise, and avocados stuffed with a seafood seviche. Citrus is often used to sauce the entrées: orange butter on the local petrale sole, lemon on the grilled leg of lamb and the roast chicken. Complete dinners, with soup and salad, are only $10 to $14 and include no less than four vegetables served with the entrée. But don't ignore the à la carte desserts, especially the homemade ice creams. Sunday brunch is also very pleasant here, particularly on a nice day when there's a flute player on the deck. Service can be slow at times but it doesn't seem to matter, as this is the sort of place to while away an evening or an afternoon.

VALLEY INN, 625 San Geronimo Drive (off Sir Francis Drake Boulevard), San Geronimo. Telephone: (415) 488-9233. Hours: 6–10 Friday–Sunday, brunch 11–2 Sunday. Cards: MC, V. Reservations advised. Beer and wine only. Parking lot.

THE WINE COUNTRY

Napa Valley/Sonoma County
THE WINE COUNTRY

The Napa and Sonoma valleys have been a wine lovers' paradise since the early settlers discovered their wine-growing magic. But, curiously, the wine country has always been something of a gastronomic purgatory. The few restaurants that dappled the countryside mostly served up "Greyhound bus station" fare. There are no documented cases of anyone actually expiring from wine-country food, but certainly there was a fortune to be made by offering Bromo-Seltzer on tap from roadside stands. However, things have changed. In the past decade there has been a migration of talented chefs to Napa Valley, and today the valley may well be the epicenter of California gastronomy. And there is accumulating evidence that the epicenter may be spreading to include Sonoma Valley.

French cuisine used to dominate wine-country fare, but California cuisine is getting increasingly more space on many menus. At the gastronomic shrines you may find your check being brought to your table by forklift, however; for a comparable meal in San Francisco or Los Angeles, the management would require signing over your life insurance and stock portfolio before even being seated. Not all wine-country restaurants cater only to the bullion and ingot set. There are many modestly priced restaurants that serve exciting and innovative fare with a heady, if less elegant, lacing of wine-country atmosphere. And it is virtually impossible to find a restaurant without a good wine list.

All of the well-known restaurants require reservations, and new restaurants that are good rapidly become well known. If you don't bother to make reservations you probably will find yourself dining in your car at Maison A & W.

A perfect day in the wine country begins with a top-down drive through the vine-carpeted countryside, with stops at a few wineries to taste and perhaps buy a few flagons of "bottled poetry." Then settle in at a charming country inn or bed and breakfast, poach for a half-hour in a hot tub, take a refreshing shower, and go out for a memorable dining experience. Life holds few greater pleasures!

Napa Valley: Calistoga
ALL SEASONS CAFE AND WINE SHOP
California Cuisine $

The All Seasons Café is a small charcuterie with 16 small marble-topped tables along one wall. The charcuterie specializes in fresh produce, much of it from its own four-acre garden, and fresh seafood mostly from north-coast waters. Mark and Alex Dierkhising, who also own the Silverado Tavern and Restaurant across the street, are the owners and operators of the All Seasons whose offerings include an assortment of gallantines, pâtés, smoked fish, and fresh seafood dishes. Specialties are offered each day and dishes are imagina tively prepared and presented. Part of the Silverado Tavern and Restaurant's wine collection is stored at the All Seasons. In the "wine cellar," a small rear room, customers may choose from some 800 labels for a modest $3 corkage charge. Also available is wine tasting by the glass, and usually about 15 choices are available. All Seasons also makes its own ice cream that's possibly the richest available anywhere! For an inexpensive dining adventure, All Seasons stands high on the list in all of the wine country.

ALL SEASONS CAFE AND WINE SHOP, 1400 Lincoln Avenue, Calistoga. Telephone: (707) 942-9111. Hours: 9–9 daily. Cards: AE, MC, V. Reservations suggested for large parties or special dinners. Beer and wine only. Public parking nearby.

Napa Valley: Rutherford
AUBERGE DU SOLEIL
French   **$$$**

Auberge du Soleil (Inn of the Sun) is unsurpassed for elegance, cuisine, ambience, and view in all of the wine country. The $3 million restaurant and inn is located high on the east wall of Napa Valley above the town of Rutherford. From the balcony is a panoramic view of the lush vineyards of Napa Valley set against a backdrop of the dramatic Mayacamas Mountains. Dining on the balcony at sunset when the valley is bathed in golden hues is a memorable experience. The decor of Auberge du Soleil is best described as "rustic elegance," a subtle blending of elements of Mediterranean and California design. The restaurant opened with Masa Kobayashi— a legend in his own time—as chef, and gained instant fame. In late 1983 Kobayashi left and the chef duties were taken over by Michel Cornu, who came from France by way of the Adolphus Hotel in Dallas. Cornu's kitchen continues the tradition of offering beautifully prepared and presented nouvelle cuisine with a prix-fixe dinner menu ($42). Outstanding among the half-dozen hors d'oeuvre choices is the seafood terrine with scallop mousse and artichoke sauce, or, when offered, the mussel soup delicately flavored with saffron. The nine entrée selections include a very exciting presentation of duckling: rare cooked breast slices of locally grown duck are served with yellow plums and capers in port wine. If your tastes focus on seafood, the salmon and turbot in puff pastry with cilantro and saffron sauce is a showstopper. An array of lovely desserts provides a perfect end to the dining experience. Auberge has an excellent wine list heavily weighted toward Napa Valley's two finest varieties, Chardonnay and Cabernet Sauvignon. Service on a busy weekend evening can be less than ideal. Lunch is served from 11:30 to 1:30 and there are two seatings for dinner: one at 6 pm and one at 9 pm.

Experience has shown the early dinner seating to be the best choice. One gets a sunset as a bonus, and occasionally at the 9 pm seating the kitchen may run out of some dishes.

AUBERGE DU SOLEIL, 180 Rutherford Hill Road, Rutherford. Telephone: (707) 963-1211. Hours: 11:30–1:30, dinner seatings at 6 and 9 daily. Cards: AE, CB, DC, MC, V. Reservations advised; 24-hour confirmation required. Full bar service. Parking lot. Jackets preferred for men. Private banquet facilities: 20–80.

Les Hors d'oeuvres

Pâtes fraîches Primavera 6.50
FRESH PASTA GARNISHED WITH VEGETABLES

Salade frisée et epinard aux croûtons et bacon 4.50
CHICORY AND SPINACH SALAD WITH CROUTONS AND BACON

Boudin de fruits de mer, au coulis de crustaces 7.–
SEAFOOD SAUSAGE, COULIS OF CRUSTACEAN

Mousse de foie de canard 5.50   **Potage du jour 4.50**
DUCK LIVER MOUSSE   SOUP OF THE DAY

Le Dejeuner

La pêche du jour Basquaise 12.50
DAILY FRESH FISH, ONION BELL PEPPER TOMATO SAUCE

Tortellini aux crevettes 12.50
FRESH TORTELLINI WITH SHRIMP

Coquilles St. Jacques meunière au gingembre 14.50
SAUTÉED SCALLOPS MEUNIÈRE WITH GINGER

Demi poulet de grain de la Vallée, mayonnaise à l'estragon 10.50
LUKEWARM, GRAIN-FED NAPA VALLEY CHICKEN, TARRAGON MAYONNAISE

Salade de canard confit, aux mangues 11.–
SALAD OF DUCK CONFIT WITH MANGOS

Jolie de petites salades 11.50
ASSORTMENT OF VEGETABLE SALADS

Lapin grillé, persillade et moutarde de grain 12.–
GRILLED FARM RABBIT, PARSLEY AND MUSTARD SEED

Le foie de veau aux échalottes et persil 11.50
CALF'S LIVER WITH SHALLOTS AND PARSLEY

Bavette de veau au soja et gingembre 13.–
VEAL SKIRT MARINATED WITH SOY AND GINGER

Sonoma County: Sonoma
AU RELAIS
French/Continental

$–$$

In the historic town of Sonoma, there are two "musts" for every visitor: a tour of General Vallejo's old barracks and a meal at Au Relais. Both are local landmarks, but that wasn't always the case. Chef Harold Marsden started luring serious diners to Sonoma at a tiny roadside café back in 1968. Within three years his clientele had grown so large that he moved the restaurant to an old farmhouse, restored with redwood siding and art nouveau nuances, and a lovely garden for al fresco meals in balmy weather. A recent addition is the Gazebo Room, named for a colorful canopied ceiling, that has little to do with art nouveau or old Sonoma, but it works. Although Au Relais's menu lists a few high-ticket items, most of the fare is moderately priced and the prudent diner can leave with a satisfied appetite and a smiling wallet. (The pastas, priced at $7, are especially good buys.) In addition to the rather standard meat and fish dishes listed on the regular menu, Chef Marsden each evening prepares several specials, most often seafood, that do justice to his skill and imagination. The wine list, which is heavy on Sonoma offerings with a few French bottlings, is well selected. Au Relais is a good choice for pleasant dining at modest prices.

AU RELAIS, 691 Broadway, Sonoma. Telephone: (707) 996-1031. Hours: 10–10 Monday–Saturday, 9–9 Sunday, closed Wednesday and Thursday during the winter. Cards: MC, V. Full bar service. Reservations advised. Street parking.

Napa Valley: Napa
BOMBARDS
Cajun-Creole

$–$$

In 1985 Bombards quietly opened its doors for business and the lovely aromas of Cajun-Creole cooking wafted up and down the valley. The locals followed their noses and a successful restaurant was born. Bombards was named after the famous European balloonist, perhaps with the hope that he will one day come to Napa Valley where balloons dapple the skies on summer mornings. The restaurant's decor is typical of a no-frills Cajun country restaurant where the energies are spent in the kitchen first and the dining room second. The stark white walls are hung with an assortment of Cajun country photographs and one wall is painted with a colorful balloon-theme mural. Tables are set with white linen and guests are seated on ladderback chairs. The Bombards menu offers some 50 selections. The heart of Louisiana-style cooking is the seasoning and Bombards uses spices judiciously. If you wish to incinerate your palate, however, the chef will be happy to accommodate your wildest death wish. In the appetizer department the andouille pig tails are a culinary delight; the sausage is rolled in short bread with a purée of herbs, parsley, mushrooms, and cheese, quickly oven-browned and served with a red-pepper chutney sauce. In the entrée department, the crawfish pie is a handsome and delicious dish, arriving in a generously sized ramekin with a crawfish breaking through the crust; the filling contains various seafoods, chicken, and ham in a beautifully spiced cream sauce. The Cajun green pork is another authentic dish that Bombards does exceptionally well, served with the classic accompaniments of black beans, corn, and a polenta-stuffed tomato with a spicy sauce. Desserts, too, are faithfully Cajun: bread pudding with bourbon sauce, pecan-praline-chocolate torte and white-chocolate lemon pudding. The wine list is modest but carefully crafted and wines are fairly priced. Bombards also offers a good selection of beer, which generally is more efficient in quenching a Cajun throat fire.

BOMBARDS, 4050 Byway East off Highway 29 just north of Napa. Telephone: (707) 224-8717. Hours: 4–9 daily. Cards: MC, V. Beer and wine only. Reservations advised. Parking lot.

Napa Valley: Calistoga
BOSKO'S
Italian $

A fun pastatorium, usually jammed with both locals and tourists from 11 am to 10 pm every day. The pastas of various sizes and shapes, including linguine, fettuccine, spaghetti, ad infinitum, are made in a gleaming pasta machine, a marvel to watch. Sauces heaped on or tossed with the pastas include a marinara (a spicy tomato-based sauce), Alfredo, basil cream, or whatever comes to the chef's mind on any particular day. The glorioso, an olive oil, garlic, mushroom, and chili sauce on a shell pasta, is outstanding. Also offered is a variety of Italian sandwiches. A good selection of wines is available by the glass and an even better selection by the bottle. The ambience is informal with sawdust on the floor, but not between the owners' ears. They know exactly what they are doing: offering wonderfully fresh pastas at wonderfully attractive prices. A perfect wateringhole and eatery for those who wish a change from the ultra-elegant dining that Napa Valley offers.

BOSKO'S, 1403 Lincoln Avenue, Calistoga. Telephone: (707) 942-9088. Hours: 11–10 daily. No cards. Reservations not accepted. Beer and wine only. Street parking.

Napa Valley: Calistoga
CALISTOGA INN
Seafood   **$$**

In 1979, Phil Rogers, who perfected his culinary wizardry
at the stoves and ovens of Scott's Seafood Grill in San
Francisco, bought the decrepit Calistoga Inn and gave it
new life. Roger's heroic efforts have resulted in one of
Napa Valley's most successful restaurants. The atmos-
phere is "Calistoga laid-back," which means unpre-
tentious, relaxed, and friendly, with an adjoining bar that
is a popular wateringhole for locals and tourists. In the
dining room linen-covered tables are widely spaced to
allow room to flail your arms if you are an animated
conversationalist. The decor is simple: bare floors, a few
tasteful pictures and posters on the walls, café curtains,
and ceiling fans, which on a warm summer evening
maintain a modicum of air circulation. Service is accom-
plished by bustling young women who glow with pride in
serving the restaurant's excellent dishes. Although the
selection changes daily, two appetizers usually offered
are tender calamari lightly sautéed in butter and a
creamy Oregon blue cheese mousse. The portion is so
generous and rich that it is wise to share a single order
between two persons. Dinners include soup or salad.
The salad is always good, but the soups are spectacular!
Even a mundane-sounding pea soup arrives seasoned
with such skill that it is transformed into ambrosia.
Rogers is at his best preparing the seafood dishes that
dominate the menu. All the fish is fresh and mostly from
north coast waters. Imaginative sauces, such as herb,
nut, garlic, or ginger, give the fish dishes a special
succulence. For the nonseafood diner, there is an
excellent roast duckling, an always-good veal dish, and a
steak. Unlimited servings of a marvelously crisp french
bread are heaped on every table. The wine list is
carefully selected and fairly priced and about 60 brands
of beer are stocked. The Calistoga Inn is a popular
gathering place for local winemakers, who can usually

be spotted by the armloads of wine they carry to their tables.

CALISTOGA INN, 1250 Lincoln Avenue, Calistoga. Telephone: (707) 942-4101. Lunch: 11:30–2 Friday–Sunday. Dinner: 5:30–10 Tuesday–Sunday. Cards: MC, V. Reservations advised. Full bar service. Street parking.

APPETIZERS:

Seafood Terrine with Lobster and Crab		$6.00
Bluepoint Oysters on the Half Shell	each	$ .95
Fried Virginia Oysters with Tartar Sauce		$5.50
Hot and Spicy Crab Cakes with Avocado Butter		$4.00
Smoked Pacific Salmon with Dill Mustard Sauce		$4.50
Fried Calamari with Aioli Sauce		$5.50
Ipswich Steamer Clams with Drawn Butter & Broth		$5.50
Blue Cheese Mousse with Garlic Croutons		$2.50

SOUP AND SALAD:

Portuguese Chicken Soup	$2.50
Tossed Green Salad	$2.50

ENTREES: (served with soup or salad)

Fish Stew Calistoga Inn	$10.50
Grilled California Halibut with Sorrel Sauce	$14.50
Grilled Redfish, Chive Butter	$12.50
Grilled Idaho Trout, Pecan Brown Butter	$14.50
Grilled Haddock, Bearnaise	$13.50
Grilled Striped Bass, Mushroom Cream Sauce	$14.50
Grilled Mako Shark, Tomato Herb Sauce	$13.50
Grilled Boston Sole Meuniere	$13.50
Grilled Swordfish, Tarragon Mustard Sauce	$14.50
Steamed Sea Scallops, Saffron Sauce	$14.50
Poached Norwegian Salmon Hollandaise	$15.50
Sauteed Veal Scallops with Shiitake Mushrooms & Marsala	$15.00
Sauteed Ribeye Steak, Blue Cheese Butter	$15.50
Fettuccine with Crab, Mussels, Tomatoes, and Curry	$14.00

DESSERTS:

Strawberry Shortcake	$4.00
Black and White Chocolate Mousse	$3.00
Italian Cream with Raspberry Sauce	$3.00
Frozen Amaretto Souffle	$3.50
Creme Caramel	$2.50
Dark Chocolate Rum Cake	$4.00
Cantaloupe Sorbet with Fresh Fruit	$3.00
Strawberry Ice Cream	$3.00

Napa Valley: Napa
D.D. KAYS
UPTOWN BAR AND GRILL
California Cuisine

$–$$

Art deco decor of the 1930s and California cuisine of the 1980s. D.D. Kays does both spectacularly. This storefront restaurant offers imaginative cooking and an upbeat ambience that is unequaled in the lower Napa Valley. The long, narrow dining room has banquettes along one wall, tables in the center, and a long bar always bustling with activity. Toward the rear a small platform hosts jazz artists Thursday through Saturday evenings. The D.D. Kays menu is a compendium of exciting dishes; in the appetizer department, for example, beer-steamed cockles and spinach tagliarini with pear vinaigrette; arugula and slivered smoked duck; or sage sausage with sautéed spinach, minced fruit, and walnuts. The dozen entrée offerings include a beautiful Chilean sea bass grilled and stuffed with asparagus and parmesan cheese, roast Petaluma duckling with raspberry-currant sauce, and a smoked turkey and brie sandwich with bermuda onions and sage mayonnaise. The fresh pastas are marvelous mélanges of harmonizing and contrasting flavors and textures. The soups and salads are always exciting adventures into new tastes. The wine list is very good and service is as upbeat as the food.

D.D. KAYS UPTOWN BAR AND GRILL, 811 Coombs Street, Napa. Telephone: (707) 224-5925. Hours: 11:30–2:30, 5:30–10 daily. Cards: MC, V. Full bar service. Reservations advised, especially on weekends. Street parking.

Napa Valley: Yountville
DOMAINE CHANDON
French $$$

The Domaine Chandon restaurant is located at Napa Valley's famous champagnery (although they insist on calling their wine "sparkling wine" rather than champagne) and since opening has been a star in Napa Valley's restaurant firmament, with first-magnitude brilliance. The restaurant decor is one of austere elegance. The building materials are unfinished concrete, laminated wood beams, and glass. The dining rooms overlook emerald-green lawns broken by water-lilied ponds and stately oaks. The Domaine Chandon menu is nouvelle French. The truck-driver set might complain that the portions are not life sustaining; however, nouvelle cuisine is characterized by Lilliputian portions. Of course it is obligatory to start either lunch or dinner with a bottle of Domaine Chandon sparkling wine to fine-tune the palate for the gastronomic experience to follow. Obligatory also is la crème de tomatoes en croûte, a silky cream of fresh tomato and leek soup served in a deep bowl

★　POUR COMMENCER　★

LE POT-AU-FEU DE POISSONS ET CRUSTACES A MA FACON　　S7.
Fish and Shellfish Soup in the style of Southern France

LA SOUPE DE HOMARD AUX POMMES DE TERRE A LA BRETONNE　　S8.
Lobster and Potato Soup with Shellfish Essence

LA CREME DE TOMATES EN CROUTE　　S5.
Cream of Tomato Soup in Puff Pastry

LA SALADE MELANGEE DE HOMARD ET FOIE GRAS D'OIE　　S12.
Composed Lobster and Foie Gras Salad

LA SALADE TIEDE DE RIS DE VEAU A L'HUILE DE NOIX ET POMMES DOREES　　S8.
Warm Sweetbread Salad with Walnut Oil and a Hint of Orange

LA SALADE DE CANARD FUME COMPOSEE A L'HUILE DE TRUFFES　　S7.
Smoked Duck Salad with Truffle Oil

LES ESCARGOTS ET PATES FRAICHES DANS L'HUILE D'OLIVE AU BASILIC　　S6.50
Snails with Pasta tossed in Basil Olive Oil

LES SAINT-JACQUES GRILLEES DANS LEUR NAGE AU CORIANDRE FRAIS　　S7.
Grilled Scallops in their Nage with Cilantro

216

canopied with a flaky, golden-brown puff pastry. If you lunch at Domaine Chandon the l'oeuf moscovite is a dish often served guests at Möet et Chandon in Epernay. The dish is a variation of eggs Benedict. Instead of Canadian bacon, fresh smoked salmon is used, and the hollandaise sauce is topped with fresh golden caviar. Another exquisite lunch offering is le feuilleté de ris de veau au jus de truffes, cameo-white sweetbreads served in a puff pastry with truffle sauce. The dinner menu offers a selection of beautifully prepared and presented nouvelle dishes. The fresh salmon with champagne and sorrel sauce and the lamb noisettes with rosemary and vinegar are good choices. The desserts are outstanding, and the wine list is carefully compiled to include many of Napa Valley's finest wines.

DOMAINE CHANDON, California Drive, Yountville. Telephone: (707) 944-2892. Lunch: 11:30–2:15 daily. Dinner: 6:30–9 Wednesday–Sunday. Closed Monday and Tuesday during the winter. Cards: AE, DC, MC, V. Reservations advised. Wine only. Parking lot.

★ LES RAFRAICHISSEMENTS ★

LE SORBET AU PAMPLEMOUSSE ET ESTRAGON AVEC CHARTREUSE $2.
Grapefruit and Tarragon Sorbet with Chartreuse

LE SORBET AU BLANC DE NOIRS ET MARC DE CHAMPAGNE $2.
Chandon Blanc de Noirs and Marc de Champagne Sorbet

★ LES VIANDES ET VOLAILLES ★

LE CHATEAU DE BOEUF A LA MOUTARDE DE POIVRE VERT ET PERSIL $19.
Tournedos of Beef with Green Peppercorn Mustard and Parsley Sauce,
Sweet Potato Angel Hair

LA LONGE DE VEAU ET SA FRICASSEE DE CHAMPIGNONS DES BOIS $19.
Loin of Veal with Fricassee of Wild Mushrooms

LES COTELETTES D'AGNEAU AU ROMARIN ET VINAIGRE BALSAMIQUE $19.
Lamb with Rosemary and Balsamic Vinegar Sauce

LES FRICASSSEE DE RIS DE VEAU AU BEURRE D'ECHALOTTES ET JUS DE TRUFFES $18.
Veal Sweetbreads with Shallot Butter and Truffle Juice

LA POITRINE DE PIGEONNEAU AVEC SA CHARTREUSE D'AUBERGINES $18.
Squab Breast with Eggplant and Zucchini Chartreuse

217

Napa Valley: Yountville
THE FRENCH LAUNDRY
California Cuisine $$$

The French Laundry is a charming old brick building at the intersection of Washington and Creek streets in Yountville. There is no sign to indicate the building is a restaurant, but warmth and hospitality seem to radiate through the bricks to announce its presence. The interior is simply but tastefully decorated to give a country cottage feeling. There is only one seating, and host Don Schmidt greets his guests by telling them that the table is theirs for the evening. The pace is leisurely and relaxed and conducive to unhurried dining and good conversation. The French Laundry prix fixe five-course menu ($38) changes weekly. The cuisine is "Napa Valley country," which means simply but beautifully prepared foods from the bountiful valley, or, in the case of seafoods, fresh from Pacific waters. The excellence of the food is attested to by the fact that reservations, particularily on weekends, are booked for many weeks in advance. Cancellations always occur, however, and it's worth a phone call to test your luck. Don Schmidt chooses his wines with great care and offers them at minimal markup. The French Laundry is a wine-country dining tradition. Perhaps its only shortcoming is that the fixed menu offers no choices, except for dessert. But the regular patrons of the French Laundry know that the food is so well prepared and the dinners so well balanced that dining here is guaranteed to be a satisfying experience.

THE FRENCH LAUNDRY, 6640 Washington at Creek Street, Yountville. Telephone: (707) 944-2380. Hours: one seating at 7 Wednesday–Sunday. No cards. Reservations essential. Wine only. Parking lot.

Sonoma County: Santa Rosa
JOHN ASH & COMPANY
California Cuisine $$

For total immersion in imaginative food and a staggering selection of fine wines, served in a delightful atmosphere by waiters and waitresses who are truly knowledgeable in wine as well as in food, John Ash & Company may stand at the top of the list in the wine country. About a hundred small windows in two walls give the restaurant an airy, open feeling. One enters the dining room through a retail wine store with a tasting bar that also offers a fine selection of wines by the glass. The restaurant is a favorite for lunch with the locals. The appetizers and light luncheon dishes include an array of pâtés, soups, innovative salads, and entrées that range from fettuccine with a four-cheese sauce (outstanding) to smoked salmon, sautéed fresh fish, or filet americaine (a hamburger with succulent cheeses, chilies, proscuitto, onions, and honey-cured bacon). Dinners at John Ash & Company are always exciting events with each dish a new adventure in subtle tastes and textures. The kitchen does exceptionally well with veal, and a different preparation is offered each evening. When available, the veal may be served with butter-sautéed fresh chanterelles. Also highly recommended is the pork loin, which is marinated in red wine and herbs. The entrées include seasonal vegetables which are prepared with skill to intensify their natural flavors and textures. The desserts are as good as any in Sonoma County, and a fine by-the-glass dessert wine is usually available. On Tuesday evenings the restaurant is closed for dinner, and a serious wine tasting is held which may include vertical or horizontal tastings of a famous or obscure California winery (usually the winemaker is present), or comparisons of California and European wines. There are also regularly scheduled special adventures in wine and foods. The restaurant may be called for information on scheduled events.

JOHN ASH & COMPANY, 2324 Montgomery Drive, Santa Rosa. Telephone: (707) 527-7687. Lunch: 10:30–2:30 Sunday–Friday. Dinner: 6–9:30 Tuesday–Sunday. Cards: MC, V. Reservations advised for dinner; accepted only for parties of 6 or more at lunch. Wine and beer only. Parking lot.

DINNER MENU

APERITIFS: Cinzano Formula Antica, Lillet Blonde, Kir or   2.25
           Kir Royale, Sandeman Character Sherry

FIRST COURSES/LIGHT ENTREES:

American Sashimi - made from the best and freshest fish   6.95
  available with salmon caviar, ginger shoyu, braised
  leeks

Fresh oysters on the half shell (priced individually)   1.10

French Escargot with garlic and herb butter   4.95

French Escargot with roquefort butter   4.95

Baked Brie with sundried tomatoes, wilted fresh spinach,   6.50
  tomatoe coulis and butter croutes

Special Soup (changes daily)   2.95

Rillette of Duck with green peppercorns   whole   5.95
  (a country-style pate made without liver)   half   3.50

Bismark Herring with tart apple, sweet red onion and   6.50
  creme fraiche

Seasonal greens salad made with local greens and served   4.50
  with Oregon Blue, Basil cream, Chinese orange or Balsamic
  vinaigrette dressings

Fresh spinach with French roquefort, roasted walnuts and   5.95
  walnut oil

Summer picnic salad of watercress, tart apples, Vermont   6.95
  white cheddar cheese, smoked chicken and fresh chutney
  with a light fruit vinaigrette dressing

MAIN COURSES:

Fresh boned quail stuffed with a sweet cornbread, pecan   14.95
  and mushroom stuffing and finished with a port reduction
  sauce

Boneless breast of chicken sauteed with French feta   11.95
  cheese, kalamata olives and tomatoes with a mustard
  beurre blanc

Tenderloin of pork "Kobe style" -- grilled with ginger,   14.95
  sesame and soy

Napa Valley: St. Helena
KNICKERBOCKERS'
California Cuisine

$–$$

Tony and Leann Knickerbocker have been Napa Valley caterers for over a decade. In 1986 they opened a restaurant, invited almost everyone in the valley to sample their food, and Knickerbockers' became an instant success. It is a clean, well-lighted place for dining that offers imaginatively prepared food at very modest prices, friendly service, and a good wine selection priced a dollar or two over retail. The à la carte menu allows the diner to dabble here and there according to his wishes and his gullet. Some dozen choices of appetizers include a beautiful ginger-flavored Thai-style chicken salad, a fresh seafood ravioli in a silky saffron broth, and carpaccio marinated in olive oil and served with grated cheese that will set the salivary glands gushing. Main courses list squab, duck breast, a superb pork loin cooked with fennel and black pepper, plus steak and lamb dishes. Pissaladière elevates pizza from the mundane to the exotic, with changing fillings for the individual pies; a favorite is the version with coppa, three kinds of cheese, and capers. Side dishes include artichoke with aioli, and grilled polenta. Each table is presented with a basket of oven-fresh bread and each time the basket is emptied, another basket appears with a different bread. One could live on bread alone at Knickerbockers'. A good selection of house-made desserts includes tortes, cakes, and ice creams. After a strenuous day of wine tasting, ballooning, or mud-bathing in the Napa Valley, Knickerbockers' is a great place to kick back, and enjoy an unhurried, informal, and delicious meal.

KNICKERBOCKERS', 3010 St. Helena Highway North (in Freemark Abbey shopping complex), St. Helena. Telephone: (707) 963-9300. Lunch: 11:30–2:30 Monday–Friday, 11:30–3 Saturday–Sunday. Dinner: 6–9:30

Monday–Friday, 6–10 Saturday–Sunday. Cards: MC, V. Reservations advised on weekends. Wine and beer only. Parking lot.

Napa Valley: St. Helena
LA BELLE HELENE
French $$–$$$

La Belle Helene has a special distinction among Napa Valley restaurants: It was the first to offer fine dining in the area and its success paved the way for all that followed. Located in a century-old stone building that was once a chicken hatchery, the restaurant has had several owners, but present proprietor Marc Dullin, a young Frenchman, is perhaps the most talented chef of them all. His French country cooking is prepared with loving care and beautifully presented. Excellent choices among the appetizers are the duck and pistachio pâté or the sautéed snails and wild mushrooms tucked into a fresh artichoke bottom. A half-dozen entrées are offered—Norwegian salmon on a bed of aromatic herbs sauced with butter and pernod is a seafood favorite. And another winner is a fork-tender fillet of beef with a sauce of roquefort, shallots, and pine nuts. Accompanying the main dishes are fresh seasonal vegetables, such as baby carrots or a colorful beet cake about the size of a Little League hockey puck. House-made desserts range from tarts and sorbets to profiteroles. The good food, attentive service, and an adequate wine list make La Belle Helene a pleasant wine-country dining experience.

LA BELLE HELENE, 1345 Railroad Avenue, St. Helena. Telephone: (707) 963-1234. Hours: 6–9:30 Thursday–Monday. Cards: MC, V. Reservations advised. Wine only. Street parking.

Napa Valley: St. Helena
LE RHONE
French

$$$

Le Rhône is the most recent star in Napa Valley's great restaurant constellation. Owners George (he's the chef) and Eliane (she's the hostess) Chalaye were the proprietors of a restaurant of the same name in San Francisco, where it was acknowledged as one of that city's finest French restaurants. The Chalayes closed their San Francisco place some years ago to return to France, where George developed new ideas and skills to add to his already impressive culinary repertoire. Le Rhône is a very intimate and beautifully decorated eight-table restaurant on Main Street in St. Helena with the decor of a dining room in an elegant country house in the Rhône Valley of France. The stark white walls are decorated with fine copper cooking utensils, photographs of vineyards of the Rhône Valley, and scenic paintings. The linen-covered tables are set with Villeroy & Boch china in the Alt Amsterdam pattern and huge, dramatic wineglasses that serve as candleholders. The prix-fixe menu ($45) includes hors d'oeuvres, soup, salad, an entrée (usually four choices), and dessert. George Chalaye describes his cuisine at the new Le Rhône as "French modern," a style characterized by light dishes with intense, natural flavors and silky textured, delicate sauces. Although Chalaye obtains many of his ingredients from local farmers, he seeks out the unusual, such as exotic game or fish, and has built a smoker to smoke Norwegian salmon. The same dish on two successive evenings may be very different here because he cooks by inspiration rather than recipe. Dining is always a gastronomic adventure that extends to the desserts, which may be some of the most spectacular in the Napa Valley. In addition to an enticing array of cakes, berries in season are presented in beautiful tortes and pies. The Le Rhône wine list is an impressive selection of

California wines plus a few wines from the Rhône Valley. Service is excellent under the watchful eye of Madame Chalaye. All dishes are brought to the tables under gleaming silver cloches, which adds an additional note of elegance to the gracious atmosphere. If your budget is too tight to allow a weekend jet trip to sample the beautiful cuisine of central France, a dinner at Le Rhône is a very satisfactory substitute.

LE RHONE, 1234 Main Street, St. Helena. Telephone: (707) 963-0240. Hours: 6–10 Wednesday–Saturday, 4–9 Sunday. No cards. Reservations advised. Wine only. Street parking.

Sonoma County: Healdsburg
MADRONA MANOR
California Cuisine $$–$$$

This century-old mansion on a wooded knoll above the Russian River Valley was built as an elaborate summer home for a San Francisco financier. Now Carol and John Muir (a distant cousin of the naturalist) have turned it into a delightful country inn with a restaurant that would stand out in a big city. The kitchen is the domain of the Muirs' son Todd and his sous-chef Mark Holmoe, both protégés of Alice Waters at Berkeley's Chez Panisse, and their cooking reflects the principles of the new California cuisine. Fruits and produce come from the manor's own gardens; salmon, trout, chicken, and duck are smoked on the premises; and unusual pizzas are turned out in an oak-burning brick oven. The menu changes nightly with both à la carte and five-course prix-fixe dinners ($37.50) offered. Among first courses, favorites include the garlicky fried Sicilian cheese, Alice Waters's baked goat-cheese salad, and fettuccine with smoked salmon, caviar, and cream. Some representative entrées are grilled pork loin stuffed with pistachios and dried fruit; entrecôte of beef with cognac, shallots, and green peppercorn sauce; and grilled rib eye of veal with apple chutney. Luscious house-made desserts and pastries conclude the meal. When dining here, you might want to consider arriving early for a stroll in the lovely gardens and an aperitif in the manor's stately music room. After dinner, there's a possibility of a round of billiards in an adjoining game room. Or you might even want to stay all night in one of the upstairs bedrooms, which still contain the splendid original furnishings. On Sunday mornings a champagne brunch is served; bring along your swimsuit for a dip in the pool.

MADRONA MANOR, 1001 Westside Road, Healdsburg. Telephone: (707) 433-4231. Hours: 6–9 daily, brunch 10:30–2 Sunday. Cards: AE, MC, V. Reservations advised. Wine and beer only. Parking lot.

Napa Valley: St. Helena
MIRAMONTE HOTEL
French $$$

There are those who insist that when the moon and stars are just right, a dinner at the Miramonte can be the supreme dining experience in the Napa Valley. Others claim that astrological phenomena are not dependable and that great evenings here can often be marred by cold and indifferent service. Also, the cost of the announced prix-fixe dinner is inflated by additional charges for special sauces and special dishes. But, indeed, on a good night when the astrological signs are favorable and the wallets bloated, the Miramonte experience can be memorable. The Miramonte Hotel is located on a rather unscenic street overlooking an unscenic railroad spur with a shopping center as a backdrop. Inside, however, the ambience is elegant. The main dining room has two magnificent stag-horn chandeliers, which give a hunting-lodge feeling. In the second dining room, walls are hung with handsome prints of Napa Valley's finest grape varieties, and on summer evenings dinners are served on the patio which is dominated by a huge, 100-year-old fig tree. Chef Udo Nechutnys was a student of the great Paul Bocuse and his culinary brilliance suggests he must have graduated summa cum laude. In addition to being an outstanding chef, Nechutnys is a master at orchestrating each dish so that there are intriguing harmonies and contrasts of flavors and textures. The Miramonte prix-fixe dinner is priced at $30 (see above) and usually changes weekly and occasionally more often depending on the availability of ingredients—of which Nechutnys demands the highest in quality. The dinner usually consists of five courses, and there are several choices in each course. With added specials each evening, not on the menu, the choices offered are very extensive. The poultry and fish dishes are particularly outstanding. The wine list is carefully chosen and always includes some of Napa Valley's best wines.

MIRAMONTE HOTEL, 1327 Railroad Avenue, St. Helena. Telephone: (707) 963-3970. Hours: 6:15–9 Wednesday–Sunday. No cards. Reservations essential. Full bar service. Street parking.

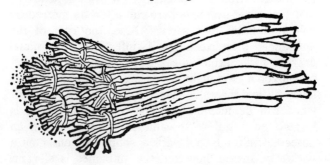

Napa Valley: Calistoga
MOUNT VIEW HOTEL
California Cuisine

$$

Ask any Calistoga chef: "Next to you, who is the best chef in town?" The answer will probably be Diane Pariseau, executive chef at the Mount View Hotel where the food, ambience, and service add up to a total dining experience as good as any in the northern Napa Valley. In the past year the restaurant has also lowered its prices, making it unquestionably one of the best values in the area, and it also has one of the best wine lists in the country. The entire hotel is done up in impeccable art deco motif, which is emphasized in the dining room by an outstanding collection of framed *Saturday Evening Post* covers from the 1930s. The menu offers both à la carte selections and a four-course dinner for $22.50 and is changed daily in accordance with the availability of fresh seafood and of produce from local farms. A typical prix-fixe dinner might include steamed mussels or confit of duck with arugula, salad, lamb roasted with oregano and garlic or broiled yellowfin tuna with chili butter, and a selection from the dessert menu. It is imperative to reserve room for the latter, especially the chocolate-apricot-pecan cake, which has enough calories to fuel a team of sled dogs for a dash to the North Pole. Equally disastrous to a diet is the frozen honey-cream soufflé with fresh raspberry sauce. After dinner, check out the Mount View bar, which is the action spot of the northern valley. A small band offers sounds of the thirties and an opportunity to dance away the calories gained at dinner.

MOUNT VIEW HOTEL, 1457 Lincoln Avenue, Calistoga. Telephone: (707) 942-6877. Breadfast and lunch: 7:30–2 daily. Dinner: 6–9 daily. Cards: AE, DC, MC, V. Reservations advised. Full bar. Parking lot. Private banquet facilities: up to 30.

Napa Valley: North of Yountville
MUSTARD'S GRILL
California Cuisine $$

When it opened in 1983, Mustard's instantly became the most popular dining place in the Napa Valley. Though a number of restaurants have tried unsuccessfully to imitate its format, Mustard's is still the "in" place. (Reserve at least a week in advance during the tourist season.) This restaurant's overwhelming success is due to imaginative food, a bustling ambience, unbelievably reasonable prices, and an excellent selection of Napa Valley wines affordably priced. The menu is the same at lunch and dinner and offers à la carte selections of appetizers, dishes from the grill and wood-burning oven, sandwiches, sides and condiments, and desserts. Daily-changing specials are listed on a chalkboard. It's hard to name favorites because Mustard's is one of those rare places where everything is well prepared. Especially popular, though, are the half slab of baby back ribs, the grilled prawns with lemon and tarragon, and the Sonoma rabbit with salsa and black beans. Do try the side dishes, too. The onion rings arrive thread thin and piled high on the plate and the whole head of roasted garlic is sweet and marvelous. Portions are generous and the service ends up being remarkable considering that every table is always occupied. Perhaps that is one secret of their success: They always have their act together.

MUSTARD'S GRILL, 7399 St. Helena Highway, north of Yountville. Telephone: (707) 944-2424. Hours: 11:30–9 Sunday–Thursday, 11:30–10 Friday–Saturday. Cards: MC, V. Reservations advised Wine and beer only. Parking lot.

Appetizers, Soups and Salads

Different Soup every day..$2.50
Skewered Pork and Chicken filets with Shiitake mushrooms.............. 4.55
Cornmeal Pancake with housemade sour cream and Topiko caviar.......... 4.80
Three Cheese Croquettes with tomato chutney vinaigrette............... 3.25
Smoked Beef Tenderloin, mustard and chives........................... 3.95
Spicey Provimi Veal Ribs, herb cured and smoked...................... 4.60
Grilled Sweetbreads with lemon, parsley, caper brown butter.......... 5.35
Warm Goat Cheese, almond coated, with sun dried tomatoes and chives... 4.40
Limestone and Butter Lettuces with seasoned pecans and bleu cheese.... 3.50
Baby Greens and housesmoked Bacon with roasted garlic dressing........ 4.95
Wild and button Mushrooms, greens and endive, creamy dijon dressing... 5.10
Chinese Chicken Salad.. 7.35

From the Wood Burning Oven

Half slab Barbequed Baby Back Ribs................................... 8.65
Smoked Chicken, chipotle marinade, orange-tomato-basil salsa.......... 7.85
Grilled Quail with mixed pepper chutney.............................. 9.90
Tarragon and Lemon Prawns, lightly smoked then pan fried in the shell.12.45
Rib Eye Steak, mixed pepper cured, with Shiitake mushrooms...........12.50

From the Grill

Fresh Fish (see chalkboard)
Whole Chicken Breast with avocado salsa.............................. 8.25
Pork Chops with many mustards.. 7.90
Calf's liver with caramelized onions, bacon, and housemade ketchup..... 8.70
Sonoma Rabbit with red tomato salsa and black beans.................. 9.95
Marinated Skirt Steak on grilled bread............................... 8.90
Pounded Veal Chop with pan fried tomatoes, basil and garlic...........12.75

Sandwiches

Hamburger or Cheeseburger.. 5.50
Barbequed Brisket of Beef.. 6.25
Smoked Ham and Jarlsberg cheese, grilled, with tomato chutney........ 5.85
Smoked Turkey Salad with cheddar and walnuts......................... 6.30

Sides and Condiments

Onion Rings.. 1.95
Grilled Eggplant and red onion with ginger butter.................... 3.30
Roasted Garlic... 1.00
Tomato Chutney.. .75
Onion and Orange Jam.. .80
Polenta... .95
Housemade Ketchup... .50
Avocado Salsa... .85
Black Beans with chopped red onions, sour cream and chives........... 2.10
Grilled New Potatoes... 1.85
Grilled French Bread, garlic and herbs............................... 1.90

Desserts

Chocolate Pecan Cake, chocolate sauce................................ 3.65
Ice Cream.. 2.50
Espresso Cheesecake.. 3.80
Caramel Custard with pistachios and cream............................ 2.95

Napa Valley: St. Helena
ROSE ET LA FAVOUR
CAFE ORIENTAL
French–Asian $$–$$$

An iron-clad axiom in the restaurant business dictates: If you have a successful formula, don't tamper with it. But in Bruce La Favour's breast beats the heart of an adventurer. His Rose et La Favour Restaurant Français in St. Helena was an enormous success that garnered rave reviews nationally. But in 1985 he closed the place and traveled to Nepal to hike and meditate about his all-consuming passion—cooking. He returned and reopened his restaurant with a new concept, a new image, and a new name: Café Oriental. The place is still small (13 tables) but it has been completely redecorated. From the lofty ceiling now hang colorful flags of Southeast Asian nations and the walls host a variety of photographs of Asian scenes, Asian paintings, and Asian artifacts. "Oriental" was added to the name to stress Bruce La Favour's constant quest for lighter, yet full-flavored, foods. He found a partial answer in the cuisines of Southeast Asia that somehow had been missed by western chefs. This is not to say that the Café Oriental food is now Asian, for La Favour's dedication is really to French cuisine, but cooking techniques and seasonings do have an Asian influence. Indeed, some of his old dishes, still served, already hinted at his new direction. The dispassionate diner can have a satisfying experience for a modest price, but the true epicure most likely will lose all sense of fiscal responsibility after the first taste and plunge through the à la carte menu with such wreckless abandon that the tab must be brought by sedan chair. Highly recommended among the cold first courses is the exquisite salad of mussels on butter lettuce with threads of leeks and fragile wild onion blossoms dressed with a silky saffron-flavored vinaigrette. In the warm appetizer department, a terrific choice is

FIRST COURSES, COLD

Mussel Salad with Saffron 7.00

The Hot and the Cool 8.00
Spicy squid salad tempered with green papaya salad.

Three Rich Salads 11.50
Lobster, partridge and foie gras.

The War of 1905 . . . . 9.50
Tuna Japanese style and filet of beef Russian style.

Terrine of Fresh Duck Foie Gras 22.00
Our grand service with beet soup, small salad and grilled bread.

One Portion Served for Two 25.00

Glass of Sauterne with Foie Gras Service 6.00

FIRST COURSES, WARM

Fresh Asparagus Vinaigrette 4.50

Rabbit Loin with Wasabi and Ginger 9.00
Lightly-cooked rabbit loin with Japanese pickled ginger and horseradish.

Poached Farm Eggs with Fennel 4.50

SOUPS

Range Hen in Coconut Milk with Galanga 8.50

A Soup of Fresh Snails from Mrs. Herb's Garden 6.50

Maine Lobster and its Jelly Served Chilled
with Herbs and Young Vegetables 10.50

FISH

Rhode Island Select Oysters with Creamed Leeks 6.50

Steamed Mendocino Coast Rock Fish
with Oriental Vegetables 9.50

Eastern Black Sea Bass in Champagne Sauce 14.50

POULTRY

Muscovy Duck Breast in Papillote with Orange and Ginger . . . 16.50
The breast roasted in paper served with a julienne of vegetables.

Duck Leg in Green Curry Sauce 9.75
Served with rice and raw vegetables.

Grilled Squab with Bitter Greens and Beurre Blanc 16.50

Roast Chukar Partridge Breasts and Partridge Sausage
Served in a Sabayon Sauce 17.50

Poached Range Hen Breast in Blood Orange Sauce 12.50
Served with a variety of young vegetables.

the rabbit loin with wasabi and ginger accompanied with a delicate array of crisply cooked vegetables. And don't miss the soup of fresh locally grown snails poached in chicken stock. The adventures continue like bullets from a machine gun throughout the menu: medallions of venison with ginger and Belgian endive, rabbit sausage with creamed parsley and a watercress sauce, duck leg in green curry sauce served with raw vegetables, to name a few entrées. The desserts, by pastry chef Ann Kathleen McKay, add a pyrotechnic finish to dinner. Café Oriental's wine list is perhaps the richest in the valley, if not the entire state. Next to falling into a vat of Cabernet Sauvignon, dining at Rose et La Favour Café Oriental is probably the most exciting adventure one can have in Napa Valley.

ROSE ET LA FAVOUR CAFE ORIENTAL, 1420 Main Street, St. Helena. Telephone: (707) 963-1681. Hours: 5–10 Wednesday–Sunday. Cards: MC, V. Wine only. Reservations advised. Street parking.

Sonoma County: Sonoma
SONOMA MISSION INN
California Cuisine and Spa Food $$$

The Sonoma Mission Inn is a zillion-dollar spa in the grand European tradition, where one can unwind, relax, dine on low-calorie cuisine, and "take the waters." Or one can do some of these things, dine on exquisite (and more caloric) cuisine, and "take the wines." The Grille at the inn has recently been enlarged and remodeled with one area enclosed by large french doors that offer a view of the pool area. The room is bright and airy infused with a rosy glow from shades of pink, peach and mauve. It combines an aura of early California with French Provincial accents. The extensive menu offers an impressive selection of appetizers, such as Pacific calamari marinated in herbed olive oil and lemon, and tiny Petaluma snails with a garlicky cream sauce and shiitake mushrooms. Wonderful choices among the salads are the romaine and radicchio with a Caesar dressing or the toma-toes and goat cheese dressed with garlic and basil. Pastas challenge anything found on the Via Veneto with fresh noodles and interesting sauces like lobster, asparagus, shallots, and cream. From the mesquite grill, the plump Sonoma quail with a raspberry-vinegar sauce is especially satisfying. The seafood entrées for the calorie-counters tend to be bland, but the Pacific salmon with a piquant citrus butter is a sure winner. Vegetables are as crisp as glass, as is the service. The wine list, skewed chauvinistically toward Sonoma wines, is extensive and the wine prices apparently include the rental of a Rolls Royce to drive around the county collecting the bottles. But all in all, the Sonoma Mission Inn offers a totally lovely dining experience.

SONOMA MISSION INN, 18140 Sonoma Highway, Sonoma. Telephone: (707) 938-9000. Hours: breakfast 7–10:30, lunch 11:30–3, dinner 6–10 daily. Cards: AE, CB, DC, MC, V. Reservations advised. Full bar service. Ample parking on grounds. Private banquet facilities: 20–175.

Napa Valley: St. Helena
STARMONT RESTAURANT
California Cuisine $$–$$$

Open your thesaurus to "idyllic." All of the listed synonyms apply to the new Starmont Restaurant at the Meadowood Private Reserve (previously the Meado-wood Country Club), 256 acres of sylvan beauty broken only by a golf course, tennis courts, and a swimming pool. Though only about two miles from St. Helena, the Reserve is located in a canyon where vines give way to oaks, redwoods, and pines to provide one of Napa Valley's loveliest restaurant sites. In 1984, the old Meadowood Restaurant burned to its foundations and, like the legendary Phoenix, its replacement rose more beautifully from the ashes. The glass-walled dining room overlooks the golf course and on summer nights tables are set on a deck where you can watch families of deer emerge from the woods to stare enviously at the diners. Chef Hale Lake (a native Hawaiian whose athletic build suggests he would be more at home on a surfboard than in a kitchen) creates some of the most imaginative dishes in the Napa Valley. At dinner, both à la carte items and a five-course prix-fixe dinner ($38) are offered on the daily-changing menu. Standouts among the appetizers have been a fork-tender carpaccio served with mango chutney, and a corn pancake with asiago cheese and chanterelles. The fresh mussel soup flavored with saffron is true ambrosia and the salad of mixed greens with candied papaya, walnuts, and Montrachet cheese is in the best nouvelle tradition. Making a selection of entrées is also difficult, but if the fillet of sturgeon with roasted sweet-pepper butter sauce is listed among the seafood choices, go for it. And the breast of Long Island duckling with guava and mango sauce is reason enough to have granted Hawaii statehood. Desserts are magnificent, too. Hale likes to use fresh berries and he does beautiful things with them, as he does with homemade ice creams and a variety of nut sorbets. The Starmont wine list is one of the best in the valley, for good reason: Many winery owners are Meadowood members and they make sure that the restaurant has a good allocation of their best bottlings.

STARMONT RESTAURANT, 900 Meadowood Lane, St. Helena. Telephone: (707) 963-3646. Hours: 11:30–2:30, 6–9:30 daily. Cards: AE, CB, DC, MC, V. Full bar service. Reservations required. Parking lot. Private banquet facilities: 12–110.

SOUTH BAY

South Bay: Mountain View
CHEZ T.J.
French $$$

If you're looking for a gracious evening of good dining, Chez T.J. is the place to go. Situated in a restored 1902 Victorian, the restaurant is the creation of two men. Chef Thomas J. McCombie oversees the culinary aspects of the evening while his partner and co-owner George Aviet concentrates on service, waiting on tables himself. The menu changes every two weeks to accommodate McCombie's desire for fresh ingredients with three prix-fixe dinners each evening. Menu Pichune is a four-course meal, Menu Moderne is five courses and Menu Gastronomique is eight courses. The portions are scaled according to your menu, so you can go all out without making a glutton of yourself. An example of McCombie's innovative culinary artistry can be found in a fillet of salmon poached in romaine lettuce, which delivers a fresh, flavorful fish inside a still-crispy wrapping of lettuce. Escallops of pork loin, served with sour cherry sauce and cream cheese pancakes, is equally flavorful, the pork almost melting on the tongue. A nice option is the choice of French cheeses or a salad on two of the menus; you get both on the third. And the homemade desserts are exquisite confections ranging from fresh raspberries to a chocolate walnut torte. From the fresh flowers on each table to the color-coordinated green china and green napkins, an evening at Chez T.J. is pleasurable to both the eye and the palate.

CHEZ T.J., 938 Villa Street, Mountain View. Telephone: (415) 964-7466. Hours: 5:30–9:30 Tuesday–Saturday. Cards: MC, V. Reservations required. Wine only. Street parking.

CHEZ T.J.

MENU GASTRONOMIQUE
@$38.00

Goat Cheese in Sauce of Port and Pink Peppercorns, or
Soup of Asparagus, Creme Fraiche and Peanuts, or
Smoked Trout with Coriander and Beets
*

Saute of Soft Shelled Crab with Sauce of Eggplant and Herbs, or
Salmon with Tomatoes, Rock Salt and Chives
*

Melon Sorbet in Champagne Float
*

Breast of Chicken Stuffed with Apricots in a Sauce of Ginger and Almonds, or
Imported Morels Stuffed with Veal Mousseline, or
Fillet of Beef with Shiitake Mushrooms
*

Salad of Spinach and Watercress in a Minted Vinaigrette
*

Selection of French Imported Cheeses
*

Petite Dessert Before Dessert
*

Choice of Homemade Dessert
*

French Roast Coffee

MENU MODERNE
@$32.00

Goat Cheese in Sauce of Port and Pink Peppercorns, or
Soup of Asparagus, Creme Fraiche and Peanuts
*

Salmon with Tomatoes, Rock Salt and Chives
*

Imported Morels Stuffed with Veal Mousseline, or
Breast of Chicken Stuffed with Apricots in a
Sauce of Ginger and Almonds
*

Spinach and Watercress in a Minted Vinaigrette, or
Selection of French Imported Cheeses
*

Choice of Homemade Dessert
*

French Roast Coffee

MENU PICHUNE
@ $25.00

Soup of Asparagus, Creme Fraiche and Peanuts
*

Salmon with Tomatoes, Rock Salt and Chives, or
Breast of Chicken Stuffed with Apricots in a
Sauce of Ginger and Almonds, or
Saute of Soft Shelled Crabs with Sauce of
Eggplant and Herbs
*

Spinach and Watercress in a Minted Vinaigrette, or
Selection of French Imported Cheeses
*

Choice of Homemade Dessert
*

French Roast Coffee

South Bay: San Jose
EMILE'S
French/Swiss

$$$

When Emile Mooser opened his small restaurant more than a decade ago, he had no competition to speak of. Today, Emile's has company when it comes to fine restaurants in Santa Clara Valley, but it still sets the standard by which other restaurants are measured. Mooser was trained in Lausanne and has more than 30 years of experience. He personally trains those who cook for him. He is not content with a stagnant, never-changing menu and his specials take advantage of what's fresh in the marketplace. The small foyer attests to Mooser's talents, with awards and articles singing his praises displayed prominently. There is even a small trophy case at one end. The dining area itself has an airy look, thanks to light mauve walls and a few large prints of flowers. The menu choices range from emincé de veau à la crème et aux champignons, finely sliced veal sautéed with assorted mushrooms and cream, to la poitrine de poulet aux morilles, braised breast of "naturally raised" chicken in a morel sauce with buttered vermicelli. For those who desire a lighter cuisine, Emile's offers "minceur" selections. The appetizers include an excellent les crevettes sautées bordelaise, prawns sautéed in butter, white wine, garlic and lemon, as well as gravlax à la française, house-cured salmon, sliced and served with a sauce of yogurt. The salads are very good and in addition to a consommé, there is a soup of the day. The Grand Marnier soufflé is almost de rigeur here, but if you'd prefer something lighter, the sorbets are wonderful. While Emile's is a pretty, intimate restaurant, that is also its one drawback. On a crowded evening there is no avoiding the conversations at the next table, or the smoke should they decide to light up. Emile's is without a no-smoking section, but the hostess does make an effort to separate the smokers from nonsmokers when possible. Unfortunately, it's not always possible and cigarette smoke does not enhance Mooser's delicate sauces.

EMILE'S, 545 South Second Street, San Jose. Telephone: (408) 289-1960. Hours: 11:30–2, 5–10 Tuesday–Sunday. Cards: AE, CB, DC, MC, V. Reservations advised. Full bar service. Valet parking.

Le Diner

Choice of soup or salad

EMINCÉ DE VEAU A LA CRÈME ET AUX CHAMPIGNONS
A Swiss specialty. Finely sliced veal sauteed with assorted mushrooms and cream

LE POISSON GRILLÉ A LA JAPONAISE
Marinated and grilled seasonal fish with ginger and Japanese mushrooms

ENTRECÔTE GRILLÉE, BEURRE CAFÉ DE PARIS
Dry-aged New York cut steak with an herb and curry butter

ESCALOPES DE VEAU, "SCALLOPINI"
Traditional veal scallopini served with fresh vermicelli

Nos Specialities

a la Carte
The Menu according to season and selection at the Market

LE POISSON FRAIS SELONS LES PRODUITS DU MARCHE
The fresh fish of the day. Please ask your waiter

LA POITRINE DE POULET AUX MORILLE
Braised breast of "naturally raised" chicken in a morel sauce with buttered vermicelli

LE PIGEONNEAU FARCIE AUX VINAIGRE DE FRAMBOISE
Roasted boneless squab filled with wild rice, in a raspberry vinegar sauce

LES GRENADINES DES TROIS ROIS
Filets of beef, veal and lamb, each with its own sauce

LES RIS DE VEAU AUX CABERNET
Veal sweetbreads in a cabernet sauvignon sauce with shiitake mushrooms

LE FILET DE BOEUF BEARNAISE ET LA FEUILLETTÉ DE CREVETTE
A filet of beef with bearnaise sauce and sauteed prawns in puff pastry

ESCALOPE DE VEAU AUX CHAMPIGNON FORESTIÈRE
White veal sauteed with wild mushrooms

RÖSTI
A Swiss specialty potato (for two)

South Bay: Menlo Park
FLEA STREET CAFE
California Cuisine $$$

Chef Jessie Cool takes whatever produce is local and seasonal and transforms it into a memorable meal, which is one reason Flea Street has a loyal and enthusiastic following on the peninsula. Most of the fruits and vegetables come from local, organic gardeners or from her own market garden. But there are a few exceptions like the papaya slices that garnish the smoked breast of chicken served with raspberry mint sauce. Another fine dish is grilled fish with Moroccan cumin paste baked in parchment paper and served with black beans and fresh tomato sauce. When figs are in season, you'll find them as an appetizer, perhaps served with goat cheese. Cool is concerned with taste above all else, eschewing such trendy things as baby vegetables for the sake of baby vegetables. Interestingly, the menu is composed primarily of homemade pasta, fish, or fowl. Very little red meat will be found on her menu, and when it is, it's usually something she's created herself, such as homemade sausages or a bit of bacon. Flea Street is a particular favorite among vegetarians. Jessie's husband Bob Cool oversees the wine selection, and the two also own another restaurant, Late for the Train, in Palo Alto.

FLEA STREET CAFE, 3607 Alameda de las Pulgas, Menlo Park. Telephone: (415) 854-1226. Hours: 11:30–2:30, 6–10 Tuesday–Saturday, 9 am–2 pm Sunday. Cards: MC, V. Reservations advised. Wine and beer only. Street parking.

South Bay: San Jose
GERVAIS
French $$$

In a city dominated by shopping centers, it's fitting that one of the best restaurants around is located in one, right alongside a laundromat with drug, liquor, and convenience stores nearby. But don't let the exterior put you off: Gervais is well worth a visit, particularly if you are a fan of classic French cuisine. Chef Gervais Henric has invested a lot of time and talent in his restaurant, making each succeeding visit more pleasurable. Dinners are priced on two levels, entrée alone or with a choice of soup or salad. If your dining partner is willing, order one of each and share. The green salad with Gervais' house dressing makes for a tangy beginning. And the soups are a pleasure to smell as well as sip—a good example is the shrimp bisque, which has a smooth-as-silk consistency and a fresh, nonfishy taste. Also in the shellfish line, the shrimp in bordelaise sauce is wonderful, either as an appetizer or as an entrée. Chef Henric's talents are not limited to seafood. The lamb with herbs and butter is moist and flavorful. There are also beef, pork, and veal dishes to chose from. For dessert, the crowd favorite is the Grand Marnier soufflé, served with a combination of the traditional cream sauce. The one jarring note at Gervais is the decor: low ceilings, less-than-appealing chandeliers and a chilled storage locker for the white wines inexplicably located in the main dining area. But it takes only a taste of the fine food to quickly overlook these minor drawbacks.

GERVAIS, 1798 Park Avenue, San Jose. Telephone: (408) 275-8631. Lunch: 11:30–2:30, Tuesday–Friday. Dinner: 5:30–10 Tuesday–Saturday. Cards: AE, DC, MC, V. Reservations advised. Full bar service. Parking lot.

South Bay: San Jose
HI-LIFE
American (Barbecue) $

The Hi-Life presents a rather low-life profile, but push past it if barbecue is among your loves. That's all the Hi-Life does, and it does it well. The menu is posted on a wall in the entry area bar: top sirloin, beef brochettes, New York steak, ribs, chicken, and teriyaki. Pick up a well-worn number from the box near the menu and sooner or later, usually later, a waitress will call your number and take your order. There's another wait beyond that and you'll soon understand why the Hi-Life has put comfortable padding around the center pillar, a consideration for those who wait. The entrée is the only variable of the meal. When you're seated, you'll find a salad of lettuce and one beet slice waiting on a Formica-topped table set with one fork. The dressing choices are italian, Thousand Island, or blue cheese. As you finish your salad, the waitress will appear with a large platter holding your entrée, accompanied with a huge baked potato smothered in butter, a steak knife, and a new fork. A basket of garlic bread is on every table. The waitress is also likely to plop down a large pile of paper napkins, which you will eventually be grateful for. The entrées are smoky but still tender and juicy. The pork ribs are a particular favorite of many patrons, but the steaks have a strong following as well. (There is the option of ordering a side of mushrooms, but if you're doing it for additional bulk, don't bother.) The chef is visible in front of a large, open-pit barbecue in the main dining room, and he's fascinating to watch as he wields enormous knives, occasionally douses flames with a spray of water, and works non-stop to produce one platter after another of delicious barbecue. The portions are more than generous, and the waitresses have take-home bags in their aprons. Even with a healthy appetite, it's difficult to finish everything off. Coffee is available after dinner, but there is no dessert. Lingering is not encouraged, although it is tolerated. Finding the Hi-Life is similar to working a maze puzzle. You'll have to navigate at least one one-way street to locate this gem. It's a secret that few people like to share, but it has been shared enough over the past 40-plus years that it's crowded even on a weeknight. The restaurant is sometimes referred to as Henry's Hi-Life, in honor of owner Henry Puckett who opened it here in the former Torino Hotel. The post-Prohibition bar has some nice Moderne touches to it.

HI-LIFE, 301 West St. John Street, San Jose. Telephone: (408) 295-5414. Hours: 5–10 daily. Cards: MC, V. Reservations not accepted. Full bar service. Parking lot.

South Bay: Saratoga
LE MOUTON NOIR
French   **$$$**

Le Mouton Noir is anything but a black sheep when it comes to restaurants. Located in the older, village section of Saratoga, this pretty dining place is inside a cozy country cottage. The interior is divided into several dining areas. Tables set with pink linens, flower-patterned china, and small mixed flower bouquets are placed so that nearby diners don't intrude. Even in the largest dining room, you still retain a sense of intimacy. One of the nicest aspects of Le Mouton Noir is the light-hearted staff. Although their French pronunciations are impeccable, you'll find none of the hautiness or pretension that is so often grating in French restaurants. As for the food, it's excellent. The chef's special presentation of fresh duck may be prepared with kumquat sauce and julienned kumquats one night and the more traditional orange sauce the next. One regular entrée is the prawns and scallops combination in a flavorful sauce. In selecting an appetizer, pay particular attention to the other daily changing chef's special, which is pasta. The desserts are seasonal and invariably tempting. Besides being pleasing to the palate, dishes at Le Mouton Noir are also visually pleasing. Everything is arranged in an artful manner when it arrives at your table. It's not surprising that Le Mouton Noir is a favorite place for celebrations—birthdays, anniversaries, promotions, and an occasional wedding dinner. But saving it for special occasions is a mistake, since a meal here can turn your whole day into a special occasion.

LE MOUTON NOIR, 14560 Big Basin Way, Saratoga. Telephone: (408) 867-7017. Hours: 11:30–1:30, 6–9:30 Tuesday–Saturday. Cards: AE, CB, DC, MC, V. Reservations advised. Wine only. Parking in rear.

South Bay: Sunnyvale
LION & COMPASS
California Cuisine
$$$

While many Santa Clara Valley residents cringe at the area's Silicon Valley nickname, it's a fact of life. And for the person seeking *the* Silicon Valley restaurant, the Lion & Compass has no competition. Nolan Bushnell, the man who brought you video games, is the founder and continued part-owner. And to top it all off, the *New York Times* anointed it in print: "The Lion & Compass is to the computer world what Sardi's is to New York's theater district." It is also one of the best restaurants around. Chef Steven Goodwin produces a long list of daily specials that take advantage of seasonal items. Plus, he gives a Chinese influence to many of his specials such as grilled five-spice quail; venison stir-fry with black mushrooms, soy, cilantro, and chilies; or soft-shell crabs sautéed with ginger and scallions and served with pan-fried noodles. Fresh fish is always featured and a good bet. Desserts include a flourless chocolate cake that is a local favorite and magnificent sorbets made from seasonal fruits. The interior of the Lion & Compass is a mélange of California greenery and decor based on the original English pub that gave the restaurant its name. The bar is a must, your chance to observe the titans of Silicon Valley. If they tire of discussing the semiconductor industry, they can always peruse the electronic New York Stock Exchange ticker along one wall. Should they but ask, a waiter or waitress will produce a phone at their table and they can call their stockbroker while sipping on English brews such as John Courage or Watney's.

LION & COMPASS, 1023 North Fair Oaks Avenue, Sunnyvale. Telephone: (408) 745-1260. Lunch: 11–2:30 Monday–Friday. Dinner: 5:30–9:30 Monday–Thursday, to 10 Friday–Saturday. Cards: AE, CB, DC, MC, V. Reservations advised. Full bar service. Parking lot and valet parking.

South Bay: Palo Alto
MACARTHUR PARK
American $$

In 1981, San Francisco's popular MacArthur Park (q.v.) opened a slightly larger branch in Palo Alto with an almost identical menu, featuring first-rate barbecue and other all-American specialties.

MACARTHUR PARK, 27 University Avenue, Palo Alto. Telephone: (415) 321-9990. Lunch: 11:30–2:30 Monday–Friday. Dinner: 5:30–10:30 Monday–Saturday, 5–10 Sunday. Brunch: 9:30–2 Sunday. Cards: AE, MC, V. Reservations advised. Full bar service. Valet parking and parking lot. Private banquet facilities: 25–40

MADDALENA'S
Continental   **$$$**

Comfortable ambience, quality service, and excellent food come together beautifully at Maddalena's on a consistent basis, resulting in memorable dining. Located in downtown Palo Alto, the main dining room of Maddalena's has dark wood wainscoting with a wall of beveled glass mirrors atop it. The smaller, upstairs dining area is much like a comfortable living room, with wingback chairs. Antique china cabinets and sideboards are sprinkled about, now serving as wine cupboards and storage tables. Small mixed bouquets grace the tables. It is obviously the home of a discriminating host. A central preparation counter in the downstairs room is a fascinating, ever-changing tableau, as zabaglione is prepared for one table, followed by the tossing of Maddalena's salad for two for another table. When it is time to serve, extra waiters appear instantly. Then they vanish to reappear only as needed. While the setting and service are faultless, the food makes the picture complete. Offerings include veal, lamb, beef, fowl, seafood, and pastas. The veal dishes are considered the best on the peninsula, and the tournedos of beef with roquefort sauce invariably elicit praise. With your dessert, consider a cup of cappuccino or an after-dinner liqueur. A particularly nice touch at Maddalena's is the live music, which may be a strolling violinist one evening and a harpist another.

MADDALENA'S, 544 Emerson Street, Palo Alto. Telephone: (415) 326-6082. Hours: 6:30–10 Monday–Saturday. Cards: AE, CB, DC, MC, V. Reservations advised. Full bar service. Parking lot. Private banquet facilities: 10.

South Bay: San Jose
ORIGINAL JOE'S
Italian $$

Since opening in May of 1956, Original Joe's has been a fixture on the San Jose restaurant scene. It's a bright, noisy oasis in the downtown area, one of the very few establishments to survive the ups and downs of this part of town. The secret of Joe's, as the regulars call it, is that it serves good food and a lot of it on a consistent basis. The menu is primarily Italian, and a pick from the pastas is a good bet. It's also a good bet that you'll find it difficult to finish a plate of spaghetti and meatballs or ravioli or any of the combinations offered. Veal is another specialty, and there are some people who plan their dining around the osso buco offered on Wednesdays and Saturdays only. In addition to the many Italian offerings, there is some plain grub—steaks, hamburgers, and a Joe's Special of ground meat, spinach, and eggs. You won't find a better hamburger in Northern California than at Joe's, a fact borne out when a local magazine held a hamburger contest and Joe's won first place. The hamburger is so good that it's possible to eat it just as

it's served on a hunk of crusty bread, without any condiments at all. Because of its proximity to the Civic Auditorium and the Center for Performing Arts, Joe's is a place where you're likely to see politicians, celebrities, and common folk all rubbing elbows and waiting for a place to sit. It's a cash-only business with no reservations, but there are those who willingly wait for hours. The tuxedo-clad waiters are slightly incongruous in a restaurant that is primarily booths and Formica tables, but for the most part they are a jolly group and quick with the food and take-home containers. In addition to the booths, there is a long counter along one wall where you can dine and watch all the meals being prepared by the high-hatted chefs.

ORIGINAL JOE'S, 301 South First Street, San Jose. Telephone: (408) 292-7030. Hours: 11 am–1:30 am daily. No cards. Reservations not accepted. Full bar service. Parking lots.

South Bay: Santa Clara/Los Gatos/Palo Alto
PEDRO'S
Mexican $

Pedro's is legendary, both for good food at inexpensive prices and for the wait. Both are directly attributable to Peter Ramirez, owner of three Santa Clara County restaurants bearing the Spanish translation of his first name. Borrowing a small sum of money from his mother and drawing on cooking skills he learned from his grandmother, Ramirez opened a small restaurant on Los Gatos's North Santa Cruz Avenue. Like Topsy, it just grew, through three remodelings and expansions. Running out of room, Ramirez erected a striking Spanish hacienda-style building in Santa Clara off Highway 101, near Great America amusement park. Most recently has come the third Pedro's in Palo Alto at Stanford Shopping

Center. The menu is Mexican food familiar to Californians—tacos, enchiladas, tostados, and chiles rellenos. Both the chile verde of pork and the chile colorado of beef are dinners with succulent chunks of their respective meats. Pedro's own creation is a special crab enchilada. The universal favorite, for nibbling while you wait in the bar or as a complete meal, are the nachos. Ramirez may not have invented these, but he's helped make them famous. Fried tortilla chips form the basis for mounds of refried beans, cheese, guacamole, and sour cream. Because the three restaurants serve more than 3,000 patrons a night, service may not always be perfect. But Pedro's is an experience, and it attracts a genial crowd that tends to be good-natured about the long waits.

PEDRO'S RESTAURANT & CANTINA, 3935 Freedom Circle, Santa Clara. Telephone: (408) 496-6777. 316 North Santa Cruz Avenue, Los Gatos. Telephone: (408) 354-7570. 2 Stanford Shopping Center, Palo Alto. Telephone: (415) 324-1510. Hours: 11–10 Sunday–Thursday, 11–11 Friday–Saturday. Cards: MC, V. Reservations not accepted. Full bar service. Parking available.

South Bay: San Jose
VICTORIAN HOUSE ANTIQUES & GARDEN RESTAURANT
Italian/Continental $$–$$$

As its name implies, Victorian House is a unique combination of restaurant and antique store. If a carousel animal, hanging lamp, or the table you're seated at catches your fancy as you dine on fettuccine Alfredo, owner Patrick Morman will be happy to add it to your bill. Morman combined his loves of fine antiques and fine foods when he opened this restaurant in June 1975 and he's been fine-tuning them ever since. Because it is a popular and convenient place for before and after the theater, you'll usually be asked by the host if you have a curtain to make. If you do, service will be speedy and they'll help you watch the clock. If not, you'll find service attentive but not intrusive or rushed. There is an obvious Italian bent to Victorian House, and the pastas are an excellent choice. Dinners offer a choice of a side of pasta or a vegetable and also include soup and salad. A nice touch is peeled tomatoes, with a freshness you'll instantly recognize. The basket of warm breads offers a variety of choices. Dinner offerings include several seafoods, with an emphasis on scampi. The chicken Sicilian is an intriguing blend of flavors that includes brandy, garlic, and olive oil. Although not all chicken dishes are boned, the waiter will usually offer to have that chore performed in the kitchen if you'd like. The dessert menu is varied and surprisingly negotiable. Ask how fresh raspberries or strawberries are served and you'll be asked how you'd like them. If the options offered aren't satisfactory and you can give the waiter an idea of what you'd like, chances are excellent that you'll get it out of the talented kitchen. With advance warning, Victorian House will arrange a special "chef's table" meal for a party of four or more—a memorable experience. The wine list is a comprehensive one, with an emphasis on white wines. There is a pleasant garden in the rear, filled in summer with greenery and flowers. Surrounded by buildings on all four sides, it is reminiscent of those tiny garden restaurants you'll find hidden away among the concrete canyons of New York City. The garden area is a particularly nice place to lunch.

VICTORIAN HOUSE ANTIQUES & GARDEN RESTAURANT, 476 South First Street, San Jose. Telephone: (408) 286-1770/6187. Lunch: 11–3 Monday–Friday. Dinner: 5–10 Monday–Thursday, to 11 Friday–Saturday, 3–10 Sunday. Brunch: 10:30–2:30 Sunday. Cards: AE, CB, DC, MC, V. Reservations advised. Full bar service. Parking in motel lot next door.

INDEX

ETHNIC INDEX

AMERICAN

See also Cajun-Creole,
  Barbecue, and Burgers.

BASQUE

CAJUN-CREOLE

CALIFORNIA CUISINE

CHINESE

See also Dim Sum and
  Asian Noodles.

256

ALPHABET SOUP

ALFRESCO

ASIAN NOODLES

BARBECUE (AMERICAN)

BREAKFAST, BRUNCH

ABOUT THE AUTHORS

The genesis of this guidebook was the publication in 1968 of California's first statewide restaurant guide: *101 Nights in California,* which in 1972 spawned a monthly restaurant newsletter, *California Critic* (a three-time winner of the Newsletter Clearing House's grand award as the best consumer newsletter in America). Meanwhile, in 1975, *101 Nights in California* was reformatted as *Best Restaurants San Francisco,* with a companion edition, *Best Restaurants Los Angeles.* In subsequent years this series was expanded to cover almost every major city in America, with top local restaurant critics contributing the reviews.

JACQUELINE KILLEEN is a restaurant critic for *San Francisco Focus* magazine. She has been writing about California restaurants since 1968 as the author of the original *101 Nights in California,* co-author of the *Best Restaurants San Francisco* guides and co-publisher of the *California Critic* newsletter. She also writes the San Francisco restaurant section of *Fodor's San Francisco.* For this edition of *Best Restaurants San Francisco,* she reviewed most of the larger restaurants in the city, along with some in the East Bay and in Marin County.

SHARON SILVA is also a restaurant critic for *San Francisco Focus.* She has been editing the 101 restaurant guides since 1969, was associate editor and a reviewer for *California Critic,* and has been a co-author of *Best Restaurants San Francisco* since 1977. Through her extensive travels in the Far East, she brings to this book a special expertise on Asian cooking and is responsible for almost all of the reviews of San Francisco's Asian restaurants, as well as the majority of the small ethnic places. She has co-authored articles on Asian restaurants for the Sunday magazine section of the *San*

Jose Mercury News, the *California Living* section of the *San Francisco Examiner,* and TWA *Ambassador* magazine.

CAROL WARREN, a former Los Angeles resident now living in San Francisco, helped to select the Southern California restaurants for the early editions of *101 Nights in California* and has been an avid discoverer of dining places since moving to the Bay Area. To this book she has contributed several reviews for San Francisco and Marin County.

MARY GOTTSCHALK is presently fashion editor for the *San Jose Mercury News,* but for many years was a feature writer there with a penchant for articles on food, and served as scout for *California Critic*'s reviews of Peninsula restaurants. She contributed the South Bay section of this book.

GEORGE STARKE was the Orange County restaurant reviewer for *California Critic* for a number of years and was also a co-author of the 1978 edition of *Best Restaurants Los Angeles & Southern California.* In 1980 he moved to the Napa Valley, where he became one of the owners of a small winery and presently teaches wine appreciation at Napa Valley College. He reviewed the wine country restaurants for this book.

ROY KILLEEN is an architect, formerly with Anshen & Allen of San Francisco. He has been illustrating the 101 restaurant guides—along with many other books— since the initial publication of *101 Nights in California.*

LET THESE GUIDES LEAD YOU TO THE BEST RESTAURANTS OF OTHER AREAS

The widely acclaimed series of Best Restaurants guides is a reliable source of dining information in the most traveled areas of America. Each is written by a leading local restaurant critic and each is the same size and format with menus reproduced. Guides to the following areas are either presently available or will be published soon.

____ CHICAGO & SUBURBS By Sherman Kaplan $4.95

____ HAWAII By Dorja Leiso $4.95

____ LOS ANGELES By Colman Andrews $4.95

____ ORANGE COUNTY By Herb Baus $4.95

____ PHILADELPHIA & ENVIRONS By Elaine Tait $4.95

____ SAN DIEGO COUNTY By Jeanne Jones & Dick Duffy $4.95

____ SAN FRANCISCO BAY AREA By Jacqueline Killeen et al $4.95

____ SOUTHERN NEW ENGLAND By Patricia Brooks $4.95

____ WASHINGTON D.C. & ENVIRONS By Phyllis C. Richman $4.95

These books are available at bookstores or may be ordered from the publisher, 101 Productions, 834 Mission Street, San Francisco, CA 94103 Please add 75¢ postage and handling for each book.

Name_____

Address_____

City_____ State_____ Zip_____

Check for $_____ enclosed.